deflowered
my life in Pansy Division

deflowered
my life in Pansy Division

by jon ginoli

CLEIS
PRESS

Cover design: Scott Idleman
Text design: Frank Wiedemann
Cleis logo art: Juana Alicia
First Edition.
10 9 8 7 6 5 4 3 2 1

Contents

Prologue

Our rental truck was packed and loaded, sitting at the cavernous loading dock inside Madison Square Garden. We started it up, drove down a couple floors of exit ramps, and headed for the Lincoln Tunnel. How the hell had we managed to get there?

It wasn't planned, that's for sure. If we had planned to get to Madison Square Garden, we wouldn't have taken anything resembling the path we took. We certainly wouldn't have formed a gay rock band. The truth is we got there by *not* planning to get there at all. Not that we headlined, mind you—we opened for the massively popular band Green Day, then at their first peak of popularity. But it was being ourselves that got their attention in the first place, and led them to ask us to do a tour that changed our lives, changed our band, and provided a bird's-eye view of how society was changing for gay people. But I'm getting ahead of myself here.

Rock and roll has been around for more than fifty years. It's one of the linchpins of modern American culture. From its controversial origins, which exposed the fault lines of race and class in America, it became a populist, mainstream music, becoming big business in the process. As a defining cultural moment, it set standards and expectations. As it became normalized, it was by default heterosexual, regular guy music; at the same time, rock and roll was androgynous. Think of Elvis Presley's makeup. Little Richard's flamboyance. The Beatles's groundbreaking effeminate haircuts. David Bowie's and Lou Reed's taboo-breaking gender-bending. Freddie Mercury's flouncing. Mick Jagger tongue-kissing Ron Wood on *Saturday Night Live*. The homoeroticism of '80s hair metal bands, all that pretty, pretty hair, but with macho jerk attitudes. Morrissey's seen-it-all-before jaded queen act. Prince, Judas Priest, Style Council, Soft Cell, Skid Row…a seemingly endless list of performers that gave off a gay vibe, toyed with effeminate or homosexual imagery, but weren't gay, wouldn't come out, or came out but then retreated into the closet.

That was where rock music stood as it entered the '90s. It was time for a gay rock band—so I formed one. I called it Pansy Division. This book tells how and why we started, and where we went. It's a story about coming of age sexually versus coming of age culturally. It's about punk and queer simultaneously going mainstream, and the meeting of gay subculture and the rock subculture. For years, when I've spun tales of my experiences with Pansy Division, people have often suggested that I write a book about them. Here it is.

When we began, we were the first gay rock band we

knew of, apart from some contemporaries appearing at the same time. I thought that as we carried on and met more people we might hear of earlier such bands too obscure for us to have discovered on our own. Though we didn't hear of any entirely gay bands, we heard about a number of gay musicians. It reminded me that a lot of gay history is hidden and inaccessible, and that we should write our own stories ourselves instead of waiting for historians and fans to do the archaeology. As for the complete history of gay rock and roll, that's another book, but here's our story.

CHAPTER 1

We Had to Come from Somewhere

Explaining how I got from Peoria to Pansy Division requires that I back way, way up. I think it's important to point out that I did not grow up in San Francisco—I was a refugee from Peoria, Illinois, the heartland of the country. Long a butt of jokes ("Does it play in Peoria?" as a barometer of Middle American tastes and values), politically it's very middle of the road. I lived there until I went to college, a mere hundred miles away.

I was born in December 1959, lived a normal life in a normal place in a normal family with two parents and a younger sister. Dad was an accountant, mom was a home-maker, all very stable, very comfortable, very nice. We weren't a close family; everyone sort of did their thing, and I was a fairly independent kid. Just before I turned six, in the fall of 1965, my family built a nice new house on the outskirts of town, in a new subdivision that had been farmland a few years before. There were very few houses or other kids nearby. That's when I made friends with the radio. I discovered WLS-AM in Chicago, and listened to it practically all day and night.

From the ages of five to ten, I completely absorbed Top 40 pop radio. Staying in my room with the door shut, I would stare at the 45s I had going around and around on my tiny record player, daydreaming about music and wanting to someday be in what I then called "a singing group." I had a few albums (The Monkees and The Mamas & The Papas were early favorites, and I still love them today), and would look at the time listings for each song and guess that that was the time of day when it was recorded. The songs were all short, so I figured that between two and three o'clock was, for some reason, the time of day when things sounded the best for recording.

I was lucky to be raised without religion. I never set foot in a church until I attended a wedding when I was eleven or twelve. As a kid I'd been to Chicago (three and a half hours away) with my family many times, so I'd seen a big city. But it seemed too alien, too far removed from my suburban experience for me to envision myself living there. I had the idea that Peoria was just like most places, so I might as well stay there. (Peorians looked down on the smaller, even more provincial towns in the area, like all-white Pekin, Illinois, named after Peking, China, whose high school sports teams were called the Pekin Chinks until the late '70s.)

But while Peoria was not Pekin, it was certainly not Chicago. On a visit there in 1970, my family was walking across a bridge when a tall, purse-swingin' drag queen approached from the other direction. Hemmed in by traffic, we couldn't escape. As he came sashaying past us, we all stared, and my mom nervously said, "He's one of those swishy guys." I bet we looked every bit like the All-American nuclear family, and I would love to know now the reaction of the drag queen to us.

As a kid, I was a loner but I wasn't completely isolated. At the age when boys tend to hate girls, I liked them. I had girlfriends at age six and age eight. Most of my friends were girls. Boys, however, were frightening—they always seemed to be a lot rougher than me. I was small and had asthma, but I had a big mouth and thus I used words to mouth off, which led to low marks for conduct. Because I had good grades, teachers would look past this; my grades gave me the opportunity to attend a gifted school in seventh and eighth grade, which was great. It was there that I met the smart and savvy Dena Smith. A year older than me, she was also a loner. Through her I was turned on to glam rock, especially The New York Dolls. I loved music and had been buying 45s since I was five, but suddenly, this exciting new music sent me off in a new and different direction, one that felt right for me.

I remember the first guy I was ever attracted to. I was twelve. My family had gone out for an afternoon boat ride on the Illinois River, on the boat of a friend of my dad's. Also on this boat was another family, a recently divorced man and his two sons. The younger son was my age, and as the afternoon wore on I couldn't keep my eyes off him. I was mesmerized, and surprised at myself. We didn't really speak to each other, but my eyes were glued to him as we walked back and forth across the deck of this little boat. I remember consciously thinking, *I really want to kiss him…Can guys even kiss?* I was totally naïve about anything gay at that point, completely unaware of the concept. It was very confusing, because I had always liked girls; now I was at the age when I was supposed to like girls but was starting to realize that I liked guys.

As Peoria had no gifted high school I was forced to reenter the public school system in ninth grade, where my education took a step backwards. It wasn't until junior year that we even got around to reading books I'd already read in eighth grade. I had been hearing from my parents for most of my life how much fun high school would be, how it would be the time of my life. Both of them had been popular, and my dad had even been a star athlete. I was neither athletic nor popular and except for a few teachers, I truly hated high school.

P.E. was hell. Like my dad, I enjoyed running, but my asthma prevented me from excelling even at that. When we had wrestling my sophomore year, I got physically sick in anticipation of the first day and stayed home; this was a bad move, since I wasn't weighed with the rest of my class and the coach put me in a weight group one step up from my actual weight. I lost every match for six weeks and got a D-. Making this worse, sophomore and junior years I had my locker next to this totally foxy, skinny, long-haired guy who I was sure was going to give me a boner one day. Checking out guys in the shower? Apart from the occasional peek, I averted my eyes as much as humanly possible for the sake of my survival.

Obviously I didn't get along with the jocks; there was the smoker/burnout crew, but they seemed so pathetic. It was the mid-'70s and I wanted nothing to do with hippies. Smoking pot? Forget it. Drinking? My parents did that, and gave me beer at home, but I didn't want it. My rebellion was *not* drinking. I did have a small group of friends (more or less three guys, three girls) that I made my sophomore year; that was the year Monty Python began airing in the United States, and our group had a similar weird sense of humor that united us. I did make one fairly close friend, Rick, who I invested a lot of hope in—he was able (though reluctant) to understand me. He and Dena are the only high school friends I still know today.

During this time it was Dena, again, who led me towards punk rock, which became my salvation. It was crude and clever and asked questions I could relate to. She bought the first Ramones album the week it came out. We poured over magazines like *CREEM, Circus, Hit Parader*, and *Trouser Press* to find out about this music. While in high school I mail-ordered import punk and new wave 45s from New York City (there was no place to buy them in Peoria)—Sex Pistols, The Damned, The Saints, The Vibrators, The Clash, The Jam, Wire, X-Ray Spex, Nick Lowe, Graham Parker, Elvis Costello, The Adverts, The Buzzcocks. Dena had purchased the first Blondie album just as she was going out of town for the weekend with her family, so I got to borrow it. The first song, "X Offender," was so great I played it five or six times before I could even listen to the rest of the album. The whole album was great, but I played that one song twenty times that weekend and bought a copy for myself as soon as I could. It's still one of my favorites.

I remember getting my copy of the first Sex Pistols 45, "Anarchy in the UK," in the mail. At first I was unsure, but by the third spin I was converted. Liking this music made me more of an outcast at school; I was conscious that this would further alienate me from the people I knew, but it felt urgent and important to listen to it. It was angry, but really fun and funny at the same time. It articulated an anger I felt but couldn't really spell out; I was still learning how to think, and I hadn't yet figured out how to phrase my discontent.

Patti Smith was the first (actually, the only) rock star I tried to look and dress like. My hair was almost the same length as hers in the cover photo on *Horses*, and I wore white button-down shirts with the sleeves rolled up. Dena and I were definitely the only students roaming the halls of my high school in the fall of 1975 wearing white button-down shirts. We also liked David Bowie, Mott the Hoople, and especially Roxy Music. I was really into Bruce Springsteen's *Born to Run* album; I recall that it was one of the first records whose sadness I could relate to, and he was one of the few musicians I was into that my other friends liked too.

Inspired by the music I was hearing, I began putting out a rock/punk/new wave fanzine called *Hoopla*, to which Dena contributed. Isolated in Peoria, and lacking contact with anyone else into this new music, we made pen pals via our zine. Between June 1977 and September 1978, I put out nine issues. Looking back through those issues now, I notice that they lack the self-protecting, limiting elitism that the punk scene came to develop later; we wanted these bands to be *popular*, dammit! They were great bands, and they deserved to be heard by everyone. We wanted The Ramones and Sex Pistols and Plastic Bertrand to knock the fuckin' Eagles and Boston and REO off the radio!

There was one openly gay rocker that I listened to—Tom Robinson. He was British, got swept up in the punk/new wave thing, and recorded a few songs about being openly gay. I bought his first album my senior year of high school, and I made sure nobody I knew saw me buying the record. I actually wrote him a fan letter, and he wrote back! (Sadly, I've lost the letter.) But his stuff was too specifically British—lots of local topical references—and seemed very, very distant from my life. Still, in purchasing that record I was taking a tentative first step. But I said nothing about my doubts and confusion to my friends.

A memorable incident occurred when I was fifteen. It was the summer after my freshman year of high school, and I had few friends. I went to the County Fair with my mom and my sister, and I felt rather pathetic. I separated from them and walked around by myself for a while. Watching a comedian on the entertainment stage, I turned around to look at the crowd and spotted a guy whose good looks stopped me cold. He was so beautiful, with straight, longish red hair and brown eyes, that I could not stop looking at him. He was sitting a medium distance away, with friends, and I don't think he saw me watching him. I lost interest in the comedian and kept turning around to catch glances of him. After a while, it saddened me to think that if he got up and left, I might never see him again—which is exactly what happened. I still love brown-eyed redheads (a rare combination). Though it may seem like I was already a budding queer just waiting to burst out, I stayed in denial for a very long time, well into college. I kept kidding myself that it wasn't guys in general that I liked, just this or that particular one, and that when I got a girlfriend those feelings would disappear.

My parents wanted me to be going on dates. I had feelings for boys, but I also liked girls at the time, which made it more confusing and easier to deny. I wasn't having luck with either sex. Naturally, I was in love with my straight best friend; so cliché! I finally told him of my feelings the night before I left for college. At least I said something, and he was still my friend afterwards. He was really understanding, and not completely surprised. (Twelve years later, after I'd gotten over him, he entered a bi-curious phase and we actually slept together, a great experience.) Years later I realized that my two favorite high school teachers had been gay; the lightbulb just went on one day. But I didn't have any reference points back then.

Music helped me survive these years and gave me hope; I got into movies as well. Though there isn't one individual record that changed my life, there is one movie—*Network*.

I saw it in January 1977 and it totally blew me away. It confirmed my nascent cynicism (which my friends seemed too afraid to admit), and like "Anarchy in the UK," was another wedge between myself and the mainstream—embracing this movie and its worldview made me feel even more of a social pariah. To me, it's the great punk rock movie—articulate yet profane, angry, funny, and not condescending. The characters were intelligent and didn't apologize for it, didn't care what anybody else thought. Seeing it was a liberating moment.

One day during my junior year we had a school assembly. The program was preceded by the Pledge of Allegiance, which we were forced to stand and recite. I was livid; it felt like punishment. It was the cold war era, and we were told that America was so much better than Russia because we were free, and all they learned in school was propaganda. If America was so great, I thought, why did we have to continually take this loyalty oath? Telling my fellow students and teachers that the Pledge was our propaganda would have fallen on very deaf ears. I just stood there and took it, seething all the way. Had I refused to stand up—and I considered it—I felt like no one would have supported me. Not my teachers. Not my parents. Certainly not other students. For the small group of friends I had, it would have been way too much, going way too far. I felt completely alienated.

By February, with three months of school left, frustrated as hell, I contemplated ditching the few friends I had and just being alone. But I just couldn't do it. Dena, a year ahead of me, had already graduated and gotten the hell out of Peoria. I remember stomping down the school halls singing Elvis Costello songs to myself, like "I'm Not Angry," "Mystery Dance," and "Waiting for the End of the World." I couldn't stand the company of the lunchroom anymore, so when the weather was halfway decent I'd take my food and walk into the big open field across from my high school and eat by myself. In the spring the weeds grew high, and I could lie peacefully hidden in the tall grass, staring at the sky. There was a church next to it and I'd sit on the grass behind it, away from everyone else. The churchyard had these craggy, short gnarled trees, and it reminded me of that line from the Eno song "Burning Airlines Give You So Much More" about "strangely stunted trees." My records were my friends, my records got me through. These are my favorite memories of high school.

While I struggled with my own sense of self and frustration there was actually an openly gay guy my age at my high school. He was such an effeminate doormat that I just couldn't relate. I hated seeing him picked on, and I considered trying to be friends with him, but he just seemed too pathetic. When I would half open my mind to the idea that perhaps I was gay, I would think of him and realize how utterly different he was from me, and if *that* was gay, I certainly wasn't *that*. Ironically, I had first noticed him in seventh grade when we were both enrolled in a "social dance class" at the YMCA. The nicely dressed boys and girls were segregated on different sides of the room. We were schooled in such niceties as signing a girl's dance card. We learned to do the box step and other simple formal dances. Apart from one "ladies" choice, the males did all the choosing. It was heterosexist patriarchal propaganda, and though I felt completely ill at ease, I coped better and stood out less than him.

My mom was really good during these years. I think she wanted to get me out of my room and out from under my headphones, so she would let me borrow the car when I wanted and even kept the gas tank full. I drove all over Peoria and the surrounding area, looking for something, anything interesting. Though I rarely found it, at least I could get to the record stores and escape into my music.

She also put up with all my anger and frustrations, but somehow managed to assuage me enough to get me through things. Once I told her that I was so pissed off with school that I would refuse to smile for my senior yearbook picture. I told her I didn't want to look like just another happy student at my wonderful suburban high school. She threw a major fit, so I fucking smiled, goddamn it. That made *her* happy; at least one of us was. I told her that I didn't want to go through cap and gown graduation ceremonies; it was another way of removing our identities, identical sheep sent off to the slaughterhouse of adulthood. She totally freaked out. We had a major argument; I asked her, "Would it *really* make you that happy if I put on this little costume and went through this silly ceremony?" "*Yes!!!*" she shrieked. My mom rarely shrieked. "All right," I said, "I'll do this for you." Superficial appearances had triumphed again. I graduated with a B+ average. It was May of 1978, and high school was finally over.

Mom wanted me to get out of Peoria, but I was so disillusioned that it just didn't matter to me. They pushed for me to go to college, again saying it would be the time of my life, but I had heard that about high school and was definitely suspicious. Without other alternatives, I passively went along and didn't resist. I went to college at the University of Illinois in Champaign, Illinois. By the second day, I felt liberated and free. College was much better than high school. I got involved with the student radio station and wrote record reviews for the college paper. I ended my high school zine but contributed to others. I had some great classes but did most of my learning at the radio station. I was on the air at least fifteen hours a week my last three years and was music director my final year there. The station was an odd hybrid—a 3000-watt commercial station with a fifty-mile radius, run by students. We played mainstream and underground stuff, from REO to R.E.M. It was shitty having to program Whitesnake in between Nick Lowe and The Buzzcocks, but its crossover audience gave it local influence far beyond most college stations.

During that time I started playing guitar and writing songs, which I'd wanted to do for ages. I bought my first guitar and came out of the closet six weeks apart in 1980, when I was twenty. The two events are intertwined; I was finally doing the things I wanted to do but had felt unable to do before.

It took me a while to figure out the gay thing. A turning point came when I met an incredible girl. She was smart, cute, and British, and quite knowledgeable about the music happening there. She tortured the girls in her dorm with X-Ray Spex's "Oh Bondage! Up Yours" single, just as I had tortured my freshman roommate with their single "Identity." Here was the person I'd been waiting for, and I just couldn't be more than friends. That's when I really knew for sure. Turned out she was a lesbian; I came out shortly thereafter, and we had a good laugh. She later became the head of the Women's Studies department at a large West Coast university.

My first sexual experience was right after I turned twenty-one, with a guy I met at an Ultravox concert. He invited me over to his attic apartment. It was February and cold, so we got down to it pretty quick. I thought it would be awkward fucking another guy—positions and everything—but I was amazed how easy it went and how natural it felt. I remember that once I was inside him, I was off to the races, pumping as fast as I could. "Slow down!" he counseled me, and it was great. I was naïve in that I wasn't even sure two guys could fuck face-to-face; I was romantic and wanted to kiss while fucking, and learning it could be done that way was a great relief. Had the

Internet been around back then I would have done plenty of watching before doing, but like Lou Reed said, "Those were different times."

It was the only time I had sex with that guy; we got together one other time but didn't really do much. As it turned out, he had a boyfriend—and they were both born-again Christians. What's more, his boyfriend also worked at my college ratio station—he did the Sunday morning Christian show! To be with me, he was cheating. So much for Christian values!

Coming out was a rude awakening for me. I knew about The Village People, but I didn't realize gay culture meant you had to like disco *or else*. When I began visiting Champaign's biggest gay bar (called, er, The Bar) in 1981 and quickly discovered that my tastes were considered different, I naïvely figured I'd be accepted because there weren't that many of us around; we'd have to support each other. Ha! I couldn't believe I was being ostracized for liking The Psychedelic Furs and The Clash, but I was. So I stopped going there. I already had my own tastes and opinions; I wasn't about to change them to suit somebody else's notion of correctness.

Champaign's underground music scene, however, was turning out to be more productive and successful for me and more accepting of my tastes than its gay scene, so I turned my focus there. After having played and written for a couple of years, I decided to put together a band called The Outnumbered. We were inspired by a terrific local band called The Vertebrats, who basically invented the local music scene in Champaign. They had great original songs, but broke up too soon; their best known song "Left in the Dark" was covered by The Replacements and Uncle Tupelo, and at one point Courtney Love was performing it live. Over their three-year lifespan I saw them at least a hundred times.

In The Outnumbered I was the main songwriter and singer,

but the only gay member. I wasn't in the closet, but I didn't want to sing directly about being gay. The clues were there, albeit lurking between the lines. I recall talking on the phone to Dena about being more open in the lyrics. She pointed out that were I to be more out, we'd be known as "that gay band," immediately consigned and filed away. Although I wanted to be out, it didn't seem fair to the straight band members to throw away any possible success for that reason alone. Besides, I couldn't see any potential audience for such a move; I could think of a mere handful of people who might like it, no more. Since our lyrics strove to be as honest as possible, it was painful to hold back speaking directly about a subject so important to me. If I was honestly happy I'd write about being happy, but if what I was feeling was depressing, so be it; I didn't want to censor those feelings, but to get to the core of the matter. I wanted to communicate true emotions, but I still couldn't say all that I would have liked.

The Outnumbered was fairly successful during our years together from '82–'87. We were '60s influenced, mixing garage-rock and British Invasion with punk; our idea was to fuse The Byrds with The Ramones, a jangly crunch. We were ambitious and managed to record and release three albums, two of which were released on the influential indie label Homestead. They'd heard a song of ours we'd done for a compilation, and when we sent them a demo they liked it and signed us. Our label mates at the time included Sonic Youth, Nick Cave, Big Black, Dinosaur Jr., and Swans (none of whom we ever played with). We played shows as often as we could, did several short tours, and managed to see a lot of the country. We didn't sell a lot of records, but a few people liked them, and it felt important to do them. My favorite write-up, from an album review in *Spin* magazine, called us "a feminist garage band." We were a really good band, and I look back on that music fondly. Though other musicians in town were more talented, we had more moxie to get off our asses and get things accomplished.

After graduating college in '83 (with a degree in Communications), I worked in a record store and pursued my musical interests. I even ended up co-deejaying a Tuesday New Wave Night at The Bar thanks to a supportive dyke who recruited me. It was a great experience, and we packed the club with a very mixed crowd, which not everyone liked. I earned enmity from some of the gay in-crowd and was dumped when the club was sold that summer. This furthered the disconnect between who I felt I was and who I was supposed to be as an out gay man.

I was out of the closet but still leading a double life. I'd come out to my friends (some of whom were very surprised to find out I was gay, though others had figured it out) and band mates (it didn't matter either way to them), but I didn't "look" obviously gay. Though open about it, I wasn't broadcasting it. My gay life and straight life were almost totally separate; I didn't wish for such a distinction, but overlap was minimal. I thought I might meet other gay guys by doing what I did, but in five years of playing over two hundred gigs with The Outnumbered, I met only two. My straight friends and acquaintances were accepting of (or at least not bothered by) my gayness, but my involvement with rock and punk music made me feel like a pariah in Champaign's gay scene. I never liked disco or '80s dance floor stuff, and that's what I felt you were supposed to like if you were gay. A friend of mine overheard a bitchy gay coworker from the record store where I was working tell a table of gay friends that I couldn't really be gay because *I liked Bob Dylan*!

I felt like I had to make a choice between leading a gay life or a musical life, and for the next five years music won. Though I tried finding ways to blend the two, it seemed to be either/or. When I was in high school and college, liking punk rock would sometimes get you called faggot. But if you *were* a faggot, well, fags generally hated punk, although some fetishized the punk look—which I didn't have, and had never had, even when I was first listening to punk. Trying to look like Johnny Rotten or Joey Ramone seemed pointless to me. Maybe gay guys living in New York liked punk rock, but I wasn't living there.

In 1985, when I was twenty-five and still working at the record store, I started booking occasional rock shows in Champaign. I was tired of having to drive two and a half hours to Chicago to see the bands I liked, so I brought Jonathan Richman, The Replacements, The Feelies, The Del Fuegos, Robyn Hitchcock, The Minutemen, Guadalcanal Diary, Dumptruck, Volcano Suns, and other groups I liked. Since Champaign had a good college radio station but not so savvy club bookers, booking agents were happy to help me bring their smaller bands. The shows were mostly successful (I even made a little bit of money), and that was The Outnumbered's best year too. I was having a great time except for one thing—I didn't have sex the entire year I was twenty-five.

By the latter half of '86, I decided to give the gay bar scene another chance. I was a bit more successful this time around, finally getting laid once in a while but not having any luck in the boyfriend department. Case in point: in the summer of 1987, I briefly dated a really cute guy who was part of the "ruling clique" at one of the gay bars. During this time, The Outnumbered was winding down, and we were playing our final shows before disbanding. I badly wanted this guy I liked to see me play, and on several occasions he'd promised to go, each time failing to show. On the night of our last show, a friend spotted him dancing at the gay bar instead, and once again it illustrated the glaring gap between my musical life and gay life. I felt like I had to make a choice between them. Thus, with the band broken up, it seemed like time to work on the gay side of my life. For years I'd tried and failed to combine these major urges, so I gave up music, even though I'd wanted to do it since I was a little kid. I was tired of being lonely, and it seemed like I had no other choice. In 1988, I sold my amps and guitars and moved to Los Angeles, where I hoped a gay life could be successfully led. I consciously thought I'd never play in a band again, unless it could be a gay rock band. That idea was so preposterous that I was sure I'd strummed my last note. And when I wrote these lines in a notebook, I was certain they'd stay there:

We're the buttfuckers of rock & roll
We want to sock it to your hole.

CHAPTER 2

California and the
Birth of Pansy Division

In August 1988, I moved to Los Angeles not to play music, but to work in music. Tipped off by an Illinois friend and ex-roommate then working at Aron's Records on Melrose, I got a job as a sales rep at Jem, an independent record distributor. During the nine months I lived there I still wasn't able to bridge the gaps in my life; I found no passage to any hidden gay rock underground, and couldn't find any gay music scene without that disco thump thump thump. I discovered well after the fact that there was a sort of queer punk scene (more of an art scene, really), but I never ran across it. It was too underground for me to have stumbled across, and that brings up the major problem with living in L.A.—it is so vast and spread out that it makes it difficult to discover like-minded people.

It was the first big city I'd lived in, and it was hard getting the hang of meeting people. I met a couple of guys via the personals who shared my frustrations (one of whom had been in a band in the early days of L.A. punk), but I still felt pretty isolated. While there I had some "only in L.A." experiences. I ended up on a date with a blond wannabe actor who'd just appeared on "Solid Gold," and went on another date (to see the movie *Child's Play*) with a guy who was *so* into dolls that he made them for various movie and TV productions. One guy I met particularly exemplifies my L.A. experience. He was a good photographer; an artsy guy, needy but all right. Through his photography he had managed to become acquainted with Hope Sandoval from Mazzy Star and Exene from X. Over a period of months, every conversation with him of at least five minutes in duration included at least one reference to one or the other, if not both. Living vicariously through them, he attached way too much importance to knowing them. It got to be a joke. It was nice to get laid once in a while, but I wasn't really connecting.

I never really did feel in synch with L.A. I joined ACT-UP L.A. at the beginning of '89, and was just getting to know people there when I moved away. Jem was slowly going out of business, and I got laid off. I applied for a job with another indie record distributor called Rough Trade, but I didn't get the L.A. gig. They liked me, though, and offered me a position at their office in San Francisco, so I moved there in May 1989, where I discovered *Homocore*, a great San Francisco zine that was radical, sexual, political, and punky. Around that time I also discovered *JD's*, another great homocore zine, done out of Toronto by G.B. Jones of Fifth Column (the only queer rock/punk band I knew of predating Pansy Division) and Bruce LaBruce. I had doubts about the word *core* part of *homocore*—I've never been into hardcore punk.

And the version of punk I liked was Version 1.0—the late '70s originals, before it became a routine. Queer punk zines existed before there were queer rock bands; the concept preceded the reality. If any bands existed at that point, they were so low profile as to be invisible, like Fifth Column, whose records I'd never seen in any store, and I was definitely looking.

Rough Trade was a great place to work. One of my coworkers was Donna Dresch, who later formed the dyke rock band Team Dresch. There were some queer musicians on the label—the dyke folk-rock band Two Nice Girls, and the British rock band Kitchens of Distinction, whose bassist/singer was that rarity, an out (rather than coyly androgynous) gay musician. Kitchens had a few songs that were gaily suggestive, but it wasn't the main focus of the band; still, drawings of muscle men graced their record sleeves. Two Nice Girls bridged the gap between tame Women's Music traditions and a more lively rock sound; it was their loudest songs like "She-Ra" and the in-your-face "The Queer Song" that I found most exciting.

The AIDS crisis was the most urgent gay issue of the day, so I joined ACT-UP San Francisco, finding others who had just moved to the city and were looking to make a difference. I had moved to San Francisco at a propitious time; a friend who had moved to the city in 1986 said AIDS had made the city seem like a morgue. By 1989, a lot of younger gays had moved to town, rejuvenating the scene. I attended ACT-UP meetings nearly every week, going to demonstrations and other meetings outside the weekly group. Being here gave me the opportunity to be influential in a way I couldn't have been in the Midwest; what we were doing in ACT-UP was resonating all over the country. At this point I had no musical ambition; I was extremely surprised when someone I knew slightly from Illinois came to an ACT-UP meeting, and recognized me from The Outnumbered. What were the odds of that?

After several smaller demonstrations, my first large ACT-UP demonstration was October 4, 1989. This was the infamous ACT-UP police riot, where police blocked off Castro Street, arrested marchers, and declared martial law—keeping Castro Street sealed off for forty-five minutes, not letting people go in and out of shops and restaurants, detaining people who had no involvement with the demonstration. It was a total show of force, a giant fuck-you to ACT-UP and to gay activism. I saw a protestor who was newer in town than me (from a Utah Mormon family he wasn't out to) take too long to heed a police demand to move back onto the curb, get clubbed, and have a newspaper stand kicked over on him. Afterwards, I spoke to our toothless local Police Commission to give my version of the events, and discovered that the official report said the protester had been on top of the newspaper box and fallen off, which he hadn't. The cop knocked him down, then deliberately kicked the box on top of him. I gave my testimony, my word against the cop's. They believed the cop, of course.

ACT-UP gathered gays and lesbians angry at right-wing homophobia and the government's lack of response to the AIDS crisis. Though AIDS was the focal point, the brazen take-no-prisoners approach inspired other activism and art. So many people involved in the group had an enormous creativity and determination that it felt like the vanguard of the moment. I was still a ways away from creating my own inspiration from all this when I heard that a gay rock band was putting out an album.

In the autumn of 1989, Rough Trade carried a new album by a Milwaukee duo called The Frogs. I'd heard about them; they were described to me as a gay supremacist band. Their album, *It's Only Right and Natural*, was, ironically, on Homestead, The Outnumbered's old label. The cover had an adorable picture of a little boy wearing a pink triangle button. As I anxiously played the album, it quickly became clear that the band was straight and was using the gay shtick as a joke. (They later put on blackface and pretended to be black; a subsequent album from that period, *Racially Yours*, took over a decade to get released.) The lyrics were rife with potty humor, like something you'd expect from a couple of thirteen-year-olds who had just discovered dirty words.

It was *so* disappointing—and the music was dull, dreary folk-rock, very unexciting stuff. But it pointed up one thing: *straight* musicians had realized it was time for a gay rock band, even if gay people hadn't. It didn't bother me that they were straight; if it had been truly funny and clever, I'd have given them credit for the concept and laughed right along. But their jokey condescension was exploitative, making fun of the idea of being gay. It was as if they assumed no one would call them on their insincerity. With no gays visible in rock music, who would raise a fuss? (I later met gay guys who'd been desperate enough to find an out gay group that they bought the fraudulent thing, since the real thing was nowhere in sight).

By 1989, it seemed like you could do anything in popular music but be gay. It was the last taboo. N.W.A were violent and homophobic and number one on the charts. Then, within a year, the atmosphere suddenly changed; straight bands were doing gay-friendly songs (The Mekons's "Empire of the Senseless," Billy Bragg's "Sexuality"), or singing songs, covers usually, which were sung to a "he" (The Lemonheads's version of "Different Drum," Superchunk's "Train from Kansas City"). One of my favorite bands, The Fall, did the thoughtful "Van Plague." But after investigation, it appeared they all were straight. The time was so ripe that enlightened straights were singing gay-friendly lyrics, but where were the open queers? Oddly, bands that I believed had gay members, like The Smiths, Hüsker Dü, and R.E.M. (a guy I'd slept with claimed to have slept with their singer in 1986) were neither specific nor open at that time.

Rock was one of the major American cultural forms of the twentieth century. Why weren't queers doing it? Had gays decided to stick to the margins because the margins were where we were better accepted? Had we segregated ourselves, disallowing rock as a gay activity? This was the music I (and millions of others) had grown up with. Why shouldn't I want to play it?

There had been queer rock stars, but they were always cloaked in an air of ambiguity, and they all later renounced their queer club memberships. David Bowie retracted his bisexuality, claiming he was just experimenting. Lou Reed went from singing "no kinds of love are better than others" in 1968 to "only a woman can love a man" in 1982. Prince asked the musical question "Am I straight…or gay?" then emphatically answered, I'm straight, I'm straight! Freddie Mercury, who my friend Alex (cover star of our first album) used to see with boyfriends in gay bars in L.A. in the '80s, finally came out as bisexual on his hospital bed the day before he died. Everywhere I looked, gay meant Stigma Attached.

Rock was heterosexual by default. You were assumed to be hetero unless stated otherwise. Only in the uncontested terrain of disco and show tunes were things different. People like Jimmy Somerville (Bronski Beat, Communards), Andy Bell (Erasure), and Sylvester, all of whom I respect for being out, made out gay dance music that ironically made me feel marginalized and isolated. It was gay bar music, and in the gay bar setting disco transformed gay men from people into product, a soundtrack for conformity. All of this was reinforcing my *Invasion of the Body Snatchers* theory of gay men.

As soon as they realize they're gay, they become pod people who suddenly start spouting catty movie dialogue, keep poodles as pets, and buy disco and Judy Garland records. *That* was "gay culture." It just didn't make sense to me. Shortly before I left Illinois, I had dated a twenty-year-old who had all these qualities and it totally depressed me. How had he gotten so indoctrinated? How had I become such a freak? I wasn't ashamed of being gay, but I was ashamed at the irrelevance of gay culture to my own personal experience. I wasn't willing to give up my identity and individuality for the sake of being what other people thought being gay really meant. I rejected "gay conformity" just as I did "heterosexual conformity."

Gay culture seemed so second rate; we were supposed to like it 'cause it was gay. Fuck that. I was stubborn and demanded the impossible. I wasn't getting much out of gay culture. Instead of adjusting to gay culture, I wanted gay culture to adjust to me. But I hadn't figured out how to do that…yet.

The activist crowd from ACT-UP spawned a social scene. First was Club Chaos, a Thursday night club full of people who had just come from the ACT-UP meeting. After we'd outgrown that space, Club Uranus was born, and lasted for a couple of years. Uranus was a very popular underground club that happened on Sunday nights. An alternative to the regular gay dance club scene, it was performance art, drag, activism, and sex all rolled into one. This was where I went to meet guys, though I was only somewhat successful. It was fun, but as with all scenes, to succeed you have to make yourself into a product. I remember someone telling me I looked too Midwestern. I took it to mean I didn't look contrived, and I liked that.

The music here was better than at other gay clubs, but

it only went so far. They played some good songs, but they played them every week—"Kerosene" by Big Black, "Stigmata" by Ministry, and Anthrax's cover of Joe Jackson's "Got the Time." Then it would be back to industrial/early techno stuff. My least favorite song was "Cubik" by 808 State, which sounds like a car alarm and a garbage truck fighting it out to see who can be the loudest and most annoying. When I think of bad, numbingly loud and repetitive electronic dance music, this is what comes to mind. They played it every week (the "dance mix," of course), and eventually I started to take it personally. It represented the aural assault I had to endure in search of lust and/or love.

As had happened earlier in my life, it was women who started to inspire me. In December 1990, on my thirty-first birthday, Two Nice Girls performed at the Great American Music Hall in San Francisco. They played "The Queer Song" and asked for male go-go dancers from the crowd, so I climbed onstage and it felt great. The crowd loved it. Why the hell weren't guys doing anything like this? Though they crossed over into the Women's Music scene, Two Nice Girls also understood punk rock, though it was only occasionally reflected in their sound. Here was a group of women breaking the boundaries...where were the men?

Another woman I was quite inspired by around this time was artist/performer Karen Finley. I'd also seen her perform in San Francisco, and her LP *The Truth Is Hard To Swallow* was a favorite of mine. She opened her mouth and said whatever the fuck she wanted. She was righteous, fearless, uncensored, and spoke truth to power. Her critique of sexism and patriarchy was right on. I was waiting for a gay rock band to be as bold and forthright.

I had been searching for a band that would combine certain elements in a particular way. I suddenly realized the synthesis I wanted to hear—the brashness of "The Queer

Song," and the freedom of expression and total fearlessness embodied by Karen Finley. It finally dawned on me that the only way to hear such a band was to start it myself. The day after the 2NG show, I wrote the first lyrics I'd written in a couple of years. The song was called "Fem in a Black Leather Jacket." It named the desire and got specific. And it was funny; it wasn't a worthy but dull political treatise you could agree with but would never *love*. I sat in my room giggling as I worked. I wrote three other songs in about a week, on a borrowed acoustic guitar (I'd sold all my guitars two years earlier), laughed my head off, and pushed myself further with each one.

Around the same time, several other bands whose musical simplicity was refreshing, also became musical rejuvenators for me. The songs I was writing at the end of The Outnumbered were mostly in minor keys and had more complicated chord progressions. Listening to Galaxie 500, Beat Happening, and Jesus & Mary Chain, I felt confident that simple was okay. Given the kinds of themes I was now coming up with, I didn't want the music to overwhelm the words, but to complement them.

On a different tangent, I was also thinking about Malcolm McLaren. When he put together The Sex Pistols, he had the concept for a type of band he wanted to see that didn't yet exist. He helped make it a reality, and history changed. (Of course, I wanted to skip the part of the story about the lawsuits and mismanaged funds.) And I knew from my experiences in Champaign that being a great musician wasn't necessary for success if you had ideas, and I thought I had a great new idea.

In the first week of 1991 my roommate helped me record the first four songs on his four-track tape deck: "Fem in a Black Leather Jacket," "ANTHEM," "The Story So Far," and "Curvature." When I told my friends about the tape, some remarked that they hadn't even known I played music. I was expecting the worst, and I was quite startled by the response—it was overwhelmingly, gushingly positive. People said they were important songs, but all I knew was that they were important to me. Encouraged, I wrote several more.

The first straight people I played the tape for were my Rough Trade coworkers. Their enthusiasm and support surprised me. At this point I realized that the project needed a name. Above my desk was a bulletin board listing upcoming releases, including one by a dance act called Third Panzer Division. Glancing up at it, I misread it as Pansy Division, and chuckled to myself. I asked my office mates, "How about Pansy Division?" "That's really good!" they agreed. I liked it, and thought I'd use it until I came up with something better, but I was soon satisfied with it. I like that it borrows the name of a military tank from Germany, a country that systematically exterminated queers, and transforms its meaning.

All of this felt very freeing. I grew my hair long, which I had wanted to do for quite a while but had lacked the confidence. I wanted more of a rocker look. This happily coincided with the gay long hair moment, which I couldn't believe was happening—all the cute guys were growin' out this foxy hair. This lasted less than a year, and was quickly usurped by the goatee decade. (As I prefer androgyny over a masculine look, this was a setback.) But I wasn't yet ready to form a band. My experiences with The Outnumbered left me wanting to be less dependent on other people to make music; besides, I hadn't lived in San Francisco very long and I hardly knew any musicians. I thought Pansy Division might be just me, the same way Matt Johnson was The The. I continued writing songs, and by April I had ten of them, as well as a newly purchased Fender Stratocaster amp, so I invited about twenty people over to my house for a party/

concert. It was a great success and that night I was asked to play my first public show, at a benefit for the newly formed activist group Queer Nation.

The San Francisco ACT-UP chapter, which had grown tremendously since I first began going to their meetings, bitterly split into two factions in the fall of 1990. The split was in large part over development of AIDS drugs and who should get them; at that time, AIDS drugs were being tested but none had yet proven effective. One faction, mostly gay white men with a sense of entitlement, wanted drugs in bodies *now*. The other faction, which included most of ACT-UP's women and people of color as well as a certain number of GWMs, questioned who would have access to these drugs, and who these drugs would be tested on (would it just be rich white men?). I could understand both sides, but when one side (the white men) basically took their marbles and left, continuing with it seemed futile. If we couldn't agree, how could we fight our enemies? The whole thing was very dispiriting.

Queer Nation was in its ascendance at this point, a development I had hoped would take pressure off of ACT-UP. Much of what happened at ACT-UP meetings consisted of people bringing up issues that were gay-oriented rather than AIDS-oriented. As it was the most visible and successful gay activist organization, people flocked to it for the possibility of airing their grievances and sharing their ideas. This was necessary in a larger context but sidetracked us from focusing completely on AIDS issues. After two years of ACT-UP meetings, my patience for group process was low, so I went to just a couple Queer Nation meetings (though I attended their actions, such as the kiss-ins).

I felt that forming Pansy Division was my way of doing activism, albeit cultural rather than overtly political. My ACT-UP and Queer Nation experiences made it seem like now was the right time and place to do what I'd thought of a few years before. When I played at the Queer Nation benefit, I could see that not everyone was ready for this. Though loved by some, my rendition of "The Cocksucker Club" helped clear the room (especially of dykes, sadly). However, soon after that I met some dykes on the same wavelength; my next appearance, at the queer underground cabaret Klubstitute, was with a group I hadn't heard of, the all-dyke band Tribe 8. It was my second public appearance, and it was theirs as well. But they had a whole band! It was crude but effective, and I was blown away. They were a perfect female parallel to what I was trying to do; to hell with the hopeful maybe of "Somewhere Over the Rainbow," we wanted it *now,* not some indefinite someday.

At the Klubstitute show, a couple of guys volunteered to go-go dance. They went over well, and then it wasn't just me up there with a guitar. I asked them to dance at future gigs, and for a while we were known for our dancers as much as the music. But I was still leery of forming a band; I knew how much work it took, and I feared this specific, pure concept I had would get watered down.

Pansy Division happened at the moment when the word *queer* was suddenly on everyone's tongues. It reclaimed an epithet and brandished it as a weapon. PD is a product of that moment, but as we carried on we also helped define the moment, hastening its evolution. When I came to San Francisco in '89, the word *homocore* was being spread; by '91, it had evolved into *queercore,* with which PD was tagged. Doubtlessly this book will be described as being about queercore band Pansy Division, but since we began a further evolution has occurred, and we don't use it to describe our band anymore. It presents a misleading image of raw noise with gay lyrics that doesn't take into account the pop qualities of our sound. While too raw for mainstream rock, we're way too poppy and wimpy for many punk fans. I'm comfortable in that spot, but it makes for a less snappy description.

At the beginning of '91, I began a DJ night with a couple of other queer rockers, including Don Baird, the rock columnist for the *San Francisco Bay Times*. (A gay paper with a rock column? I wasn't in Peoria anymore. Or L.A.) It was called Faint of Heart, then later Rock & Roll Queer Bar. Successful as a monthly club, we went weekly about halfway through the year. My idea was that if gays would go to clubs to dance to music whose performers they were unaware of, they'd do the same at a gay rock club. We played a number of danceable but often obscure songs we liked, many of which were current. We didn't want to do an oldies night, but we'd have drawn better if we had played more early '80s stuff. Just as we were getting the hang of it, our bar got sold, and we were orphaned. Though we hunted for another location, the project dribbled to a halt as I got busier with Pansy Division.

During the time of Rock & Roll Queer Bar, I had planned a trip back to Champaign for a wedding. I had been sending my four-song tape around to various friends, including an old pal from the Champaign music scene, Kent Whitesell. He loved the demo and was the first person outside a close circle of gay friends in San Francisco who saw its potential. He seemed to think it could be huge, which I found preposterous; I thought maybe *some* people would like it. Since he'd just opened a recording studio, he had offered to record me for cheap if I ever got back to Illinois. I took him up on his offer, thinking this would be a good opportunity to get together with people from back home to make a demo to play for any prospective band mates. I also had the idea that I could use the bass and drum tracks as a backing tape for playing live; it would buy me some time before I figured out what to do next. Also, I rewrote The Ramones song "Rock & Roll High School" as a theme song for my club, called

"Rock & Roll Queer Bar," and couldn't wait to get back and blow people's minds with it.

Kent got our friend (and his ex-band mate) Chris Bowe to play bass, and recruited a drummer I barely knew to play drums (little did I know that this first drummer would put in motion a revolving door of drummers who'd come and go). Even though Patrick Hawley (drummer number one) had no rehearsal before we went in to the studio—I discussed arrangements with him the day before, but we didn't have a chance to practice them—he was so great that what had begun as a demo came out as finished product. Of the thirteen songs we recorded, nine were used on the first album: "Versatile," "Bunnies," "The Story So Far," "Hippy Dude," "The Cocksucker Club," "Crabby Day," "Luck of the Draw," "Rock & Roll Queer Bar," and "ANTHEM."

Returning to San Francisco, I discovered the backing tracks didn't work out well in a live situation. It was tough coordinating the cues, especially in little clubs with meager sound systems. I played a few shows that summer by myself, sometimes with dancers, sometimes not. A friend of mine got me a free show at the place he tended bar. I did two sets alone (no backing tapes), learning a few covers to fill out the set. One of my best friends attended, and by chance he ran into a straight couple he knew who were there to see another act on the bill. I got up there, played my songs—in a straight bar—and they were, as he put it, "absolutely astounded." The subject matter was so out there, but delivered in a casual, forthright manner, and his friends were stunned and amazed. Given the social atmosphere of the time, they said I had a lot of guts to do what I was doing—that I was really putting myself on the line. At this point I felt driven; this was a time when underground gay cinema was on the rise, gaining bigger audiences partly as a response to the dearth of real gay characters in movies and TV. I was wondering why there hadn't been a musical equivalent, and felt determined to make that happen.

By now I was ready to look for a band. This was a sign of my own evolving ambition and sense of possibilities. However, even in San Francisco I'd had trouble meeting queer rockers, so, doubting I'd get a response (and expecting prank phone calls) I placed this ad:

> Guitarist/singer looking for bassist and drummer
> to form openly gay rock band. Influences:
> Ramones, Buzzcocks, early Beatles.

The ad ran in the *San Francisco Bay Guardian* and *SF Weekly*, two alternative weekly papers. (The gay papers didn't have Musician Wanted advertising; the *Bay Times* tried putting my ad under Help Wanted, which I resisted as it was hardly a paying gig. They didn't even have a Hobbies/ Shared Interest section, so I had to convince them to create one.) The puzzle pieces were about to come together.

CHAPTER 3

The Band Takes Shape:
Chris Freeman

Chris Freeman answered my ad. He said he'd been waiting ten years to read an ad like mine. We'd had similar experiences being gay in a predominantly hetero rock scene. He had moved to San Francisco from Seattle in 1987, after toiling in various bands there for almost a decade. Shortly after he'd left Seattle, which had been very dead for music in '86 and '87, the scene there exploded. Chris was sorry that he hadn't been there to witness it firsthand, but he'd tried out for some of those bands and had never gotten the gig, being as out as he was. He even knew a number of the people involved early on in Sub Pop; a lot of them worked together at Muzak! He had actually hired Mark Arm of Mudhoney to work there. Though it's now a hip, happening place on the international rock scene, Chris's experience with Seattle in the '70s and

'80s was of a narrow-minded provincial city without much going on, "like a Mayberry with skyscrapers," he called it.

I gave him the demo, which he then took on a European trip with his boyfriend. While on a train in Switzerland, he popped the tape in his Walkman. He said he laughed so loud and hard that people stared, embarrassing his boyfriend. I took his reaction as a great compliment. Also, Chris was six foot five and a Beatles freak; The Outnumbered had a six foot three Beatles freak bassist, so I figured it was my fate, at five six, to be towered over this way.

I asked Chris to join and he accepted. He was in three rather low-key bands when we met. Now playing in four bands at once, he figured PD would be the least likely to succeed. Still, I could tell that Chris had the right personality and disposition to do these songs. Not everyone had the nerve to play them. Here were songs that were unapologetic and blunt. No hiding behind euphemism. No hunting for hints between the lines. No apologies. It was our way of fighting back at a time when gay sexuality was under right-wing attack. The Outnumbered's songs reflected the frustration and desperation of the Reagan era, where the political seemed to be crushing the personal. It was music you could respect and appreciate, but it was sometimes like embracing barbed wire. Now I wanted a band that people could truly enjoy, which would make people feel joyful. The '80s had been too frustrating; I wanted the '90s to be happier. I wanted music that would transform my frustrations into something fulfilling.

It was about freedom, too. We get the free speech idea drummed into us in school in this country, even if most people don't really want you to speak freely, but to conform and use the rhetoric of being free. (Advertising and Republicans have fully co-opted this.) I felt like I had nothing to lose, and thought I should take advantage of the fact that these things *could* be said instead of just hoping that someday someone else might eventually say them. It felt patriotic. We had freedom, so we ought to use it.

A few months after we began playing together, Chris turned to me and said, "Hey! This stuff has political meaning!" I said, "Duh, took you long enough!" My plan was to use humor and tell stories to convey the songs' viewpoints; I hate self-righteous singers for whom the message is so important and heavy that their music is like taking medicine. Another advantage of singing songs about personal politics was that they tended to age better than songs about specific topical events.

We figured our audience would be people like us, disaffected queers of a certain age who'd grown up loving rock music. The gay ostracism Chris and I had both experienced as rock-loving queers led us to believe this audience was small, but at least we'd be there for them and they'd *love* us! Maybe we could make albums, and use our annual two-week vacations to play out of town. To us that was an ambitious goal.

Still, we lacked a drummer. (Patrick Hawley back in the studio in Champaign had been a one-time thing.) The first ad hadn't turned up any, and no realistic candidates had answered a series of ads that followed. For our first show together we used taped drums, and it fairly stunk. We resolved to not play again until we found a drummer, and asked friends for leads. We had recorded one early session with Chris's roommate, Sally Schlosstein (drummer number two) who was just learning drums, but she was just temping to help us out. We located Jay Paget (drummer number three) through a friend, singer/guitarist Barbara Manning. Jay was playing in Thinking Fellers Union Local 282, and after we'd met him he agreed to join us as a side project. With him we were finally a complete band, so we had pictures taken and started hunting for gigs.

So far we had played queer venues exclusively. We were wary of "straight" music clubs; even in San Francisco we worried about gay bashings. We finally crossed the line doing a gig at the Chameleon on Valencia Street. We had worried over nothing; there were no homophobic incidents, and the reception was stunningly positive. It went so well that we got another gig there a few weeks later, this time playing with Tribe 8. With our four go-go dancers (now co-sexual), it was a watershed event.

During this set, my friend Will told me later he was seemingly cruised by a guy who had his arms around a woman. Will and this guy kept trading glances. We were playing "Versatile":

There's a few straight guys I've known
There's a few straight guys I've blown…

Will gently but swiftly turned to the guy and looked at him with some serious let's-hook-up intent, but the guy rather sadly looked at the floor and shook his head no. I loved hearing stories like this!

We got gigs in other clubs around town and started attracting a following. We were a "demo tape of the week" pick in the *San Francisco Bay Guardian,* and later on they named us "Best New Local Band." We opened for bigger local bands like Jawbreaker and Voice Farm (who had just won the *SFBG's* award for "Best Local Band,") playing at Slim's, which had just won the same paper's award for "Best Local Club." We had made cassettes of our album to sell, bringing them to several book and record stores in the Castro. What's more, people were actually buying them! Locally, we were getting on the map.

Compared to mine, PD bassist Chris Freeman's young life had been much tougher, tumultuous, and dramatic.

His conception was an accident (broken condom); there's an eleven year difference between Chris and his youngest natural sister. He didn't even know his parents well; workaholic dad, indifferent mother. Instead, he knew his sisters well, since they did the bulk of caring for him. By the time he'd reached age seven his parents were fighting really bad, and when he was ten they finally split up.

When his abusive mother was found to be an unfit parent, he was sent back to his dad, which he was very happy about. But since his dad remarried immediately, he had four new brothers and a "Brady Bunch" type situation. Two of Chris's stepbrothers would tease him mercilessly, threatening him if he mentioned anything about it to his dad. Estranged from everyone in his family at this point (his sisters had grown up and moved out of the house), Chris spent a great deal of time during childhood making friends with the radio.

His father moved the family around a lot looking for work. Chris went to nine different schools—three elementary, four junior high, and two high schools, all over Washington state, a triangle from Lopez Island, to Aberdeen, to Grand Coulee, with points in between. Realizing that he could start over each time, he got good at meeting people and figuring out who to be friends with. Still, he was teased a lot: everyone seemed to realize that he was gay before he did. Though he had girlfriends, people still called him faggot. He hit puberty very late and was teased about that in gym class; it probably helps explain his boyish looks today.

His dad advised Chris to go into the service (like he had), and become a dentist. Though he tried to get Chris interested in different things, the only thing Chris really liked was music, which his father could not stand. As a Navy man, he felt that was "one step up from being a prostitute, working in a club somewhere where there's whores—the musicians sit in back while the whores do their thing." Chris wanted to do the polar opposite of what his dad wanted, causing years of friction.

In 1974, in eighth grade, he moved to Aberdeen, later famous for being Kurt Cobain's hometown. He hated Aberdeen so much he tried reuniting with his wreck of a mother, who was living in a trailer in Grand Coulee. Almost immediately he realized he'd made a major mistake, as living on an Indian reservation made him even more susceptible to getting beaten up. He lasted four months before going back to Aberdeen.

When Chris was about fourteen or fifteen, his dad offered him his savings to either "go to college or get his teeth fixed." Chris had a bad overbite, having sucked his thumb until he was ten; since he was planning on being a musician, he would have to look good, so he chose to get his teeth fixed. Unable to afford braces, he had eleven teeth pulled, including wisdom teeth and some weird ones that were growing in wrong. He had to sit for an hour everyday pushing back on all his teeth to straighten them out, but it worked.

In junior high he started realizing what was going on with him sexually, having crushes on his male teachers. Right about that time, when he was fourteen, the movie *Cruising* had come out, and reading about it he thought that if that's what gay was, that wasn't him. So after deciding he wasn't gay, then facing that he really was gay, his solution was to give his life to Jesus Christ. He threw himself into Bible study with the aim of becoming a minister. He studied with a minister who gave him some solid advice: "Look at the history of the Bible, because you can't take it at face value." Realizing the Bible was, in Chris's words, "a ridiculous made-for-TV piece of crap—whole sections cut out, things reworded, all of Jesus's references to reincarnation cut out"—he lost his faith.

Around this time he got into Alice Cooper, Kiss, and Elton John. He liked the flashy clothes and wild haircuts, but it was really about liking the songs as well. It was Kiss, with their "comic book, horror movies, Beatle-ish melodies but still heavy," that made him realize he wanted badly to be a musician. This drew the line—it was pretty tough reconciling listening to Kiss and trying to be a Christian.

Besides, at fifteen or sixteen he realized that Christ wasn't taking away his gayness—it was getting worse. He almost had his first gay experience in the bathroom of a mall.

"I had stopped off in the mall to go record shopping, and I had to go to the bathroom. In the bathroom was this guy who was cruising me but I had no clue, just didn't know. He said, 'Do you need a ride somewhere?' and I said, 'I'm just going to my job at McDonalds,' and I just about got in the car when I realized what was really going on. And it flashed in my mind—*Cruising*! I'm going to get killed! So I fled, and I never had that experience." After that, at sixteen, he pursued having sex with girls in his high school. Despite his functioning properly, it didn't feel as exciting as he expected.

His dad and stepmother wouldn't allow him to go to concerts until he was sixteen, so reaching that age was joyous: just four days later he got to see Kiss with Cheap Trick. However, less than a month prior to that, he missed seeing Led Zeppelin, despite pleading with his stepmom that he'd be sixteen in two weeks anyway.

By now he was attending high school in Seattle. Contrary to my avoidance of the druggie crowd, Chris realized that selling drugs to people was an effective way to keep them from beating you up. He sold acid and speed, "high school shit drugs." During his junior year, his dad found a joint in one of Chris's pockets and kicked him out of the house. Just like that. Moving to the University District of Seattle, he spent his first income tax refund on a bass and did basically everything his dad didn't want him to do. He had a job at Shakey's Pizza Parlor at night, and the manager (who saw that Chris was a hard worker—though he didn't see Chris spitting on the pizzas of nasty customers) cosigned a lease so Chris could get an apartment. Having his own place made him cool with people at school—"Yeah, come on over, I'll sell you some drugs, I got my own place." By sophomore year he already realized the futility of high school—he hated being there, hated being teased. But he decided that music would be his career, so he took everything musical—chorus, piano, guitar, theory—adding basics like typing and accounting in his senior year. To keep from being beaten up, he took every class possible (no study halls), graduating early on Valentine's Day 1979. He skipped commencement and his senior picture, things I'd done to appease my mom, and went to work instead of college. He began playing music with other people, and quickly learned that there was an abundant supply of guitarists and a shortage of bassists.

He did not get kicked out of the house for being gay. When living at home, he'd been having sex with girls (with his dad giving him condoms); Chris was even engaged at one point. But when that fell apart, he had a clean slate, so he thought, *I'll try it*. He met a guy at the Arboretum in Seattle, though he didn't know it was a cruisy area, it was just where you went to go swimming. "He thought it was cool that I was a musician and we hung out a little bit, and the third time we got together to go to a Waitresses concert he sprung it on me—that he was gay, and wanted to do it with me. Here was my chance. To this day, that guy had the biggest dick I have ever had up my ass."

"During sex with him all the bells and whistles went off. Everything I always wanted happened during sex, so I thought, *I'm not going to pretend anymore, I'm just going to tell everybody and separate the wheat from the chaff.* I told my sisters, my dad, and my stepmom—I told them I was bi though—cause I didn't know it was going to be an exclusive thing, and I thought it might soften the blow. Instead my dad just went off on me, saying I was the black sheep of the family and I would end up in jail. I thought, *Fuck you, I'll show you. I'm going to be successful despite everything you said.* It took nine years for my dad and me to discuss the subject again; then I realized that what he wanted was for me to be happy, and he just couldn't see it in the choices I was making.

After deciding he was gay, coming out was not hard. "My friends had already figured it out; the ones it did matter to were peripheral friends anyway. I had a sex buddy I was pretty much exclusive with. As soon as we had sex I was like the alien on his face, I couldn't be separated from him. He would take me out to certain clubs, and I was scared because of the idea of *Cruising*—which I hadn't even seen—but the whole idea of sleazy pickup bars creeped me out. I went to a few places with him and realized, god, they play *crappy* music in here. This was '82, and why were they playing these songs that were six and seven years old? They were playing disco, and I was really surprised; I hated disco when it came out, I really did, I liked pop, but the straight-up disco shit...ugh! I was there with the burn-The-Bee-Gees-records thing on the football field at my high school; I wanted rock! To find that gay people were listening to disco was abhorrent to me.

"Then we found a great place called Tug's, and when we walked in they were playing Soft Cell's 'Bedsitter' video and Nina Hagen's 'Smack Jack' video. There were crazy dark black-light walls; it was cool, and I thought this was where I could find a home. In that place I was meeting cool people, but it was a mixed bar, not necessarily a gay bar. So I was meeting just as many women as men. The guys there were kind of twisted misfits who were goth before goth had really taken off. So I really couldn't relate in a bigger way— I like hard rock and punk rock—but I stayed away from anyone who went to the other clubs 'cause I knew they played disco."

Just as I had experienced more acceptance in the music scene than in the gay scene, so did Chris. He knew only one gay person in the Seattle music scene—the singer from a band called Mental Mannequin. "They had this weird obviously gay lead singer named Upchuck," Chris relates. "I loved their band, kind of a strange punk rock Genesis, and got to be friends with their keyboard player Gordon Raphael (later producer of The Strokes). Later Upchuck had a band of his own called The Fagz, of which he was the only gay member. He was ultraflamboyant and had leopard-skin hair, which in Seattle in 1980 was really out of control. That was my social group, other musicians."

Chris eventually landed in a band called Attachments. "We were popular in Seattle with a certain group of people; we weren't hip by any means, but I thought we were a good '80s pop band. We thought we were marrying Eurythmics and Led Zeppelin...but what came out was the new wave Heart."

Eventually, Attachments started getting popular. They came very close to being signed by A&M Records. As one of the main songwriters, and since there were two female singers (hence the Heart comparison), Chris could "write songs without changing the pronouns, which was really nice." In 1985 they made an album with Terry Date (who later worked with Soundgarden, Rob Zombie, and—eeek— Limp Bizkit) and shopped it to A&M. A&M sent up a marketing team to groom the band, and it came out that Chris was gay. They said, "Well, you're just going to keep that quiet." As he was "just the bass player," the girl singers were going to be the ones interviewed the most anyway.

Because he was so anxious to be signed, Chris held his tongue. Then it got complicated: the record deal required designating one band member as manager, and that led to a series of ego trips, jealousies, power moves, and general strife that factionalized the band, with some members being fired just as contracts were ready to be signed. Boom...no more band.

"I floundered around trying to put something together, but by 1986 people weren't getting signed and were moving away, and there was this really damaging anti-postering law in Seattle. That was the year the scene died. This left a clean slate for Sub Pop to start with a while later on, but I knew all those people and knew I wasn't going to fit into a band with them, in part because I was gay."

Chris auditioned for bands, and when they'd find out he was gay, they would always choose someone else. He lied about it to get auditions, but later it would be, "Sorry, you just don't fit the profile." Though none of these bands became famous later, some of these people ended up in bands that got signed. After the experience with Attachments, where everyone had been welcoming about Chris being gay, it was a depressing time.

Embittered, Chris decided to move to L.A. Just before it was scheduled to happen, he used his vacation time to come to San Francisco with a group of friends. Despite never having visited before, he says, "We drove up to Twin Peaks and got drunk, and I said, 'This is the most beautiful view, and I'm going to move here.'" On his birthday weekend in August 1987, he gave his two-weeks' notice and moved to San Francisco along with the two other friends who had been tossed out of Attachments.

Chris was twenty-six, and he had dedicated himself to making it in the music business.

While it wasn't music biz central like L.A., San Francisco was a much more manageable city and had a far more active scene than Seattle had at that point. During this time, the San Francisco scene (like L.A.) was full of lousy rock and hair metal. After trying out for different bands, he hit a wall. As he describes it, "The last straw was a band called Model Citizenz. Their music was so interesting on one level, but so shitty on another level—the lyrics were so banal and dumb, but it featured the keyboard player from Spinal Tap, Viv Savage (aka David Kafinetti). *Oh my god, I'm playing with a guy from Spinal Tap!* I decided I wouldn't tell them I was gay. The musicianship was solid, but it was just too stupid."

He quit the band and decided he was ready to start dating. He had spent the first year and a half in San Francisco being celibate; moving to the hotbed of AIDS, he decided to keep to himself for a while, especially since his last relationship had come to a bitter end and he needed time to regroup. Like me, Chris had not been able to integrate the gay side of his life with the music side of his life. I had quit music to pursue being gay, and something similar happened to Chris. "I met a guy through a personal ad who I went out with for about three years. He was intrigued that I was a musician, but thought it would take too much time away from the relationship. So, I stopped playing music entirely and sold a bunch of my gear. But after six months I was itching to play again." This time, it would be different. His focus had been to find a band that would "make it." Now, nearing thirty, realizing that kind of career wasn't going to happen for him, he decided just to play music for fun. It would no longer be a career goal.

He got a job as a video editor, a creative and fun position that paid well. It felt like a corner had been turned. Then, one day: "I was reading the music ads in *SF Weekly*, and here was an ad for gay musicians, and I said '*What?* There actually are other gay musicians?' I hadn't met any except Upchuck (although years later I ran into some music scene people from Seattle and realized they were gay as well, but they had been closeted back then). The ad mentioned The Buzzcocks, early Beatles, and The Ramones, which was right up my alley, and it turned out to be Jon. I was like, 'Shit, ought to be interesting.'"

"So I was along for the ride. The first year was very fun, laughing about every new song Jon would play for me, going, 'Who's going to hear this?' At my job I'd regularly see Lynn Breedlove, a bike messenger at the time, and one day she said, 'What are you doing tonight?' And I said I had plans. And she said 'Oh, I'll talk to you about something later on.' We were both tentative with each other. Later on, we both showed up at the Chameleon, and she said, 'Is this what you are doing tonight?' And I said, 'Yeah, I'm in this band Pansy Division, are you in Tribe 8?' There was this shock, and we were instantly bonded, both playing in these queer bands, their Stooges to our Ramones, an interesting scene. It was very celebratory and fun, and I just thought no one is going to get it, it would be our little thing for fun. Jon had been saying, this record's almost done, we're going to finish it, and I was thinking, *Okay! Keep your dreams, Jon!* He was very diligent, and went around to Streetlight Records and A Different Light bookstore, consigning cassette tapes of an early version of *Undressed* and keeping track of the sales. And when Jon went looking for record labels we got bites, which I was shocked about. The Dead Kennedys's label was interested in us? I started getting more excited too, but in a way I couldn't because my partner hated Pansy Division and would never come see the band. I played him the tape after I joined and he hated it. I eventually had to break up with him, in part because I realized what I was doing in this band was going to be more important. Doing a project for fun was one thing, but he never would have supported me going on a tour—which was always my dream—or putting out a record."

CHAPTER 4

Finding a Label
and the First Release

Beginning in the autumn of 1991, I began mailing copies of the Illinois recordings to independent labels in the United States and Europe. I'd lost my job in May '91 when Rough Trade went bankrupt, and had gone to work for Dutch East India, an indie distributor that owned Homestead Records. Initially the only offer we had was from a tiny gay label, Significant Other; they were very supportive, but were so small we were afraid the record would be invisible. So we bided our time, hoping for a bite from a bigger label, convinced the time was right for a band like ours and worried someone would beat us to it. There was an article in *Option* magazine that summer about nascent queer rock bands, spotlighting L.A. queer country-punker Glen Meadmore (who we had not heard of at that point), and we were chomping at the bit to get our stuff out there.

To improve the album, we recorded a few new songs and redid a couple from the Illinois session. Patrick Hawley (drummer number one) called one day to announce he would be visiting San Francisco, and would we like to do some more recording with him? Jay's commitment to us was coming to an end (this side project was now taking up too much of his time), so we finished the album in July 1992 with Patrick, rerecording "Fem in a Black Leather Jacket" and "Surrender Your Clothing." *Undressed* was now complete; we also recorded four extra songs to release as singles.

In June we had a great time playing on a side stage at San Francisco's Gay Pride event. A memorable part of the show was the lesbian sign language interpreter, who had not been told in advance what we'd be singing about. She seemed awkward and embarrassed, but she valiantly translated the songs, looking a bit mortified having to put "We're the butt-fuckers of rock & roll, we want to sock it to your hole" into sign language.

Our last show with Jay was noteworthy. A guy we knew had the notion of putting on a clothing-optional gay dance party. It would have DJs and live music, and he thought we'd be the perfect band. None of us had done anything like it. We said we'd consider playing nude, but wouldn't commit to it ahead of time; we didn't want people showing up just to gawk. So we said yes to the performance, maybe to the nudity, depending on the vibe. But when we saw the flyers, they read:

Fags Au Natural—A Nude Rave. Performing Nude: Pansy Division

Gulp. Guess we were going to show it off in public.

The night of the show we did a sound check, then went

home to eat. We waited longer to go back to the club than we ordinarily would have; we were nervous, and wanted to postpone the moment of truth. When we finally arrived, the power had gone out to the sound system (the DJ setup was using too much juice). Ugh. The brightly lit room was two thirds empty, with maybe fifty people confusedly milling about. As we walked up the stairs we heard what sounded like live music, though we were supposedly the only live performers; to fill the silence, one of the go-go boys had gone onstage and, playing my guitar, sung a song called "Homo Truck Drivin' Man." More people gradually arrived, and by showtime there was a nice crowd of one hundred and fifty mostly nude men.

Tickets were ten dollars nude, fifteen clothed, with a limited number of clothed tickets available. Unfortunately, it was billed as a rave (a trendy phrase at that time in the Bay Area), though it wasn't in the slightest; you could sense this disappointment in some of the crowd. After working out the technical problems, we took off our clothes and went onstage to an enthusiastic response. Once we began, most of our nervousness disappeared. It also helped that the guitars covered most of our bits anyway (Jay had his drums to hide behind). Nonetheless, it was pretty damn weird seeing a crowd of nude men dancing with each other to our music. It was great! I even managed to get through it without sporting wood. (The irony is that certain band members later got into the habit of showing their members onstage, but you gotta start somewhere.)

Signs were posted throughout the club that read NO SEX. This was obeyed less and less as the evening went on. The night turned out well for me; I went home with a guy I'd been wanting to get in the sack for months. He told me he had attended because he couldn't pass up a chance to see me naked; I told him all he'd had to do was *ask* and he wouldn't have had to pay to see it. Though he soon left San Francisco, he turned out to be a long-term, long-distance fuck buddy of mine.

When we did wear clothes onstage, we dressed fairly ordinarily, usually in jeans and T-shirts. I was against being costumed. If you imagined what a gay band might look like, you'd probably think of something more flamboyant. We took a different approach—we might blend in with the crowd visually, but our ideas, our substance would be flamboyant. I thought it more subversive to hide in plain sight than to strut about like a peacock. Some people who don't like us have called us a novelty band, but we would probably have been far more successful, at least in San Francisco, if we'd been more gimmick conscious. If we'd worn wigs, costumes, and makeup, and camped it up, we could have attracted a much larger audience. As the band evolved, we took an interest in developing more of an image, but at that time a non-image was what we wanted. We may have formed in San Francisco, but I was from Peoria, and Chris was from Aberdeen. We didn't want to throw off our backgrounds; we wanted to subvert them, so we literally wore them on our sleeves.

Also, I wasn't interested in creating a mystique about the band. That was a lesson learned from punk. Don't be up on a pedestal, constructing some larger-than-life myth, be down to earth, matter of fact. Put another way, I was against being grand and dramatic. Drama is tiresome. Get to the point, cut to the chase, don't play games, don't waste the audience's time. Remember the scene in *Hairspray* where the white kids are hanging out in the black record store listening to the dirty blues? That's the kind of band we wanted to be, the kind of music we wanted to make—music that would be passed on with a whisper, saying, you gotta hear *this*!

Word of mouth was spreading. An interview with us ran in punk bible *Maximum Rock 'n' Roll*. We had managed to sell two hundred and fifty cassettes in town, and suddenly, three labels were interested in us: Lookout, Alternative Tentacles, and Bar/None. Bar/None had considered signing us earlier, but label honcho Glenn Morrow played us to some gay rockers he knew (who were affiliated with the indie rock club Maxwell's in Hoboken, New Jersey); their appalled and offended response gave him pause. By the time he'd reconsidered, we'd already signed with Lookout.

A.T. said yes first, but we wanted to release a single right away, and they said they couldn't fit it into their schedule. We had a 45 ready with a Christmas song on it, and we wanted it out that year. Lookout said they could do it, so we went with them. Either label was fine for us; both were local labels with a reputation for being artist-oriented and honest, so we felt it would be an honor to be on either one. As it turned out, going with Lookout proved beneficial for our band in ways unimaginable at the time.

Actually, we didn't really "sign." We insisted on having a contract with Lookout; it was the first time a band on their label had asked for one. I liked the punk ideal of a verbal agreement, but being a student of rock and roll, I'd heard countless stories of what can go wrong when people disagree over what their verbal agreement was. The contract was only one page long, with typos, but it spelled out in basic terms who was entitled to what and when. We licensed to Lookout the rights to the album indefinitely, as long as it was kept in print and quarterly royalties were paid on time. We got Lookout's standard deal with their bands—60 percent of profits on all record sales, minus some specific expenses. Major labels customarily offer a 5–15 percent royalty, which is calculated after ridiculously bogus "packaging charges" and inflated, unaccountable overhead expenses. Our contract was for that first album and single alone, and required no further obligations from us. (Every time we did an album with Lookout we signed a new contract for that particular record; however, over time the contracts grew longer.)

At that time, record sales were increasing for many punk/ indie labels, which led them to be more professional in their business dealings. Some punk commentators thought that any written contract was a betrayal of punk DIY ethics, but I knew that punks could be jerks like anyone else, and I wanted protection. The touching naïveté with which some punks held this attitude was ironic in its parallels to hippiedom; pointing this out to punks *infuriated* them, which is partly why I enjoyed pointing it out.

Chris had located another temp drummer for the time being, recruiting an acquaintance named Chris Wolcott (drummer number four) to play a handful of shows with us. The most exciting gig during this period occurred at Gilman Street, the legendary all-ages punk club in Berkeley. We played with riot grrl torchbearers Bikini Kill and Tribe 8, an exciting and totally packed-out show. I had previously traded demo tapes with Bikini Kill singer Kathleen Hanna, loved their music, and was thrilled to do a show with them. Their music examined society's objectification of women, critiquing the male gaze, and our music balanced the scale by objectifying men. Both of our bands were for equality in relationships, a partnership really, rather than the typical weak/strong, dominant/dominated patriarchal paradigm. We were feminists too, we just happened to be men.

The performances were great, full of determination and exuberance, but some of the audience just didn't get it. The sexist response from some of the men made clear how the punk scene (even in "enlightened" Berkeley) could be just another boys' club. Still, the infiltration by these women, crossing from audience to performer and determined to claim that space, helped change that scene. It was exciting to witness the barriers breaking down, and to see our own band as part of that change.

We were aching to get a record out. In November 1992, the first Pansy Division record was finally released—a 45 with "Fem in a Black Leather Jacket" on the A-side, plus two B-side tracks, "Homo Christmas" and "Smells Like Queer Spirit," that wouldn't appear on the forthcoming album. "Fem" was a declaration about a guy I thought was hot, in no uncertain terms. To our ears, it sounded like a hit, catchy pop with a sort of girl group/Motown-ish quality filtered through jangly, distorted guitars. When I first sat down to write a song for this new idea of a band, and envisioned what I really wanted to sing about that I hadn't yet heard sung, this is what plopped out.

Of the two B-sides, "Homo Christmas" was our wish fulfillment, since holidays and families in general can be traumatic for queers. I imagined this as a song that you could sneak off to play away from the rest of the family when you were "home" for the holidays that would make you smile and raise your spirits. I wrote it in twenty minutes one day prior to a rehearsal. It was nearly Christmas, I had an idea for a Christmas song, and we had a show that night, so I wrote the song at four, taught it to the band at five, and played it live that night. The other B-side, "Smells Like Queer Spirit," requires some explanation. We loved Nirvana, but at that time their hit song was so omnipresent it drove us crazy. Since it wasn't until well after the song had been a hit that a lyric sheet was issued for it, we had no idea what large chunks of the lyrics actually said. I thought, what if the lyrics were slurred because they were singing gay lyrics? So we wrote our own. Part of it was random: Nirvana's lyrics didn't seem to make any sense, so we threw in some irrelevancies of our own, such as the reference to Fugazi's *Repeater,* one of my favorite albums at the time. It could have been anything, but that's what I thought of that day.

Chris and I weighed the pros and cons of releasing the Nirvana cover. We figured it would get attention, but also worried that it might cast us in the wrong light. But we were insecure that our band might get ignored, so we went ahead. We decided, however, that it should be on a single, not on the album. It succeeded in getting attention, though it did give us a reputation as a parody band in some people's minds.

We also worried about getting sued over our version. Technically, you don't need permission to record someone else's song, you just pay royalties—but if your version "defames" the song in the estimation of its owner (which is most often a music publishing company, not the songwriter), they can sue. However, we felt we were obscure enough that it would slide by. Before its release, we heard of a concert in Portland, Oregon, to fight Measure 9, a right-wing ballot measure to deny full legal rights to homosexuals. To our delight, Nirvana was playing it—a chart-topping rock band explicitly supporting gay rights. Better yet, our friend (and A.T. record head) Jello Biafra was the emcee, so we had him ask Nirvana if they minded us doing a version of the song with queer lyrics. According to Jello, all gave their assent, saying they didn't mind, so we felt that much safer releasing the record.

(Later, after we became better known, and after "Queer Spirit" appeared on a CD collection of our singles, Nirvana's publishing company, EMI/Virgin, tried to sue us over our version. We'd paid our royalties, but they saw dollar signs; after they saw we'd sold only 20,000 copies, they laid off. That's what can happen when you sell your song publishing, music biz jargon for ownership of your compositions—other people decide who can do what with your songs, not you.

Nirvana's members had nothing to do with this threatened lawsuit.)

We've kept the publishing rights to our original compositions; given their content, we were sensitive about their misuse. If you want control over what happens to your songs, it's stupid to let them go for what is basically a cash advance. Also, most songs in the United States are published through two major clearing houses, BMI and ASCAP; I'd been a BMI member since I was in The Outnumbered, so Chris joined ASCAP, to see if one did a better job than the other. With BMI, I was getting small checks for airplay royalties within six months of release, but when Chris had gotten nothing after three years, he contacted ASCAP and was told that not only hadn't they collected any royalties, they hadn't gotten around to registering his songs yet! He then switched to BMI (though the jerks at ASCAP dragged out the process of switching over for nearly a year). From our experience, we would advise any songwriters to avoid ASCAP.

CHAPTER 5
Undressed

In March of '93, our debut album *Undressed* was officially released. It's the purest distillation of the original Pansy Division concept, and thus it's a *very* horny album, with a higher proportion of sexual subject matter than our later records. We refused to be cowed into worrying about what people might think about our lyrics being so blunt, whether they were right-wingers, or assimilationist gays who felt like we should behave well in order to further acceptance by mainstream society.

The album opened with "Versatile," an observation about stereotypes in gay men's roles, the sexual hypocrisy of some straight men, and a Pete Townshend reference (he had just revealed at the time that he'd had sex with men, causing consternation among the ranks of Who fans). I was tired of hearing straight people ask things like "Which one of you plays the woman," tired of stupid black and white thinking. "Fem in a Black Leather Jacket," a fun statement from the single, was included on the album as well. "Bunnies," one of our best-loved songs, was an ode to that *hot* early part of a relationship where all you want to do is *do it, do it, do it!*

"Hippy Dude," like "Fem," was about a kind of long-haired guy I desired; it's a tribute to all the long-haired beauties I used to see on Haight Street when I first moved to the city. With "Curvature," I was conscious about breaking new ground for song subject matter; if anyone else had penned an ode to curved dicks, I hadn't heard it. "The Cocksucker Club" was my response to a friend's comment that a guy we both found attractive was, ahem, *in the club*. We included "Rock & Roll Queer Bar," the rewrite of the Ramones I'd penned for my DJ nights; I'd sung my own lyrics to myself for years, so I decided to sing them to everyone else too! (Chris once handed a CD to Johnny Ramone onstage at a show in San Francisco, but we never heard what they made of our version.)

It wasn't all fun and games. "Crabby Day" was the bitterly humorous tale of a young man who got crabs, and the jerk who knowingly gave them to him. It had been inspired by a friend of ours who kept getting crabs, and us shrugging and laughing about it. But apart from the humor, there were several romantic, heart on the sleeve songs such as "The Story So Far," "Boyfriend Wanted," and "Luck of the Draw." These were more personal and introspective than the rest of the album, and some fans' favorites. "Luck of the Draw" was inspired by an awful guy I'd picked up at Club Uranus, but combines several other disastrous experiences; "The Story So Far" and "Boyfriend Wanted" document my state of mind trying to find love after moving to San Francisco. Many reviewers never mentioned that we did songs like these; they weren't as incendiary as others, but they offered balance and variety. Far too many indie/punk bands in the '80s and '90s made albums that had one sound, one tempo, and one mood spread out over an entire album; we hated that, and arranged our album accordingly.

The album concluded with "ANTHEM," our statement of purpose.

We're here to tell you, you better make way
We're queer rockers in your face today
We can't relate to Judy Garland
It's a new generation of music calling

We're the buttfuckers of rock & roll
We wanna sock it to your hole
With loud guitars we're gay and proud
We're gonna get ya with your pants down

Closeted rockers, we've heard of a few
They won't risk their careers to come out to you
We have no such deceptions, no such ploys
We make it clear we wanna sleep with boys

We're the buttfuckers of rock & roll
We wanna sock it to your hole
We don't care if you're top or bottom
Just use your butthole, everyone's got 'em

We do love rock & roll, it's true
But that boy meets girl stuff just won't do
We got our condoms, we got our lube
We know how to use 'em, how 'bout you?

We're the buttfuckers of rock & roll
We wanna sock it to your hole

Latino, Asian, white, or black
We're gonna getcha, we're gonna getcha
We're gonna getcha, on your back!

Many of the songs on *Undressed* were inspired by conversations I'd had or overheard. I wanted to document the colloquial language gay men used among themselves, to capture that vernacular. We hoped other gays would have a shock of recognition hearing them, the same way we'd have reacted to someone else doing such a record. It was important to make sure the pronouns were correct; we didn't want anyone having to guess whether or not we were gay.

The material was uncensored, and so was the album cover. Our friend Alex, who had go-go danced for us, had volunteered to pose nude for the cover. Since he was sexy and beautiful, and more of an exhibitionist than we were, we took him up on the offer. We thought having a nude male image on the cover would make a statement—there was nothing to hide. We sang about dick, and we showed it too. Alex, who has a nice-sized dick, was disappointed when he saw how shriveled it appeared in the photo, but it's still lovely. The front of the CD booklet revealed Alex's upper torso, and you had to open it up to see the rest; the LP, however, revealed all. (Before copies could be shipped to Japan, the shrink-wrap over the penis had to be whited out.) We feared that stores might be afraid to stock it, but didn't hear of any problems. However, Lookout had to switch cassette manufacturers after their usual supplier (in Alabama, y'all) refused to print the cover, despite the beauty of the photo (and a very flaccid dick).

Though there is a certain amount of shock value in this music, our initial intent was to aim it at a specific segment of the population. We were trying to reach a certain self-selected community. Apart from them, we hoped that certain straights would appreciate an open door to an area of life they wouldn't normally be privy to. Though gay, I could relate to songs about hetero relationships, and I figured if our songs were good enough, anyone gay, straight, or in between could relate. Our songs would validate and be inclusive of gays' stories, and for straights, they would illuminate a different point of view. But whoever was listening, we felt we'd done what we set out to do—make catchy, simple songs with music and lyrics that were bold and direct.

Concurrent with the release of *Undressed* was the single "Bill & Ted's Homosexual Adventure," on the fledgling Outpunk label from San Francisco. (Our arrangement with Lookout gave us the freedom to put out songs on other indie labels, which in turn have their own followings and allowed us to reach more people.) Outpunk was run by Matt Wobensmith, a young gay guy active in the underground punk scene who'd fled to San Francisco from rural Pennsylvania. Just as we thought it was time for a queer band, he thought it was time for a queer record label. All this stuff seemed to be happening in quick succession. Matt released our 45 as well as Tribe 8's first EP, and became a good friend of ours. The B-side was our version of Spinal Tap's "Big Bottom," a song that *cried out* for reinterpretation.

For a laugh, we did a video for the song, our lip-synching intercut with footage swiped from the first *Bill & Ted* movie and X-rated footage of the best *Bill & Ted* look-alikes we could find in our local video store (we did better with Bill than Ted). The single came out in an X-rated sleeve, using a shot from the video for the front cover. We went down to Chris's office on a Sunday afternoon to film the lip-synch parts, and he edited it at work after hours. Total cost: twenty dollars! (Most of which went for renting the videos we stole the footage from.)

The video screened in at least two dozen gay film festivals (including some as far away as Germany, Australia, and New Zealand), where it was greeted with enthusiasm. In Chicago, it earned a standing ovation and even got a repeat showing at the end of the program. A couple of years later we had one sent along to Keanu Reeves, through a mutual acquaintance, with a note saying please don't sue us, but we never heard back from him.

Now that we had a chance to make music people might actually hear, our ambition was to spew forth all we could— on albums, on singles, on compilations. We wanted to make the most of our opportunity, because you never know how long these things will last. Our idea was to do an album a year, and release singles at regular intervals like our favorite punk and new wave bands. In one year, 1980, Elvis Costello released more songs (forty) than Jackson Browne had in a decade. That's how we wanted to work, to be as productive as possible. Bands like Steely Dan or Bad Company or the Eagles could barely deign to put out records every three years. How urgent was your music in that situation?

Undressed received mostly good reviews. As a new band on an indie label, it got covered by a sympathetic network of fanzines, but received little coverage in the more mainstream music press. We didn't do a lot of promotion for it. Lookout mailed about a hundred and fifty copies to grassroots press and selected college radio, and very few to gay media. We wanted to see how far it would get on its own, without being pushed. We wanted it to have a life of its own, to see if word of mouth would travel. Gauging people's reaction was great entertainment. We felt the territory we claimed was unlimited; to those who said homosexuality was a limited topic, our response was that people wouldn't say that about heterosexuality, because hetero = human. We started with so many sexually oriented songs because they hadn't been done before. If we were known for our raunchier songs, we weren't ashamed, but we didn't want it to begin and end there.

The Outnumbered had been a serious-minded band without many fun songs. I wanted this new band to make people smile and laugh along, to really enjoy it, and see the fun in defiance. While this won us fans, it also won us critics who don't (or won't) see the seriousness lurking behind the humor. Utilizing humor puts you at risk for being known as a novelty, and, like our style of music or not, I'm surprised how many writers can't see beyond it. I suspect homophobia occasionally, but laziness in others; with an avalanche of releases piling up, superficial listening isn't a surprise. The truth is our reviews have been mostly good, but it's the coverage we didn't get that's significant as well.

One well-known punk rock commentator, famous for having half a thought (and for proving the truism "a little knowledge is a dangerous thing"), wrote that "any hetero band that sang about sex so freely would be pegged as sexist in a matter of seconds." He missed the point (as he usually did) that our songs are about sharing and enjoying sexuality equally, not imposing it on the other partner in a sexist "I'm gonna do it to you" kind of way. Our songs are more like, "We're going to do it together!" It's about mutual desire, not sexist conquest.

Our records were getting around, and our video had gotten around, but we hadn't. Still on the drummer hunt (Chris Wolcott had only been temporary and now he'd moved on), we dug up David Ward (drummer number five), a hunky bi-guy whose Oakland loft became our rehearsal space. With new drummer in tow, we did a handful of gigs in Washington and Oregon. A show in Olympia had us opening for a good Two Nice Girls-related dyke band Girls in the Nose, and local dyke outfit C.W.A. (Cunts With Attitude), who were *fantastic*. They were aping the whole

N.W.A. thing, and had hysterically funny lyrics that paralleled ours quite well. We even got to play a gig at Tug's, the mostly gay bar Chris used to go to when he lived in Seattle. (Tug's had video monitors in the club, so after we finished playing we aired the "Bill & Ted's Homosexual Adventure" clip to ecstatic response.)

In February 1993 we made our first trip to L.A., playing at SPEW, a queer underground fanzine convention where we met people like writer Dennis Cooper, force of nature Vaginal Creme Davis, and the riot grrl band Bratmobile. We went to Washington, DC, in April 1993 to play the March on Washington for gay rights. David couldn't afford to go (we had to pay our own way), but we were able to scrounge a temp drummer, musician and spoken word performer Juliana Luecking (drummer number six), to play two shows with us that weekend. All of these successful out-of-town appearances confirmed our feeling that it was time to do a proper tour.

CHAPTER 6

First Tour

Chris and I had two weeks vacation coming, along with an extra unpaid week we both managed to get, into which to cram a nationwide tour. We had a fair amount of trepidation about doing such a tour. We'd rarely strayed far from our safe Bay Area cocoon, and we feared for who might be lying in wait in some distant city. We were going through the South. Being out had its advantages, but we worried we might be sitting ducks; bigots and homophobes can read (well, some of them anyway) posters and gig listings too. Chris arranged to call someone at the same time every day to confirm we were safe. It was often suggested to us that we send CDs to Jesse Helms and Pat Robertson—instant hysteria, just add water! But we never wanted to have a symbiotic relationship with the right wing.

We were also concerned about our van. It was a piece of shit given to us by a friend of Chris's. The previous owner had hit a deer and wrecked the front hood, which no longer closed in the customary fashion and had to be bolted and unbolted to open (and to keep shut). It didn't have a proper grille; a friend in San Francisco donated a refrigerator grille to keep the radiator at least partially covered. It looked horrible, but it also looked like it held nothing of value. Nervous about carting around valuable musical equipment, David put curtains on the back window, padlock holders on all four doors, and constructed a comfy loft (handy having a carpenter in the band), keeping the equipment totally concealed. Worried about being given away in hostile environs, and driving such a crappy van, we kept any pro-gay or Pansy Division decals off our bumper.

For David and Chris, it was their first tour ever, and they were both very emotional the day we left. I booked the tour myself, conveniently making all the long-distance calls from my job. I had some contacts, and some numbers passed on by Tribe 8, who'd done a reasonably successful tour a few months before. The first show was in Kansas City, smack dab in the middle of the country. Our opening band had a gay drummer and they covered The Rolling Stones's long-bootlegged "Cocksucker Blues." We met James Grauerholz, longtime manager/caretaker of William Burroughs. Though we didn't get to meet Burroughs himself on this occasion, we made a pilgrimage to his house three years later when we played Lawrence, Kansas. He asked us, "What is your band's credo?" and I replied, "To bring buttfucking and cocksucking to the general public." In his slow, unmistakable drawl, he said, "Well, it's always been there, but it's always been hidden." On this first trip to Kansas City, no one was waiting to beat us up or slash our tires. About seventy-five people showed up, and we had a great time.

This trend continued as we performed in St. Louis, Chicago, Dayton (where we played with Guided By Voices, who were godawful), Providence, Philadelphia, New York, Baltimore, Atlanta, Austin, and Houston. Six years after the last Outnumbered show, I was onstage in Champaign again. We played a few college towns: Macomb, IL; Princeton, NJ; Oberlin, OH. A few shows were duds: Boston, Columbus (a last-minute addition), Norfolk; Columbia, SC. We made anywhere from forty dollars a night (Columbia) to five hundred (at the colleges), usually in the middle, plus whatever we made from selling our records and T-shirts. There weren't a ton of people waiting for us, but there were a few actual fans, as well as the curious and the supportive. Being out there, out in the "real" America was exciting, and it was great to see that we got a lot of people excited! We played with a few other gay (or partially gay) bands: Size Queen in Philly, The Peecocks in Boston, God Is My Co-Pilot in NYC, Meat in Atlanta. Some were better than others, but you could see a trend developing.

Playing out of town was a big adjustment in one sense— we didn't have dancers to provide visual entertainment. In San Francisco, any show we did would have two to eight dancers prancing around the stage, spraying silly string, waving signs, and interacting with the audience. We couldn't really move around onstage, we were surrounded! But now, we had to provide all the visual stimulus, and we were unprepared. At first we stood there fairly still, carefully trying to gauge the audience's reaction rather then "performing." I recall longtime gay activist and music biz figure Jim Fouratt telling me, after our show in New York at ABC No Rio, that I needed to shake my butt and jump around more.

We went over pretty well, but sometimes we didn't play that well. David was a source of fan interest, a big hunky guy who would play with his shirt off. He looked like he would crush the drum kit, but in reality he was a sweet, gentle guy, and that's how he played the drums. Way too nice! We wanted to rock, to kick some ass, man, but it wasn't as good as we aspired to. I thought we might get tighter playing almost every night, but we actually sounded worse at the end of the tour than at the beginning. Though David was totally supportive of our concept, and is one of the nicest guys we've ever met, by the end we knew we needed a different drummer.

All in all, we did nineteen gigs in twenty-three days, and the weather was great the whole time. This proved more fortunate than just convenient; though our van survived the tour trouble-free, a few months later it died during a rainstorm. Because the hood wouldn't completely shut, water leaked inside and soaked the engine. So thank heavens for the twenty-three days without rain. We drove 8,800 miles and took in $6,800; our expenses were $3,800, so we made $3,000. We couldn't fucking believe it! We set aside half for the band fund, and divided the rest—$500 apiece. Since we'd only been hoping to break even, we were thrilled! It was good incentive to do more touring.

Our lack of conflict, and the good reception we received, made us think that despite the AIDS crisis, things really had changed for the better for gays in this country. Neither Chris nor I could have imagined something like this occurring so peacefully in the '80s.

After coming off the road we were ready to get back in the studio as we had a single we wanted to record. "Touch My Joe Camel" is one of the silliest PD songs, one that has not aged particularly well. But it does summon an era when phallic symbolism in cigarette ads was at an all-time high, and as phallic-minded as we were, it seemed like ripe subject matter to tackle. However, it was sadly clear upon studio playback that David just wasn't cutting it as drummer. It took some trickery to make the finished product sound as good as it did. David bowed out quite gracefully. He also wanted our band to sound as good as possible, and was very supportive in making the transition.

The band needed another van. We hadn't made enough money to buy one, so I dipped into my own savings and forked out $5,000 for a beige van that had belonged to some Arizona retirees. David Ward built us another loft bed, and we were road-ready again.

We then hooked up with David Ayer (drummer number seven), who had played in Samiam and Isocracy (both early Lookout bands), and was currently in another band called Porch with a former member of Primus. We recorded a few songs and played a few shows with him, but although he was capable, it was clear his style wasn't really suited to us. He was a good heavy drummer, but was too stiff to play pop. He didn't swing enough—too much rock, not enough roll. The drummer hunt resumed.

Apart from sending promo materials to the promoters in each town in advance of our tour, we didn't make much effort to contact gay press; we felt we were at odds with the gay mainstream. We welcomed any interest, though, so when a friend at *Windy City Times*, Chicago's weekly gay paper, suggested an interview, I was happy to oblige. However, his fortyish editor, hearing our music, refused to cover us. He heard the anti-Judy Garland lyric in "ANTHEM" and huffed that we couldn't possibly be gay, because no gay person would put down Judy that way. Fear of such a reaction was why we hadn't courted the gay press in the first place. A year later we finally did get covered in that paper, but only after receiving local coverage in more mainstream (straight) Chicago media first.

I don't really have a beef with Judy Garland. Though her style of music is not to my taste, I can see that she was talented. The beef I have is with the almost saintly significance gay men attach to her. Many older gay men identify with the traumas she experienced, saying her struggles reflect difficulties gay men have had to overcome. That Garland's death was a trigger for the 1969 Stonewall riots is not to be overlooked, but to hold on to her as an icon, I feel, is to cling to the past—a past of victimization. I say enough with the self-pity already! Dramatically wallowing in the tragic is blaming others for your problems, fetishizing helplessness. (It's the same gripe I have with Morrissey, by the way, which makes him such a delicious target.) Despite my own trials and tribulations, I've had a fairly happy, well-adjusted life, and I can take responsibility for my own happiness. Judy Garland is the gay past, and while it's important to remember her, I don't think we need to dwell there.

Around this time I did one of my first interviews on behalf of the band with a gay New York writer. After discussing our album, which had just been released, I asked him to put our address at the end of the article, as it might not be easy for his readers to find our record. When I told him that it was ten dollars postpaid, he condescendingly explained that we weren't charging enough; we should charge fifteen dollars. I explained that I thought CD prices were excessive, that I hated paying fifteen bucks for CDs, and I was putting my money where my mouth is. I thought having a lower price might actually induce more people to buy it and listen to it. Over the phone I could almost *hear* him rolling his eyes; his attitude was totally materialistic.

Here again I felt gay culture clashing with punk culture—unquestioned materialism versus a questioning of capitalism. To me this was a restatement of the '70s punk versus disco argument. Disco celebrated pleasure and materialism;

punk was suspicious of it. While punk could be materialistic too, it questioned the process and considered the contradictions. Ultimately this got taken to extremes; one of the most aggravating things about punks in the '90s was their fright about making a profit. Playing the underground circuit, we repeatedly encountered the simpleminded purist view that profits—however small—were somehow wrong. We know how that battle turned out—with disco's incredible mass success, and punk being ignored and marginalized. But the issues it raised never went away.

Another New Yorker we encountered was putting together a gay musicians' guide. He wanted information from us—a photo, a copy of our CD, and a short bio. Fine. He also wanted to charge us eighty-five dollars for the privilege of being in the book. I told him no way; if he was serious about writing about gay musicians, why would he leave out anyone who wouldn't pay? Would he leave out K.D. Lang or Pet Shop Boys, just because they wouldn't pony up the money? He was just trying to get unknown musicians to send in money so they'd be represented alongside the bigger acts. The exposure would help them, he explained. Wow, what a definitive book that would be—only those who pay get included! After I chided his approach, he offered us a listing for free, since he wanted us in there. We declined, and he angrily wrote back, saying we were stupid for turning down his selfless act of charity. He said that he didn't like our attitude, and he'd gotten in trouble with his editor by sticking his neck out to include us for free. *Ooooh!* We were so concerned. (By the way, during our correspondence with him, his return letters always included an eight by ten head shot of himself.) After the book eventually came out, several fans who had bought it approached us, puzzled that we weren't in it. I explained the best I could about a certain brand of capitalism, where you get to pay extra for being gay.

CHAPTER 7

Deflowered

After that first tour, we were on top of the world (if back at our jobs). We had an album out! We'd had a successful tour! Each success was increasing our hopes and ambitions. During our time home in '93, I'd been pretty prolifically writing songs. We were anxious to get back in the studio and make a better album.

While making your debut album, you don't know how you'll be received. You never know if you'll be noticed or ignored, or if you'll even get a chance to make a second record. In its first year, *Undressed* sold five thousand copies, which was our goal. We were confident that our second album would get a hearing. Hunting for a good local studio, we found one, Komotion; looking for a good, easy to work with engineer, we found Fred Cirillo. To temporarily solve the drummer crisis, Chris recruited Lliam Hart (drummer number eight) to play drums on the album. An excellent drummer and a quick study, he was already playing with Chris in another band at the time. Since we didn't know when we would be able to record again with such a solid drummer, we decided to record nearly everything we'd written, to make an album and also have a few songs for singles. In total, we recorded twenty-three songs and knocked out the album in about a week.

We titled the album *Deflowered*. We had hoped to call it *Laid,* but the UK band James beat us to it by a few months; I prefer *Deflowered* anyway. (After naming the first LP *Undressed*, I had thought we should call the second one *Laid*, and the third *Cigarette*.) While many of our songs are proudly about sex and desire, some are about sexual politics. The opener, "Reciprocate," is a tale of dissatisfaction from one who is doing most of the "work" in bed and wants some pleasure in return. It was also a dig at the usual rock and roll paradigm, in which men demand satisfaction from women, without offering any themselves. "Anonymous" describes a situation I found myself in one night at a rock show. A cute guy was making physical contact with me—slam dancing, but salaciously. After several instances where he was clearly dancing right into me, I then explicitly grabbed his crotch, and he grabbed mine in return. But afterwards he refused to look at me or acknowledge what had happened, much less follow through. The music was as fast and furious as the song that was playing at the time of the incident.

"Rachbottomoff" humorously touches on how some guys are completely unaware of, and out of touch with, the erotic possibilities of a certain part of their bodies. "Kissed" tries to counter the frustration of going out with guys who refuse to kiss (which still boggles my mind) by offering, um, incentives for doing so. I had gone on my first European vacation the year before, and I thought of the lyrics while standing by the ancient walls of the city of Siena, wishing I had a guy to make out with right then.

A couple of songs on *Deflowered* are barbed critiques of the gay scene. "Negative Queen" describes a common gay character, a sadly true stereotype that drives us crazy. One line specific to San Francisco ("Don't put up posters on Castro Street/He'll rip 'em down so he can shop in peace") would get big cheers when we played it in town. When I first moved to San Francisco, and ACT-UP was in full force, there were flyers for various events all over utility poles in the Castro, but after ACT-UP and Queer Nation faded out there was a self-appointed cadre of neat freaks called the Golden Broom. They tore down any signs on poles to keep the neighborhood "clean." They said that people should put ads in newspapers and on billboards if they wanted to advertise and that it infringed on their personal rights. Umm, so how do people not rich enough to do this get their message out? I hated that fussy fags had already forgotten their hard-earned freedoms to such an extent that they now wanted freedom *from* things, not freedom *for* things.

"Fluffy City" summarizes my time in the plastic West Hollywood gay bar scene. Though specifically focused on L.A., the issues addressed—muscles versus brains, alienation with the "body beautiful" mentality, and a specifically gay tacky fashion sensibility—have applications for any gay scene. It names several irritating WeHo bars ("Wish I had a *Revolver*/the whole place puts me in a *Rage*"); the former actually copied the lyric sheet and artwork from the album cover for a flyer promoting the club! Rather than being satirical, the lyrics are anthropological investigative reporting (kind of like N.W.A.), but done in a humorous way that will engage the listener rather than register as dry social protest.

A few songs were more introspective. "Not Enough of You to Go Around," a song revived and revised from The Outnumbered, is a wistful, bitter recollection of a guy too popular to keep up with. "A Song Of Remembrance For Old Boyfriends" switches genders on an obscure Jonathan Richman song (his version has never been available apart from bootlegs) and is a sweet, sad, nostalgic memoir. Before the song was released, I went up to Jonathan at a show in San Francisco and told him we'd recorded the song, and asked if he had any problem with it, especially since we had switched genders. He said no, and besides, once it's out in the public there's not much you can do about it anyway, so go ahead.

"Deep Water" is a first-person tale of being queer in high school that's become one of our most requested songs. I recall sitting in algebra class at the beginning of my freshman year of high school, thinking that if I could know that I was going to go through high school without ever having a girl-friend, I'd end it all right then and there. Remembering that, and wondering how much worse my fears would've been had I been more aware of my gay feelings, I tried to write a song from that person's mindset. I wouldn't have written this song for our first album; it was the growing awareness that teenagers were becoming part of our audience that got me thinking about the issue.

Other songs were more direct in spelling out certain desires. "Groovy Underwear" is pretty self-explanatory. I couldn't think of any songs written about underwear at that point, and the subject just seemed ripe for plucking. "Beercan Boy" celebrates the biggest one I ever saw (on an Illinois farm boy). This one pushes the edge of silly (maybe over the edge), but even though I am not a size queen (honestly!) it's still a thrill to have something exceed your imagination. "New Pleasures" contemplated sex toys as a temporary compensation for singledom. "James Bondage" was Chris's first songwriting contribution, exploring his Sean Connery fantasies (circa 1975, the era of *Zardoz* and *The Man Who Would Be King*). When Chris was first pondering writing material for the band, he used the phrase one day in conversation, and I said, "That's a great title! Write that song!" This song has its own cult following, probably the PD song most often heard in leather bars.

The album closed with a version of Pete Shelley's "Homosapien," done in the style Shelley's band, The Buzzcocks, might have chosen in their earliest, punkiest phase. It was one of the first openly queer songs I'd heard, one of my favorites, and a song Chris credits with helping him come out in 1981. The original was also one of the first songs I ever liked that used programmed drums, but I always yearned to hear it done rock style.

Still, it felt slightly incomplete. We had most of the songs together for the album but it seemed like a piece of the puzzle was missing. Sex was a large part of the subject matter, but this was still the time of AIDS. I felt we should address the issue, but I didn't want to sound maudlin. My friend Trebor Healey had written a poem that described the troubles of someone infected by the virus. I put his poem into song form, dropping some lines and adding others until I got the balance I wanted. This was "Denny." Instead of expressing sentiment about a subject, I told someone's (fictitious) story instead. Bringing it to rehearsal, I was afraid my band mates might think it was too heavy; instead, they *loved* the song and enthused about it as a great leap forward. People have asked if there is a Denny, but Trebor says it's a composite of several people, one that then underwent my own changes. I wondered what the reaction of some fans would be, but it has always been very well received. Amid a batch of celebratory sex songs it gives some needed gravity.

On our first album, and on most subsequent albums, there were graphic illustrations and uncensored descriptions about what is safe sex and what isn't; it was information every high schooler should have access to but probably doesn't. Singing about sex in the age of plague, we wanted to be informative without being repetitive or preachy. On *Deflowered* there was also a nationwide list of gay youth groups and their phone numbers (this was before Internet use was commonplace). Including this information in our packaging was our attempt to get listeners, especially younger ones, to understand the context of our songs.

Our photographer Marc Geller again created a gorgeous eye-grabbing cover. It's sexy and innocent, naughty and sweet. We were extremely proud of our creation. We felt like we'd grown tremendously since the first album, and felt ready to take on the whole world, not just a corner of it.

After completing the album sessions with Lliam, we continued looking for a permanent drummer. We weren't finding the right one (trying out both men and women, gay, bi, and straight), so when some gig opportunities came up, Lliam agreed to do them. He was a bit uptight about some of the lyrics on the album we'd just recorded, but he was really freaked out about playing "The Cocksucker Club" and "ANTHEM" in front of audiences. It was too much for him, and it showed. A pivotal gig was in Santa Cruz in February 1994, where we played with Heavens to Betsy and Excuse 17, bands whose members later joined forces to form Sleater-Kinney. We did not go over well. The indie kids sat stone-faced. It was the first time we'd really flopped; we played the songs decently, but the chemistry and vibe were just not right, and the young all-ages audience didn't respond. Our songs are pretty simple and direct, and Lliam (as well as other drummers we've had at various points) had the attitude that our stuff was pretty easy to play, that "I can just knock this stuff out, I don't have to think hard about it." But getting the nuances right was crucial to delivering the songs in an effective way, and it wasn't clicking.

Despite the Heavens to Betsy experience, we asked Lliam to continue with the band. It really wasn't working; our asking was a reflection of our desperation. At this time Chris and I had the feeling that our band was on the verge of *something*. Lliam had been trying to make it in the music biz for a long time, but our hopes must have sounded rather improbable to him. In the end, Lliam lasted two more gigs before we dumped him; though surprised, he seemed pretty relieved.

At this time one of our best-received singles came out. The three-song *Nine Inch Males* EP, with a risqué cover photo mocking Nine Inch Nails, had "Fuck Buddy" as its A-side. As subject matter (celebrating someone who isn't a lover but is more than a one-night stand) I thought it was a unique and specifically gay male point of view. It was a viewpoint queers could identify with and an educational experience for our straight listeners. The B-sides were covers of a Beat Happening song and what I felt was a latent Hüsker Dü song. We'd recorded the single a few months earlier with David Ayer; the session yielded a fourth song which appeared on a 45 compilation called *Stop Homophobia, Volume 1*. One of our best-loved covers, "Cowboys are Frequently Secretly Fond of Each Other" was something I'd found on a Giorno Poetry Systems compilation LP I'd borrowed a few years earlier from the Champaign Public Library. It was a song I thought needed to be spread far and wide.

Things were happening at a brisk pace. Just as we contemplated getting a booking agent, one appeared. Jay Scott, who booked the Canadian band No Means No, had heard *Undressed* and sought us out. He was headquartered in

Vancouver, BC, and arranged for us to play a music convention/festival there in May '94. David Ayer agreed to help us out just for this occasion, and we made it up to Canada for a great weekend. But something was brewing that was going to change our lives and the fate of our band.

With *Deflowered* due out in June of '94, Chris and I had decided to quit our jobs in September and tour heavily to promote the album. If it didn't work out, we'd have to come back and get new jobs, and though I had a job I liked, it seemed to be make or break time. We felt this was the record that could somehow break through.

One day I ran into Chris Applegren from Lookout Records on a Berkeley-bound BART train. At MacArthur Station in Oakland, I caught a glimpse of Tre Cool from Green Day, getting on a train in the opposite direction. Chris said that Tre liked us and had mentioned his band would like us to open for them. We didn't know Green Day at all; I'd heard their Lookout Records albums, and I'd gone to see them play live twice in San Francisco, but they'd cancelled both shows. Through word of mouth, and touring the underground punk circuit, they'd sold nearly fifty thousand copies each of their first two albums, with barely any advertising or college radio airplay. Their major label debut album had come out three months before, and their "Longview" video was just taking off on MTV.

I got Tre's number and called him, but he sounded distracted and got off the phone rather quickly. He asked if we had a van. I said yes. He didn't seem too interested in talking to me, and I thought that might be the last I heard from him. So I was flabbergasted when, about three weeks later, he called back to ask us if we wanted to open their tour. Hell, yeah!

There was just one problem—we didn't have a drummer.

Not planning to tour until September, we were giving ourselves time to find the right one. It meant quitting our jobs three months ahead of schedule, no big deal. There was no way we were saying no.

We talked to several potential candidates, mostly people we'd played with and knew, but nobody could commit to a six-week tour. We called Butch Flowers (drummer number nine), a gay guy we'd met on tour the previous fall, who lived in Ohio. He'd said then to call him if we ever needed a drummer, and though we had only spent a couple hours in his company, we did. We sent him a tape of ours to drum to, and had him mail us back a tape of himself drumming to it. He played decently, not great, but we said yes and crossed our fingers. We *had* to take a chance. We wanted to move forward, and thought that if he worked out, we might have a permanent drummer. We flew him and his drums out to San Francisco, and rehearsed together for a few days. It didn't sound that great, but we really didn't have much choice. And then, suddenly, we were gone—on tour with one of the hottest bands in the country. I knew it was going to be a wild and memorable time, so I took along a notebook and started a diary.

CHAPTER 8

Green Day/
Pansy Division Tour Diary

(Current PD band members: Chris, Jon, and Butch on drums)

7.2.94 Vancouver, BC, Canada

Last week I quit my job so I could go on tour. I guess I'm a professional musician now. We have a few shows of our own en route to meeting up with Green Day next week. Left Seattle early today for Vancouver, to give us extra time in case there were problems crossing the border. Good thing we did—though they didn't inspect us, we had to declare our merchandise. We brought a whole tour's worth with us, so we had to pay a big tariff, and they wouldn't take credit cards, so we had to drive around Surrey, BC, withdrawing money from cash machines. Big hassle, took four hours, used up all our extra time.

Which was less than usual because we had one and a half gigs today. We were invited to play three songs at a Smugglers/New Bomb Turks gig; we borrowed their equipment, it was quite sloppy, but the crowd really liked it. Chris said a couple of guys looked very stunned. Hey, we're just being ourselves!

We had dinner at a resolutely hetero place called Planet Earth, filled with poodle-haired girls and their dumb jock boyfriends. Our official show was at the Lux Theater, part of an AIDS fundraiser that included DJs and performances. It was our first show with Butch on drums, and though he was okay for a first show, I hope he picks it up fast.

It was more queer than our usual crowd; lots of cute boys. Chris went off with a date, and Butch and I ended up staying at a punk rock dump; even though they hadn't paid rent in months, they hadn't been evicted 'cause their landlord is a slumlord. Because of my cat allergies, I slept in the van; the next morning, one of the cute punk boys came out to the van to sleep with me. This tour is going to be great!

7.3.94 Victoria, BC

Our punk pals took us to an Indian temple for excellent free food. Then we took a beautiful ferry ride to Victoria. Tonight we opened for New Bomb Turks, but Butch had a terrible show, very disappointing. We've got six days before the Green Day gigs start and we aren't ready, and I'm not sure how seriously our new drummer takes all this. We had fun after the show—the club rents (owns?) a crash pad for its touring bands, and both bands stayed there, eight beds! Wish more clubs had this arrangement (almost none do). We usually ask around for housing or stay in the occasional hotel, which we can't really afford if we want any money left at the end of the tour.

7.5.94 Vancouver, BC

We were going to rehearse today, but while we were at our booking agent's office downtown, someone busted a window trying to break into our van. They didn't succeed—the padlocks worked! But we had to find a place to fix the window, so there went the afternoon. Butch practiced by listening to tapes; we had a nice sidewalk dinner on Robson Street.

7.6.94 Vancouver, BC

The gig was pretty uneventful, but an improvement. It was a historic night for our band—all three members got laid the same night, for the first time in band history! Yippee!

7.8.94 Calgary, AB

Got our day off to a rousing start by going directly to the Laundromat. We have enough clothes so that we need to do wash every week (or week and a half if we really stretch it). There was a TV in the Laundromat, and we knew we were in another country when a folksinger did a version of "This Land Is Your Land" with Canadian lyrics.

Since it was our first show with Green Day, we headed down to the venue very early. We met them for the first time; having spoken only to Tre on the phone, I hadn't encountered Billie Joe or Mike at all. Chris hadn't had contact with any of them. They made us feel welcome and at ease and were very nice, very helpful. We thought they would be, but you never know. No rock star trip that we could see; hell, instead of a tour bus they had a converted bookmobile.

Tre told us they wanted a band that would mess with the minds of the dumb jock following they had recently acquired with their MTV exposure. Billie Joe told me he hoped people would talk about this tour for years to come—it would be so momentous that people would lie that they'd been there.

Well, maybe!

Sound check ran late (Green Day's equipment truck hadn't arrived), and we didn't get to do one until after the doors were opened. When we finally played, kids were pressed up front against the stage barrier, holding the prime spots in anticipation of Green Day. One fourteen-year-old brat gave Chris the finger during the first song. He was thoroughly pissed off but didn't want to move; he finally relinquished his spot. We played okay; the first few songs were kind of slow, but then it picked up. Still, about two-thirds of the crowd fled to the lobby, like any show where people don't care about the opening act. At least the reception wasn't too hostile.

We are being paid two hundred and fifty dollars per show. This seemed reasonable to us; it was a little more than we were averaging on our own. We heard stories about other groups in our position making a mere hundred dollars per show (or less), basically paying for the opportunity of exposure, so we were glad to be dealing with people who were fair and on the level.

7.9.94 Edmonton, AB

Went to the world's largest shopping mall, the West Edmonton Mall. It has an amusement park, a fake beach with fake ocean waves, a fake pirate ship, a tank with real dolphins, bungee jumping, an ice rink, and a scary-ass roller coaster with the most startling drop. It was overkill, but fun. There was a dumb variety store called San Francisco with tacky souvenir shit; funny, there's no store in San Francisco called Edmonton.

Tonight's gig was better than last night's in every way. We played better, and the crowd was into us; unlike last night, most of the crowd stayed for our set, and we got much more applause. Sold more merchandise too! We sell our own merchandise after we play, and a girl, seventeen or eighteen, came up to us and said she was really into anal sex, and thanked us for singing about it.

The Green Day guys have been really nice. I asked Tre today if any of them was gay or bi; he said they're not queer but bi. Oh. I think they're gay friendly; none of 'em would relate any same sex experiences they'd had, though Billie Joe expressed a curiosity about having one. (*We never did see any fooling around or any potential "situations" during any touring with them. And none with us—too bad!*)

7.11.94 Winnipeg, MB

Listening to CBC News as we entered town, we heard of a study done at the University of Colorado regarding homosexuality and child abuse. Anti-gay groups in the Hate State, where an amendment denying full rights to gay people had passed the previous year, had been urging such an investigation. The result? Out of 269 studied cases of child abuse, only *two* involved homosexuals. Chris said, "And one was Michael Jackson!" And I said, "The other was Jeffrey Dahmer!"

Tonight a few shitheads yelled *"You suck!"* We replied, "Of course we suck, that's the *point!* We suck *good*." They later changed their chant to *"You suck shit!,"* but they were far outnumbered. There was even a mosh pit for the last couple of songs, which was different. They were a bunch of girls at the foot of the stage, and they *loved* Chris, the big ham!

It can be *so* nice to be at our merch table both during and after Green Day's set. Sweaty shirtless boys come out to the lobby to cool down, and I must say it's a sight to see. It's interesting being around so many high school and college kids, not our usual company. I fell in love every, oh, five minutes or so. We had some funny conversations with the kids. When I revealed that I had never watched "Saved by the Bell," they were in disbelief. They said it was the best show, that I really needed to watch it!

To avoid potentially time-consuming border hassles, we left right after the show for an all-night drive to Minneapolis. As we were loading and rearranging our van, some kids came over to talk to us. Some were fans, but one angry guy was spewing Adam and Steve stuff. His girlfriend was defending us, but it was dark and we decided to get out quick. This angered Butch, who wanted to debate the guy, but we had to explain to him that dark parking lots were not the place to hold arguments with drunken homophobes. At the border, the Canadian customs guy took a long look at the cover of the *Nine Inch Males* EP, and read the lyrics, but sent us through.

7.14.94 Omaha, NE

Our first U.S. Green Day show, at a bowling alley in Omaha called the Ranch Bowl. Six hundred people wedged into a room designed for half that number. There was an all ages section and a drinking section. Part of the deal for the bands was free bowling. I got a 137, with 5 strikes! Chris sucked, Butch did best, Mike from Green Day did well. Whee!

Before the show, we were alerted to a guy in line wearing shorts that had WHITE POWER written on the back. Green Day and their road crew went outside to confront the guy and we followed. Billie Joe said, "We don't like your shorts." The guy said, "It doesn't mean anything." But they registered their displeasure and pointed him out to the (mostly black) bouncers. We thought that was a very cool thing to do. Luckily, there were no problems.

In a gutsy move, Tre (who had dyed his hair green and was sporting barrettes) went out into the pit (yes, there was a mosh pit) during our set. He asked a guy for a light, but the guy thought Tre was hitting on him, and acted really uptight and offended. Tre, in his oh, so subtle way, said "I'm not trying to hit on you, I just needed a light. And you're not that cute anyway!" Pansy Division—feel the tension rise among the straight guys!

We played rather sloppily but went over pretty well. Again, girls loved it; one loaned Chris her handcuffs for "James Bondage." We revamped our set, adding "Deep Water" and "Boyfriend Wanted" plus both "Curvature" and "Versatile," which we had been alternating, and it seemed to work. We had a few hecklers and quite a few middle fingers; it seemed like a more redneck crowd than the previous GD shows. Worried about this as we loaded out, a line of girls helped protect us as we carried out our gear. Grrl power! Walking this gauntlet to get out to our van (which was parked too far from the door—a lesson learned), I was reminded what women go through, fearing abusive men.

We noticed that Green Day aren't selling their two Lookout releases at the shows; since it's hard finding them outside of indie stores, many of their new fans haven't run across them. So, we asked Green Day if they'd mind us selling their CDs and LPs at our merch table, and they said okay. We had Lookout send us a few boxes, and between our own releases and theirs, our merch sales far surpassed our guarantee.

7.19.94 Madison, WI

The wild delirium of being in this great situation has not been able to mitigate the fact that our drummer is really lousy. His inconsistency is maddening; it changes randomly each night. He doesn't seem interested in getting it right, and if we're not going to have a pro drummer, I'd rather have someone less scatterbrained, more communicative and alert. It's really really getting Chris and me down. But we're doing the best we can.

After eight shows, Green Day altered their set tonight

for the first time. I'd mentioned to Billie Joe that our tour was the perfect time for them to do "Coming Clean," their coming out of the closet song. So tonight they played it and dedicated it to us! It was a wonderful moment. In turn, Green Day asked us to play "Groovy Underwear" (which we'd stopped playing cause Butch was struggling with it), and we said we would. We felt very lucky to be on tour with such a cool band.

(*Green Day never did laundry, as far as we could tell; they'd wear clothes until they could wear them no more, give them away to fans, and then go thrift shopping for more.*)

7.20.94 Neenah, WI

Last night people warned us to be careful when we told them our next show was in Appleton, Wisconsin (it was actually in the next town over). Appleton is the hometown of the late Joe McCarthy, the red-baiting paranoid 1950s senator who (with the help of self-hating homosexual Roy Cohn) did decades of damage to our free speech rights. They have a statue of him there. So we set out with trepidation.

The show was outside the city limits, in a country-looking bar called the Ridgeway. It was next to a farm, complete with a big red barn and a weathervane. The place was big, but it had only one phone—a pay phone. I tried using it about 5:00 p.m., but it kept ringing. Once I picked it up to hear the mother of a teenage girl who was to attend the concert; she wanted to know if the Ridgeway was a bar, as she didn't want her daughter to drink. "And what's the name of that band, Green Day? Are their lyrics okay?" I assured her that they were. If she only knew who she was talking to...

Word had spread that local holy rollers were going to picket the show over the mention of masturbation in the "Longview" video (they never showed). Yup, we were in Hicksville; we discussed our concerns with the promoter and security, bracing for danger. So we went on stage…to a terrific reception, our best yet! No heckling and only a few middle fingers, and lots of cheering! Tre put new heads on Butch's drums before sound check (Butch was more interested in playing video games in Green Day's bookmobile), and we sounded our best yet. If only we could be this good consistently! For a place we expected so little from, it was inspiring.

During Green Day sets we usually experience a trickle of customers at the merch table, but tonight there was no real lull all evening, and we sold a ton. Signed lots of autographs too. People seemed so happy we were there doing what we did. And, more cute guys per square foot than anywhere else we've been. Butch and I had whiplash from turning our heads so much. It was so hot that sweat was dripping off the walls, a shirtless boy bonanza! The most beautiful, completely adorable teenage boy, with girlfriend in tow, came up in the lobby and gave Butch a big hug, totally making his day.

We stayed in Appleton with a girl we met at the show. But first she took us grocery shopping (documentation of which is on the back sleeve of the "Jackson" 45) and then to Pivot, Appleton's gay club, where we had a pretty good time. We rarely get to gay clubs on the road; the hours usually conflict with our shows, it's usually a weeknight, and we're usually too tired. I slept in the van again—we keep staying with people who have cats, aaargh! At least in the van there's no one else in the room and I can jack off in privacy.

7.21.94 Chicago, IL

On our day off from the Green Day tour we played at the Empty Bottle in Chicago. We had some spare time the next day, so we went to the Shedd Aquarium, where the ticket taker recognized us from the gig the night before and got us in for free! Calculate the odds of *that!*

7.23.94 Cleveland, OH

Drove all night to get here, checking into a hotel at 9:30 a.m. We were playing one of those all day radio station free concerts, but they made us play hours before Green Day. We had been both dreading and looking forward to this—four thousand capacity, our largest venue yet, three times larger than anything else on the tour. We played at 2:00 p.m. in front of maybe five hundred people, with both fans and homophobes showing up. One irate redneck heckled us during and after our set, hassling people who were dancing and enjoying it. He picked a fight with Chris in the parking lot afterwards (security intervened just in time); he nearly talked his way backstage in order to get to us a second time. Got back to the hotel about 4:00 p.m.—individual rooms, what a luxury! Turned on the AC, made some calls (including one to David Ward regarding his future availability), jacked off, and slept. Went out that evening; some folks we'd met at the show brought a group of people to show us around Cleveland, including a supercute rocker boy I brought back to the hotel. First time I ever had sex with anyone wearing a glittery Black Sabbath T-shirt.

Since we played early in the afternoon, we missed the riot. Nearly ten thousand people tried to get into the free show, causing havoc, arrests, and cancellation of Green Day's performance. They are now *huge,* booked into venues they've outgrown in the few weeks since they were booked. It's an amazing sight to see.

A few things: 1) People are starting to tell us that they've come to the show to see us. 2) I'm starting to hear grumblings from fans that Green Day are "too rock star," but that's not fair; from what I see, they don't act like it. Unfortunately, they can't hang around outside clubs post-show like they used to, 'cause there are just too many people wanting a piece of them. 3) It's great to see a burly, potentially threatening-looking guy walk up and say, "You were fucking great, you guys really rocked!" 4) Being on Lookout has been an incredible boon. Lookout bands' T-shirts are everywhere we look. So many kids are interested or curious about us due to that connection alone; the other night we stayed in the suburbs with some kids whose tastes seemed quite mainstream, but who also owned records by obscure Lookout bands like Rauool!

7.24.94 Indianapolis, IN

Tonight a big (and really supportive) bouncer escorted me to our merch table after our set; someone yelled, "Fuckin' faggot," and I said, "That's *buttfucking* faggot, thanks!"

We stayed with fans in Carmel, out in the burbs. I was exhausted and wanted to go to bed, while everyone else wanted to stay up longer, so I crashed in their den in the basement. It was a totally dark, windowless room, and when I woke up a couple hours later it was completely pitch black and I panicked, thinking I was dead. I finally found the door and burst out, scared as hell. Everyone else was still up hanging out, and apparently this was the funniest thing they had ever seen.

7.25.94 Cincinnati, OH

The audience reaction has been improving, and so has the buzz about us. Is it 'cause we're doing bigger shows (thirteen hundred capacity tonight)? More crowds lately seem to know our lyrics and are moshing more heavily during our set. We're signing more autographs. Would we be getting this reaction in these cities if it was the beginning of the tour, or have we gotten better?

Tonight someone threw a bra (fer chrissakes!) at me during "Denny," of all songs. It was totally the wrong moment to crack up, but I couldn't help it, it got tangled with the microphone. It was a nice black bra. I felt like Tom Jones.

7.26.94 Grand Rapids, MI

Driving into town, we had to call for directions. Had trouble finding a phone—nothing but houses and churches and churches and churches for fifteen minutes. The show turned out to be in a mall, at a club that until recently had booked cheese metal. The female bartenders had fluffy perms, and the bouncers were sports bar ugly. Our set went over well, but not as well as the last two nights; Chris mentioned this, saying he was disappointed, but I replied, "You're already taking this for granted!" Next week it's back to small clubs for us. However, Green Day have said they want us back in the future, so maybe this won't be the end after all.

There was a third band on the bill tonight, a local ska band called Mustard Plug. During their set, Tre destroyed Mustard Plug's deli tray; he threw their food at the walls and ceiling, and slathered mustard all over every electrical outlet in the room. It was the first incident of rock star behavior we'd witnessed from Green Day, but it was pretty hilarious. Tre was by far the most obnoxious GD member, but he could be very generous as well. I did make a mental note to avoid getting on his bad side.

7.28.94 Pittsburgh, PA

Today we drove around Pittsburgh tracking down medical supplies for Butch. He's never played drums this many days in a row before, and he needs to wrap his wrists and take Motrin before he can play. He told us he was a professional drummer, but we didn't realize he'd really only played weddings. At least he's been friendlier lately; I don't think he likes us any better than two weeks ago, but he doesn't want the circus to end.

According to Green Day's crew, tonight's club is a sleazy

place that got booked as a favor to somebody; normally they wouldn't get such a prestige gig. Lousy sound system, terrible monitors. We got through it somehow. As we began our first song, Chris pointed out someone's shirt that said SILLY FAGGOT—DICKS ARE FOR CHICKS. He said, "We're a bunch of faggots from San Francisco, and we won't put up with this bullshit, or any other homophobic or sexist or racist bullshit." Some of the club's security guys loved it and told us we were brave; a dreadlocked black bouncer told us we were the punkest band he's ever seen.

I was glad to visit Pittsburgh because I'd had a summer romance in San Francisco with a bi guy who was now back here. Didn't get to sleep with him though (lives with his girlfriend, damn!), though I did go out with him and his friends after the show to a series of bars with names like Chief's, Luna's, and Gooski's. Could have had sex with a cute local gay rock musician, but he was obnoxiously drunk. For once, my dignity won out over my dick.

7.29.94 Buffalo, NY

Continuing our tour of rust belt towns, we played on an outdoor stage in a suburb near Buffalo International Airport. There were planes taking off to one side of us, and golf balls from a driving range on the other. I kept looking up, anticipating the collision.

Reaching so many younger people, we get asked if we want to be role models. A lot of gay artists squirm when confronted with that question. My response is, hell, yeah! I don't mean we're perfect human beings, fer chrissakes, but if we give encouragement to queers to be open, out, and to speak up for themselves, by all means yes.

7.30.94 Allentown, PA

Had to drive three hundred and sixty miles through shitty

fifty-five MPH New York and Pennsylvania turnpikes. Got up very early; it was Butch's turn to drive, and after going over the route with him, Chris and I took naps. I woke up to find us thirty miles past our exit; his only excuse was "I wasn't paying attention." Aargh! Tired of being a baby-sitter.

The venue was called Barron's Beach Club, an outdoor venue attached to a bar. We had not been included in the adverts for the show, and almost nobody was expecting us. A few brave souls got into it, but this was the most hostile reaction we'd received so far. You could feel the resentment seething below the surface, and Gordon, Green Day's merch guy, said he heard it well above the surface too. But Green Day played "Coming Clean" and dedicated it to us, and a bi girl approached us and had us sign her shirt. Many fans ask us to sign clothes; I don't understand!

Our set was fairly mediocre, but we got by. But I'm tired of getting by, I want a drummer who will sound great. Afterwards we found out that the house sound man had a homophobic reaction to us; he sabotaged our sound mix and abandoned his post two songs into our set. Green Day's soundman noticed, and he stepped in and mixed us instead. Thanks, Randy! Conversely, the guy who did the monitor mix, a big blond jockish type, loved it and said he might make it to the show in Philly.

Stayed in Green Day's hotel rooms, a first; I actually ended up sleeping in Mike's bed (he wasn't there though). A big bed all to myself! Such little things mean a lot on a low budget tour.

7.31.94 New Britain, CT

What a dump! The Sting was the name of the club, and it had two sections—a big room where the band played, and a titty bar next door with a *Saturday Night Fever*–style dance floor. There was a secret passageway between the two so the bands could sneak a peek. A bouncer wore an AIDS KILLS FAGS DEAD T-shirt. It made me realize how condemned you are to a certain reality if your band becomes popular enough—there was nothing remotely "alternative" about any of the venues we've played this week.

8.1.94 Philadelphia, PA

Our last show for now with Green Day. We have gigs of our own to get us back across the country. Walked around South Street buying going away presents for Green Day and crew; I got Tre some barrettes, Billie Joe a masturbation condom (for "when masturbation's lost its fun"), and a fridge magnet for Mike that said SMOKING POT LEADS TO…I FORGET. Went to the gay bookstore Giovanni's Room and bought the new issue of the *Advocate*, with its article on queer punk. Our venue, the Trocadero, was run-down but charming. Our set? Good songs, sloppy execution with moments of interest, and a good reception apart from a smattering of homophobes. This is what we've gotten used to by now.

Butch and I ran onstage and kissed Tre during their encore. Afterwards, backstage, we presented our gifts; they gave us a cash bonus at the end, payment for a show we couldn't play (they had added one show to the end of the tour without telling our booking agent—we have our own show that night). What great treatment! We then went to their hotel and hung out more anyway. I'm sad it's over, but anxious to play for our own audience, small though it may be. The experience went better than expected, but I know how much better we can be.

8.3.94 Baltimore, MD

Today just couldn't help but be a letdown after the last

month. The show was okay, but seventy-five people just doesn't compare to twelve hundred.

Chris sat Butch down to talk today (as casual communication has been virtually nonexistent lately), and he agreed to complete this leg of the tour and then leave. But he wants to stay on good terms with us in case we tour with Green Day again. He thought our concerns, like the sound of his drum kit, were petty and trivial, and instead of acting professionally about it, took it as a personal affront. What Chris and I recognize as day-to-day sacrifices and minor inconveniences, he sees as major bumps in the road. We are not clicking, to say the least. Eight more days till we get home.

When we first discussed having Butch play with us, we told him it was opening for Green Day, which in retrospect was a mistake. (We found out later that despite his invitation to call him, he didn't really like our music, and just wanted to go on a big tour.) We didn't get along well with him personally, and his inconsistent playing felt indicative of someone not interested enough in our music to get it right. He told Chris a few days ago that we were a crappy indie band that wouldn't get anywhere.

Leaving Baltimore, Chris wanted to stop by Ganymede Press to try to cadge some back issues of *Daddy* magazine. He did, but got more than he bargained for—they talked him into modeling, right then and there—*while we waited in the van!* (Chris still insists he needed to have his arm twisted—yeah, right!) See *Daddy #21* for the results.

8.4.94 Philadelphia, PA

Back in Philly again for our own show. Being an over-twenty-one venue, not many people who saw us open for Green Day could go. Sadly, all ages shows are not always so easy to come by.

8.5.94 Hoboken, NJ / New York City, NY

Two shows today—Maxwell's in Hoboken early evening, the gay rock club Squeezebox in New York for a late-night gig. To celebrate this hectic day, Chris and I both got food poisoning. We ordered the same chicken dish last night in Philly, at a Mexican place on Second Street. Uggggggggh.... The nausea would come and go; we were sick and stressed. We were also disappointed in the turnout at Maxwell's, maybe twenty people. It's such a great club that I'd hoped we'd do well there, but we're on the wrong label, wrong coast, wrong profile. Oh, well.

Conversely, Squeezebox was totally our scene, our crowd. Here was our first queer crowd of the tour, and it was fantastic! We forgot we were sick for a while. The DJ was good, the drag queens were great, the crowd was cute, and it was a great space. I'd go all the time if San Francisco had something like this. Played for an hour at 2:15 a.m.; at one point onstage I said, "You're the crowd we've been waiting for—a queer audience that gets it!" and a guy yelled, "*You're* the *band* we've been waiting for!" Hey, me too!

8.7.94 Dayton, OH

Played an all ages club in a suburban strip mall, and it was a blast. A gayer crowd than usual, too. Really fun, although Butch played his worst show yet. His tempos were so fast I couldn't keep up, and I had to stop "Beercan Boy" and start over. It was so bad I was laughing! Six days to go! We woke up the next day at a fan's house in suburban Huber Heights, on a street called Watergate Drive, on the twentieth anniversary of Nixon's resignation. Synchronicity, anyone?

8.9.94 St. Louis, MO

One hundred and twenty five people on a hot Monday night in St. Louis means we're doing pretty damn well. We have a benefactor here, a wild middle-aged woman named Barb. She's Catholic, but smokes pot (Arkansas Polio Weed she calls it), goes to punk rock shows, and has a house full of Dead Kennedys, Fall, and Black Flag cassettes. She lives in a respectable burb thirty miles west of town, and on our way out of town she took us out for a huge, expensive lunch. She said it was being written off as a meeting her husband had with some bankers. Thank you, Barb!

Today our latest single came out, a cover of Prince's "Jack U Off." After spending a fair bit of money to get the photography right for the *Nine Inch Males* EP, this time I stole the cover photos directly from porn mags. Included as an unlisted bonus track was a safe sex public service announcement that Anthony Kiedis of the Red Hot Chili Peppers had done about condom use. The spot was considered too frank for radio; if young people are going to get the safe sex message they'll need facts and frank talk, and this PSA was just too honest. A fucking shame. During an NPR news story about its suppression they had actually played the whole thing; I taped it and slapped it on the end of side B.

8.10.94 Wichita, KS

Chris was in a totally bitchy mood this morning. He said it was an accumulation of details. I felt he was treating me like Butch! Three more days till we're home…

On the way to Wichita I suddenly realized we're in the West again. We'd entered the empty zone, the open country, and it felt like a relief. Driving around Wichita, we were back in the typical Western/Midwestern street grid pattern. It was 95 degrees when we arrived at four, and the promoter secretly put us up temporarily in a room in the luxury hotel he works at. Stayed till seven—three sublime hours of air conditioning, rest, NPR, and free phone calls.

The club, Kirby's Beer Store, has a legal limit of twenty-seven; some club's stages are bigger than this whole club. But they crammed in way more people than that; the whole underground scene seemed to turn out, and the place was crawling with queers. The onstage sound was lousy, but the loud crowd rallied my mood. What's more, I got to go home with the cutest guy there! Er, he came back to the hotel with me—the rightful tenants of our room canceled, so we secretly got to stay there for free. Butch (who I was sharing the room with) also met a special friend, and they blessedly didn't return till 5:00 a.m. Chris and a fan broke into the Jacuzzi and stayed up till four. We hope our host still has his job.

8.13.94 Western Nevada

In Salt Lake City our opening act was a group of female impersonators(!). After the show we left directly for San Francisco, driving all night to get home ASAP. I hugged Chris, told him I loved him and how much fun I'd had despite the obvious stresses (er, the other one third of the band). Chris also couldn't wait to get home and get Butch out of our hair. So here I am at 7:40 a.m., driving though Nevada, watching the morning sun casting gorgeous light and dramatic shadows upon brown, desolate mountains. I'm thinking about how much I enjoyed the trip, but also how little fun it was at certain points. I'm sure I'll mainly remember all the good stuff as time goes by. I'm thinking about the forty things I have to do when I get home; there's always plenty to do. Mail to answer. Drummers to call. Males to call! We were in New York a week ago, and now San Francisco beckons. Whee!

Little did we know that this was only the beginning, as we were headed for even bigger, longer, and more headache-inducing tours.

CHAPTER 9

Canadian Tour

In September 1994, we went back to Canada to do our own tour with the Canadian band Chixdiggit. David Ward (drummer number five) returned to drum for us, and it was a wonderful time; he played fairly well, but more importantly, the stress level was much lower than when Butch was with us. Chixdiggit (all straight, what did you expect with that name?), who were all twenty-two or twenty-three, were like our little brothers, and we grew very protective of them during this trip. They had a soccer ball, but none of us Americans could play, so we compromised and played four-square, which none of us had played since early grade school. We made up our own rules and played just about every day the last two weeks of the tour.

It was our first trip all the way across Canada (though

we cheated and skipped the empty part in the middle, as we always did, dipping down to Chicago). As we were reentering Canada, a customs official looked at Chris's Ramones T-shirt and said, "Great band!" I love Canada!

9.24.94 Toronto, ON

Finally made it to Toronto, our first time here. Horrendous traffic—the biggest city I've ever driven in that didn't have a bypass around it. (As of 2000, they had finally built one.) The show went well, except for one incident. Chixdiggit played before us, and during their set an extremely drunk punk insisted on violently slam dancing. It was just short of assault, and it made the crowd uncomfortable; they had to keep looking over their shoulders. During our set, he began tormenting people, so we stopped and had him ejected. It took several Chix members and others to forcibly remove him, and he kept trying to fight on the sidewalk after being tossed. After that, the mood was so ebullient that the rest of the show was tremendous fun.

9.26.94 Montreal, QC

Our first visit to Montreal was a debacle. Due to miscommunication between our booking agent and the club promoter, we arrived at the club to find 1) we were getting one third of the door, but only after $315 of expenses were met; 2) we were not billed as performing at all. We guessed the promoter had agreed at one point to take our show, but held out to find something better, and then decided to take us at the last minute. We hadn't been advertised, wouldn't get a cent, and nobody, but *nobody* knew we were playing. So for once, we didn't. We decided to be tourists and went to Rue St. Catherine, a notorious street of nightclubs and gay bars. David and I didn't see any guys we were interested in, but Chris sure did, and he was determined to find someone to take him home who would take pity and house the three of us. (We didn't know a soul in Montreal, and couldn't afford a hotel.) Meanwhile, David said he was going for a short walk. Two hours later, with no sign of him, we stopped a patrol car and asked what we should do. Just then David appeared, apologized, and, out of earshot of the police, told us he'd met these kids who offered to get him high, so he hung out with them smoking the worst pot he'd probably ever smoked. (He was a connoisseur.) As it turned out, Chris did get laid, finding us a place to stay in suburban Brossard with a very nice man named Pierre. Good work, Chris! I slept in the van, but we got showers and juice and toast and conversation in the morning.

I was enjoying being on the road this time around. People have asked if I started the band to get laid, and though I didn't primarily, I was hoping it would be a secondary benefit. On the road, I was having sex on a regular basis, with guys I found really cute—the type of guy who it seemed wouldn't give me the time of day back in San Francisco. So for several years the majority of my sexual experiences happened on tour.

Back in the states, in Cleveland, we got tremendous news from Jay—Green Day wanted us to open their arena tour! We'd be on tour with them again in a month!

CHAPTER 10
The Big Time:
Second Tour with Green Day

10.31.94 San Diego, CA

We pulled our van off I-5 at the Rosecrans Avenue exit and headed to the right, towards the ocean. There it was, looming ahead. A huge expanse of pavement, and in the center, a large, tall, round cement structure. On it was a large sign in flashing lights: SAN DIEGO SPORTS ARENA PRESENTS GREEN DAY! PANSY DIVISION! TONIGHT! SOLD OUT!

How the fuck had this happened to us? A mere year before, in October 1993, we'd taken our first tentative steps into the world of touring. Now, on Halloween, we were about to play for over eleven thousand people in a huge arena, a sports arena fer chrissakes, a temple to the kinds of activities I'd spent my youth trying to avoid. A bunch of fags singing about sucking dick. Were we about to be fed to the lions?

We greeted Green Day, our first meeting since the show with them in Philly nearly three months earlier. Things had changed for them. The *Dookie* album had gone through the roof—it had now sold three or four million. A year before they were a word of mouth cult band on a small label, and by fortunate timing and a great album, here they were at the top of the mainstream music scene. And they hadn't changed their sound or lyrics! They had quite suddenly catapulted to the top, and they were dragging us along with them. Every venue we had played with them on the summer tour was too small and sold out. Now they'd made the leap to the big time, but even an arena couldn't hold all the people wanting to see them. They'd gone from traveling in their modest bookmobile to a tour bus with bathrooms and twelve sleeping berths. They'd been to Europe in the meantime (and had played the latter-day muddy outdoor festival at Woodstock '94), but this was the first big arena show they'd played.

Before the show, I asked Tre if he was nervous. "Fuck yeah!" he exclaimed. I wasn't nervous in the sense of being scared. I was nervous in the sense of being agitated and excited. We now had our own dressing room. It had food and drinks in it. We had to park our van inside the building to avoid the massing Green Day fans.

We did a sound check. The place was so big, could enough people possibly show up to fill it? The stage was enormous, more room than we'd ever had before to move around. Barriers created space between the stage and the crowd; that gap was where the crowd usually was at our gigs. Our friend Matt, of Outpunk Records, traveled with us for the Southern California shows; before we went on, we played his label sampler, *Outpunk Dance Party*, over the PA system, and it was strange and thrilling knowing that thousands of kids were waiting for Green Day listening to this. Finally, it was time for us to play.

The lights went down. Huge cheers from the audience. We walked onto the stage, the lights came on. "Hi, we're Pansy Division from San Francisco." Quieter, some cheers, a few boos. We began our set. Mobs of young guys right down front were flipping us off. We hammed it up right away. Chris was shaking his ass, saying, "We're big fags from San Francisco!" Pandemonium. There was *way* too much going on at one time to see it all from the stage. I wished I could be floating above it all taking everything in, but I had to concentrate on performing; I was unable to observe closely without screwing up. People were giving us the finger and throwing objects at us from the left. Up right and center was a group of girls slamming together, getting into it. A small number of fans were cheering us on up over there, surrounded by a mob of middle fingers down over here. Activity was happening whether songs were going on or not. Some people were moshing, but they were moshing before the song even started. Mostly, we were just *in the way*, an inconvenience before Green Day came on. Being perched at the mic a majority of the time, I couldn't see most of what was taking place on the huge stage around me; I had no idea what was happening to David and Chris at any given moment.

But hey, we did it! We made them sit through us, made them have to deal with us. Maybe it made some people think, and maybe that's what kids would be talking about the next day at school. It's cool to ponder that kind of impact. I felt like it took a lot of guts to walk out there, but I couldn't decide if it was a failure or a triumph. And even though the crowd was ten times as large as any we'd played to on the summer Green Day tour, we sold a mere $164 of merchandise, and that was at inflated prices (the arenas usually take 15–20 percent of the proceeds, so bands have to jack up the prices). That's about what we'd sold at a GD show with eight hundred people, not eleven thousand. So the crowd was not digging us. It also meant we weren't getting through; you have to learn to work a crowd when you are playing in front of people that far away from you, and we didn't do it. Green Day, who already had cartoonish, larger than life stage personas, made the adjustment well. It could have gone much worse, so that was some consolation, and it was a rush, a real thrill to play in one night to more people than we'd played to on our own just-completed month-long tour. We walked around the arena during Green Day's set, but just a little, 'cause we were afraid we'd get beaten up. (One odd note: the concert promoter was gay, and he sought us out afterwards to buy eighty dollars' worth of merchandise for himself.)

Oh, and Green Day's merch guy, Gordon, was now bringing Green Day's Lookout releases with them—no more extra merch money for us this time around. But we did get a raise, now making five hundred dollars per show.

11.1.94 Los Angeles, CA

Our show in Los Angeles was at the Palladium, a much smaller (three thousand-plus) venue. The audience tension during our set was more palpable. In the middle of one song, I got hit in the chest with a full Big Gulp–size cup of ice water. Pelted with coins, at one point I turned to David Ward midsong to see a trickle of blood dripping down from the middle of his forehead. He'd been hit with a quarter square on, but didn't know he was bleeding. Coins made big dents on my guitar. But we were defiant, Chris even more in-your-face than before, and it was exhilarating. After watching Green Day's set from the side of the stage, I walked out to where the T-shirts were being sold, and as the crowd dwindled, I saw a father buying his fifteen- or sixteen-year-old son a Pansy Division T-shirt. It was satisfying, after all that grief from the crowd, to see we'd gotten through to that one in a hundred.

After a couple of shows on our own, we returned to San Francisco, where we were joined by Danny Panic (drummer number ten), who would play the next leg of the tour with us. The drummer for Ramones-inspired (that's being kind) Chicago band Screeching Weasel, Danny was a big fan of ours, and we'd talked to him about touring with us. He agreed, but had commitments that prevented him from doing the San Diego/L.A. shows. He flew out to San Francisco, and began rehearsals with us as soon as we got home; we had a week before meeting up with Green Day again to teach him our set and get him integrated into our band.

Two days before we left, Hole played at the Fillmore in San Francisco, and the three of us went. Chris brought a *Deflowered* CD with him, and was able to give it to Courtney Love as she walked off stage. She saw it, grabbed it, and when she recognized it, held it to her chest and said, "Kurt really loved your band, thank you so much." *Wow!* I was very happy and very sad at the same time. Though you never know whether people are saying such things just to be nice, a year later I did see an interview Kurt had done with gay British journalist Jon Savage where he said positive things about us.

11.15.94 Denver, CO

The Denver show was a great start. This time, working in a drummer on short notice paid off—Danny was great. The first real rocker drummer we'd had, Danny was a pro, and we soared. We were finally getting up the sound we'd been working towards. It was great fun, and well received. I recall a few homophobic guys lurking around our merchandise table that night, trying to cause trouble, but there were a lot of girls around to defend us, telling them to fuck off. Chris was now introducing "Reciprocate" every night with the same spiel, which always won the girls over to our side. "How many girls are here?" Loud cheers. "How many girls know that all guys can be assholes!" Deafening high-pitched roar. "Yeah, we know, 'cause we have to date them too. So you're having sex with them, and you're in bed with them; all they want is to get off, and they do, and then they're *too tired* to do anything for *you*. And you're sitting there going, ahem, what about *me?*" Huge roar! "To all those selfish guys we say: *Go down or go home!* Learn how to *reciprocate!*"

11.17.94 Kansas City, KS

Our second show was in Wichita, but before we could get there, disaster struck. This was the first day our van, a used one we had bought in April, had been in cold weather (it had snowed in Denver). About an hour east of Denver, I noticed white smoke coming from our tailpipe. I checked the temp gauge, but it was normal. I figured it was condensation from the cold temperatures. But it got worse. Gauge was the same. I was getting concerned, then suddenly a cloud of smoke burst from our engine. We were nine miles from the previous city, Limon, so we tried slowly crawling back there. Bad move. Turned out the gauge was busted. The van died, we got towed in, and were told our engine block was cracked and melted. We couldn't go on, and we couldn't get it fixed quickly. We missed the show. So the next morning, we rented a U-Haul truck, crowded the three of us into the front bench seat, and drove to Kansas City, getting there right at show time. We left our van to be repaired, and would have to pick it up on the way home. So there we were, second day of the tour, in a crowded vehicle, no padlocks, no loft bed, all comforts and conveniences gone. Gulp! Welcome to Pansy Division, Danny!

11.18.94 Chicago, IL

Next was Chicago. We had to drive overnight after the Kansas City show to get there. Now that Green Day had a tour bus, their driver would whisk them overnight to the next city as they slept. We had no such luxury, and we were uncomfortable and exhausted. Without being able to sleep in our vehicle, we'd be miserable for the next three weeks. So when we got to Chicago about 11:00 a.m., I called around, rented a minivan, and Green Day agreed to help cart some of our gear around. It was still cramped, but more civilized.

The Chicago show at the Aragon Ballroom was a landmark one for me personally. Being from Illinois, I'd seen many concerts there, including The Jam, Patti Smith, and The Clash (with The Undertones!). It was a dream of mine during The Outnumbered days to play such a big place, but we never came close. But now here I was! Danny being from the Chicago burbs, his friends and relatives turned out. Being able to get a bunch of my friends backstage helped make it a special night.

MTV was on hand to film Green Day. Thanks to them, there was abundant food and drink, which we were ravenous for after hardly eating the day before and driving all night. Because they were filming, the lights were kept on during the show, so we could see the entire crowd (4,500 people). They filmed a few songs of ours, as a test run. It was hard to read the audience, to tell if they liked it or not, or if they could hear the words. They just kept moshing. Perhaps the lights prevented a more negative reaction; there was a big cheer when we announced that it was our last song. But we hung out by the merchandise table, sold lots of stuff (it had picked up considerably since the first night in San Diego, a good barometer of our adapting to the situation) and signed lots of autographs, and were thanked profusely for just being there. Yay!

11.19.94 St. Paul, MN

Now that some fans had heard of us and recognized us, we got approached by teenage girls desperate to meet Green Day. Typical was the girl who pleaded, "I know Billie Joe would like me if he could only meet me." We were venturing out into the venues more often; there isn't much to do back-stage, and hanging around isn't too thrilling after you've done it a few times. At our own shows we can interact with fans, and we were missing that.

Also, because we were so far away from a lot of the crowd, they couldn't make out our faces to recognize us anyway. In St. Paul, we got spotted in a hallway and asked for our autographs, which then drew a swarm of people. It's a bit scary. One kid, who looked to be eight or nine, meekly asked, "Are you really gay?" I replied in the affirmative. "Wow!" he said. "That's so cool!"

Danny's mild case of bronchitis had worsened, and the seven-hour drive from Chicago to St. Paul in his chain-smoking and soon to be ex-girlfriend's car contributed heavily. But Green Day were major potheads (well, so is Chris), and they tried to make Danny feel better by giving him pot cookies a fan had brought. Except they didn't tell him they were pot cookies. Then Tre offered him some rocky road ice cream. With hash in it. Immobile to the point of paralysis, Danny slept on the Green Day bus, riding with them to Milwaukee. After a fitful sleep, he looked in the mirror to find he had been garishly made up overnight. At least the lipstick was an appealing shade.

11.22.94 Cincinnati, OH

After another good time in Milwaukee—we were getting the hang of the arena thing, and Danny, despite his illness, was in top form—Green Day took six days off for Thanksgiving, and we headed out for three club shows of our own. To play our own shows, we had to cram all our stuff into our minivan, 'cause Green Day weren't there for the overflow. The contrast between one hundred fans and ten thousand was almost surreal. We played in Cincinnati at Sudsy's, a bar/Laundromat. We didn't have much laundry to do, we'd just done it two days before, so we brought just a few things in to wash while we did our sound check. After sound check, I went out to the minivan, parked behind the club, and found the door open—and the passenger window smashed. Stolen were all our personal belongings—our bags and suitcases—and all our extra merchandise, boxes of CDs and T-shirts. Oh, if we'd only had our padlocked van here! At a time when things were going so right for us as a whole, so many things on a day-to-day level were going badly. But, we had to play a show. It wasn't the most fun we've ever had. It was such a what-the-fuck mood that we even played "Smells Like Queer Spirit," the last time to date we've performed it. We hadn't even rehearsed it with Danny (though he played it perfectly!). We each had a day or two's clothes; I had one pair of underwear. Then we got back to the Green Day tour, and had no time to shop for clothes. Green Day gave us some clothing (people were showering them with all kinds of gifts), but I wasn't able to buy underwear for a week.

11.25.94 Detroit, MI

Next up was our show at Cobo Hall in Detroit, another huge arena, 12,500+ sold-out seats. I walked around the upper reaches of the arena prior to our set, and talked to some kids holding up a big Pansy Division banner—cool! As a Kiss fanatic, Chris was especially stoked to play the place where *Kiss Alive!* had been recorded. However, we were not accorded the same rapturous reception as Kiss. We had wondered if and when we would encounter a hostile crowd, and it finally happened. It was bad from the first song; the audience rained shoes, lighters, and coins on us. They were negative and loud. A larger percentage of the audience hated it more than anywhere we'd been; there was constant booing and chanting. I could see very few people applauding, and those people were getting hell from others around them. Our usual tactics, which included enlisting the girls, weren't enough that night. Though the crowd was unrelentingly negative, we didn't cut our set. If they chose to make us suffer, we'd have to return the favor. Oddly enough, we sold over a thousand dollars in merchandise, a tour high, but we couldn't see the support from the stage.

Why that night? Why that city? Was Michigan really more redneck than elsewhere? The three of us scooped forty dollars in coins off the stage. People were throwing clothes too, and as we hadn't had a chance to shop for clothes after being ripped off, we picked through those too!

Around this time, Pearl Jam had their highly publicized war against Ticketmaster. Their high "convenience fees" and bogus charges were causing ticket prices to escalate, and Pearl Jam noted that their tickets would be priced at over twenty dollars and thus unaffordable for many of their fans. I was supportive of this antimonopolistic move, but it was a little hypocritical. Tickets for the Green Day show at Cobo Hall were only $7.50. Despite taking a stand against the slimier end of the music biz (Ticketmaster's practices are now the norm), all Pearl Jam had to do was lower their goddamn guarantees if they were really concerned about what their fans were paying.

11.27.94 Fairfax, VA

Green Day's tour manager had warned us of trouble looming at an upcoming show in Fairfax, Virginia, a conservative suburb outside Washington, DC. The promoter told Green Day in advance that they wouldn't allow us to play, that we weren't appropriate; Green Day's response to the promoter was that if we didn't play, they wouldn't play. Now that's what friends are for.

The promoter backed down, but when we arrived, he pulled me aside for a lecture. In a friendly but stern way, he said our material was too mature for Green Day's young audiences. He said that there would be eight- to twelve-year-olds in the crowd. I asked why he was worried about our lyrics and not Green Day's, which also have some references that might not be suitable. And who were these kids anyway? What parents were letting their kids go to concerts so young? I told him, if they're that young, much of what we sing about is going to go right over their heads, they won't get it. But they'll know they saw a gay band, and it will get them talking, one way or the other. To us that would be a victory, meaning we'd infiltrated Pat Robertson country. This guy kept saying things like he had a lesbian sister, and he was for gay rights, but not in these circumstances. He said he was dreading the day-after phone calls from parents. I told him I had the right to sing about sex, kids had the right not to have what they heard censored, and what we sang about was part of the world we live in. To counter years of hetero propaganda these kids had heard, a few bad words and risqué songs wouldn't do them any harm. This discussion went in circles for fifteen minutes, until I finally told him it was a waste of my time. When we played, the reception was mixed but more supportive than I'd figured; it was the only show we played with Green Day in the South. Ironically, the gig was at the Patriot Center at George Mason

University whose namesake refused to sign the Declaration of Independence because it didn't guarantee enough rights and freedoms. Yet we were being asked to tone down or cut out "provocative words" from our songs; now what kind of freedom is that?

12.2.94 Uniondale, NY

We were adjusting to the big stages, and this week's shows went over better. I remember Chris admonishing some hecklers in front of the stage in Philly, and telling him not to bother, that 98 percent of the nine thousand people there couldn't see what the hell was going on up front anyway. We received a friendly reception in Canada playing in Toronto and Verdun, outside Montreal, in a hockey arena where they put rubber mats over the ice and the crowd and stage on top of it. Afterwards, we picked Canadian dollar coins out of the ice in holes of the rubber mats.

On Friday, December 2, we got to New York. We played Nassau Coliseum, in the burbs on Long Island, 14,500 seats, sold out, our biggest arena yet. Walking around backstage, some of which was dimly lit, we thought we saw Joey Ramone, and went up to say hello, but it turned out to be Howard Stern. Which wasn't as exciting, but he was nice and mentioned us favorably and repeatedly on his next show. What really blew us away with the show was the thrilling reception. When they announced our name as we walked onstage, there was a huge cheer! We looked at each other in amazement. We then proceeded to play one of the best shows of the tour, with loud applause after each song. Though we had hecklers, we were glowing at our best reception yet.

Our friend Tim was at that gig; he had just moved to New York City that year from California. Tim, then twenty-eight, had an eighteen-year-old boyfriend who had a number of younger friends. He asked if they could come to the show and meet us, and I said sure, no problem. During the evening, Tim was backstage rounding up his five friends, getting them their backstage passes. The security guarding the backstage area gave him the most disgusted looks they could—they thought Tim was procuring teenage boys for Pansy Division. He figured the guards must have seen this happening—with girls—on a regular basis with other bands, but since he had the passes they really couldn't say anything. If looks could kill...

Later that night, we had another after-hours gig at Squeezebox in Manhattan, our second this year, and were interviewed on the way there by a writer from the *Village Voice*. At the club, I announced that we had just come from playing in front of ten thousand teenagers (which caused someone to yell, "Did you bring any of them with you?") and now we're here to play for the fags. By the end of the night we were exhausted but about as satisfied as we'd ever been. We conquered the mainstream audience and underground too. We were having it both ways. This was as good as it gets.

The next day was Saturday, and Green Day played on "Saturday Night Live." We went along with them, and got to hang out backstage and see all sorts of famous folk. Most of the cast of "SNL" were short. We met Roseanne, that week's host, as well as legendary music bizzer Ahmet Ertegun from WEA, Tim Armstrong of Rancid, and an Epic Records A&R rep sporting spiky, newly dyed green hair in an attempt to sign Rancid. Mike asked me for a Pansy Division shirt to wear onstage; we didn't have any with us at the moment, but Chris was wearing his big dick T-shirt with a PD logo on the back, so we cut it up and Mike safety-pinned the logo onto his shirt. We sat in the green room and watched most of it on monitors; we weren't allowed into the audience area, though we could wander around backstage (which was surprisingly small and cramped).

Afterwards, we were invited to the post-"SNL" dinner/hangout. Green Day were driven there in a limo (which they seemed a bit amazed at); we also tried cramming into it but there wasn't enough room. We thought we'd missed our chance to hang out with the stars, but then another limo glided up, we got in, and were driven to Planet Hollywood. We sat there with Roseanne and Chris Elliott and Rancid and Green Day thinking we'd better enjoy this 'cause it wasn't gonna last! The stroke of midnight meant it was December 4, my birthday, and Chris and some of the Green Dayers got me a birthday cake. It took a while to arrive, they told me later, which was a shame, because they had arranged to have Roseanne sing me "Happy Birthday"! But she had to leave to catch a flight, so the cake arrived after she'd left. Damn! But it was a great birthday, maybe my greatest birthday ever. It was my thirty-fifth, and if you'd asked me eight months before if I saw this night coming, I'd have said, No Fucking Way! It made me feel *soooo* good to know that I had stuck to my own ways and followed my own impulses to get to this point.

We went up to New Hampshire for a show on Sunday (a pretty lackluster night for both bands), then returned to New York on Monday for the biggest and last show of the tour—Madison Square Garden.

The Green Day boys were pissed off. The show was a multi-artist Christmas extravaganza: faux "alternative" Z-100's Acoustic Christmas. But no one had told Green Day it was acoustic until shortly beforehand, or that it would be a huge multiband festival show. The show had sold out on their name alone, and then the radio station added other acts. The lineup from top to bottom: Green Day, Hole, Weezer,

Melissa Etheridge, Bon Jovi (gag), Sheryl Crow, Toad the Wet Sprocket, Indigo Girls, and us. When Green Day found out about Bon Jovi they were fit to be tied. This was everything they (and us) had ever fought against. This was an alternative station? Yeah, well we knew what a joke that was. Bon Jovi was a local hero! Green Day said they wouldn't do the show. Their soon-to-be-ex-managers talked them into it, but they were fuming. The radio station tried to throw us off the bill, but Green Day said they wouldn't do the show if we didn't get to play. We'll always be grateful for the many times they stood up for us that year.

We got a ten-minute slot at 7:00 p.m. It was amazing! We squeezed in four songs. The crowd was still coming in; the place was two-thirds to three-quarters full for our set (about twelve thousand people) and it was tremendous, loud applause and loud cheers. It was as short as a breath though, and then it was over. But we'd never dreamed of playing such a place, and it was an incredible experience.

There were a lot of celebrities backstage. I stood next to Brooke Shields (she's tall). I saw Evan Dando of The Lemonheads. He was with Courtney Love, and neither was looking very well. Courtney gave Chris a kiss. (He kept the napkin that he used to wipe her lipstick off of his cheek.) Chris saw Mike Rutherford of Genesis. (I wouldn't be able to pick him out of a lineup.) We got interviewed for MTV; they spoke to each band, and when they ran a half-hour special about this show, they aired the interviews of every performer except us. We met all of the other acts (except Bon Jovi), and everybody was very casual and friendly, no rock stars trips or egos (except Bon Jovi). Melissa Etheridge told us we had a lot of guts, and wished us good luck. We felt like we were crashing a party, but tried to soak it all up; it would be over soon enough.

The sore point of the evening for everyone, it seemed, was

Bon Jovi. Without enough dressing rooms for each band to have their own, bands doubled up—except of course for Bon Jovi. Their entourage arrived early in the day, and commandeered the largest dressing room for themselves—the only one with telephones. No other bands were permitted in their dressing room. The only other phones were two pay phones in the hallway, but it was loud out there, and there was a line for them. In those pre-cell phone days, eight bands on the road in one place meant high demand for phones.

While other acts mingled backstage, Bon Jovi's entourage was easy to spot, especially the women. One had an appalling tanning salon tan (kind of a nuclear orange) and really unnatural-looking breasts. I thought she might have been a drag queen at first (but that would be an insult to drag queens). Jon Bon Jovi stayed in his dressing room until his time to play, and then had some lackeys *clear the hallway* so he and his own personal film crew could safely get through. The only people in the hallway were other musicians and their friends, but cleared we were. We cracked open our dressing room door and saw Bon Jovi getting pumped up for his show. He punched the air like *Rocky*! He grunted! He punched the air again! He looked like a total moron. The other acts watching were giggling behind their hands. And instead of walking onstage, he went to the sound desk in the middle of the arena floor and had a spotlight put on him there. Sadly, the young crowd seemed to like Bon Jovi as much as they did the other bands.

The evening ran a bit behind schedule, but the only performer to blatantly run overtime was (guess who!) Bon Jovi. By the time Green Day came on it was 12:45 a.m.; many of their underage fans had gone home. Billie Joe was so disgusted that he returned for their encore totally naked (which earned many negative comments because, my god, there were *children* in the building!). As it was a Christmas benefit for Z-100's charities, none of the bands were paid.

We had to hit the road directly after the show to drive Danny back to Chicago, and ourselves back to San Francisco. But we can say we did it, even if it was just that once.

CHAPTER 11

Pileup

After the whirlwind of the last six months, we were glad to get home for Christmas. We got busy right away putting together our next record, which we decided should be a compilation of our singles releases.

One reason we decided to compile *Pileup* was our overestimation of how many people still had turntables and would buy vinyl. We figured our singles would sell fewer copies than the albums, but they sold substantially less. Many PD fans weren't able to find the singles or even aware of their existence, so we compiled them onto a CD. Though I like all of the tracks on it, overall it's my least favorite of our albums. Fans rate it higher than we do. Eleven of the twenty songs are covers, which were never as important to us as the original songs we wrote. It's fun, but trifling, with our most propagandistic songs ("Ring of Joy" and "CSF"), our silliest songs ("Touch My Joe Camel," "Bill & Ted's Homosexual Adventure"), and the fun but already outdated "Smells Like Queer Spirit."

However, it did contain "Jackson," one of our best covers, a duet with Calvin Johnson of indie stalwarts Beat Happening (and later of Halo Benders and Dub Narcotic Sound System). I loved the Nancy Sinatra version as a kid (there was also a good Johnny Cash/June Carter version), and though it was a last minute choice it turned out better than some songs we'd been playing for months. I'm still partial towards our version of Spinal Tap's "Big Bottom," and "I Can't Sleep," an original song we'd recorded for an Outpunk Records compilation. Based on personal experience, the song reflects on picking up the guy you want and getting him home, only to find out you don't really want him and now wish he would stop snoring and go away.

It also included our version of Liz Phair's "Flower," one of our most requested covers. During the *Deflowered* sessions, drummer Lliam was enthusing about Liz Phair's *Exile in Guyville* CD, which was already a favorite of ours, and suggested that "Flower" would be a good cover for us. We agreed, practiced it on the spot, and recorded it the next day. Even though we got some of the lyrics wrong (sorry Liz, you didn't include a lyric sheet), it was one of our best gender-bent covers. This album was also where the much-requested "Homo Christmas" found a home. Putting all this on one CD cemented our penchant for silly humor, which once established, was a hard reputation to break.

This was also our first album to have a foreign release. We set up a deal with the U.K. indie Damaged Goods; unlike some U.S. indie labels, Lookout had no arrangements for releasing their titles in the United Kingdom or Europe. We hoped that having a Euro release would put us a step closer to touring there.

Around this time, a store in Jupiter, Florida—truly another planet—was warned by the local sheriff not to display our records in view of children. The police had received calls warning that it was carrying pornographic record covers, of our band and others. The store owner, who was very cool, sent us a video of the media coverage—it was the lead story on that evening's local news on the three local stations, two of them with live reports from the store! The inaccuracies and anchorpersons' bad hairdos were just what you'd expect; one station actually gave a balanced report, interviewing a few customers, but overall it was much ado about nothing. We were mentioned by name, and one station showed a copy of the "Bill & Ted's Homosexual Adventure" 45 with certain parts pixeled out. Gotta titillate those retired folks! The clip makes for hilarious viewing, and we later included it on the *Video History of Pansy Division*. Ultimately, the store had to set up an "adults only" bin behind the counter, but they still stocked it.

Was the sleeve obscene? Not to us. Our CDs bear no Parental Advisory warning labels (which we'd be forced to use if we were on a major label). The thought of someone naïve to sex seeing a photo of two men engaging in an act of love doesn't bother me. To me, the vicious hatred displayed by Jesse Helms (may he rest in eternal torment) is obscene. The blatant corruption of senators like Trent Lott and Mitch McConnell is obscene. Lack of gun control and the hypocritical war on drugs is obscene. To have the Mormon Church donating thousands of dollars to defeat gay marriage initiatives, despite the supposed separation of church and state (and their tax-free status), is obscene. Two guys doing it in bed is charming and sweet.

Once again we decided to hit the road and we still needed

a drummer. I got down on my knees and pleaded, but Danny Panic still wouldn't permanently join our group. He wasn't ready to leave Chicago or his band. We asked anyone and everyone we knew if they knew of a drummer, anywhere in the country, and our T-shirt guy, Smelly, pointed us in the direction of Dustin Donaldson (drummer number eleven).

Dustin was about to move to San Francisco from Kalamazoo, Michigan, and we spoke over the phone and arranged to meet up once he got here. We had actually hung out a couple times before we left for the tour with Danny. Dustin had some ideas we weren't sure about (and a look that really didn't fit our style), but he nominated himself as our drummer, thus beginning a very bumpy ride that lasted nearly two years. Taking on Dustin meant abandoning the ideal all-queer band lineup, but he was a good drummer, and we needed one, and he was available. We took him on a three-week tour, and it went pretty well.

Much of this tour was in the South, which was less-traveled and more fear-inducing territory for us. We played what were to this date our only shows ever in Alabama and Arkansas (playing Arkansas' one liberal college). Booking an Alabama show was difficult—we ended up playing a house party in Auburn, something we normally don't do. But it turned out well, and the best part was a wild queer boy with several genital piercings who got naked on stage with us, and who I got very friendly with afterwards. During the show there were some rather shifty looking types milling around, who didn't seem to be there for the music. After finishing our set we hung around selling our merch, with our equipment in the next room; I looked out the window to see these losers trying to stuff our drum kit through the window and put it into their waiting pickup truck. When I asked what they were doing, they said they'd come to get their drums. Once busted, they slunk away pretty quick.

We played Phoenix on the same bill as newly signed Jimmy Eat World; it was their hometown, and their fans hated us and fled in droves. Their music was absolutely ordinary (they improved a few years later) but I guess that's what people liked about them. Billed last after them, we watched three hundred paying customers dwindle to thirty by about fifteen minutes into our set, and people hurled food at our van as we left (mashed potatoes all over the windows). In Salt Lake City, we had a heckler—a middle-aged gay guy who thought we were causing harm to the gay community by singing so blatantly about sex. Since there were only twenty people there, he stood out in the crowd. The second we finished, he rushed up to the stage to tell us we were hurting the cause and setting the gay agenda back years.

Prior to this the tour, I got a call from someone at MTV wanting to know when we'd next be in New York. They were doing a segment on queer punk and wanted to film one of our shows and interview us for MTV News. I cheerfully told them that MTV had already filmed a show of ours in Chicago AND interviewed us in New York and they should track down the footage, buster! Which they did, calling us back two weeks later to let us know that the segment was about to air. We got up at 5:00 a.m. at someone's house in Dallas to watch it. The entire piece was about four minutes long, ran six or seven times that day, and six or seven times again that weekend on "The Week in Rock." Mostly centered on us, it was intelligently done and presented us accurately. With Green Day's help, we'd infiltrated the mainstream media. The following week, *Pileup* was released, and thanks in part to the MTV exposure, sold out its entire pressing (about 7000 copies) almost immediately; in one week, it had outsold each of our previous albums.

Around this time we reaped another reward of being on tour with Green Day—product endorsements! With their encouragement and contacts, I got a much-needed new amp and guitar from Fender, Chris got a new Fender Jazz bass and a discount on an amp from Gallien-Krueger, and we all got free sneakers from Converse (which we wore anyway), three pairs a year. Every time we'd hit New York, we'd call ahead, place our order, and stop by to pick up our shoes. Dustin got drumsticks and cymbals at deep discount. All we had to do was credit them on our next album, which we did. We were doing so well I even had to change my phone number, and get an unlisted number. We were on a roll.

CHAPTER 12

Down Under

In the meantime, our attempts at doing an Australian/New
Zealand tour bore (kiwi) fruit. We had learned before the last
leg of the Green Day tour that it would happen, right before
we'd met Dustin, so we secured another temp drummer to
do the overseas shows (we had to apply for the work permits
months ahead of time). Patrick Hawley (drummer number
one returns!) had played on *Undressed* but had played live
with us only once. He flew to San Francisco, rehearsed for a
few days, and we were off on our first overseas tour.

Australia was great! Even now it seems incredible that
it really happened. None of the Lookout bands had been
there, not even Green Day. The promoter hired a top-notch
publicist, and our presence was treated like a big deal.
We got interviewed on national radio, played fairly large

professional venues, and the crowds reacted quite well. It was our first time driving on the left side of the road, and our first with a tour manager (he drove).

We played Brisbane, Canberra, Adelaide, and several shows each in greater Sydney and Melbourne. In Melbourne we were interviewed at a gay and lesbian radio station and played two nights at the Punters' Club. The first night, a cute, drunk skinny boy jumped up on stage and took off his shirt; he was hanging from a beam above the stage, kicking at people, and the bouncer threw him out. Too bad. I instructed someone in the front row to undo his pants, and if he danced naked up there I'd let him stay. Oh, well. The second night, a group of very cute boys stood right up front. They didn't strike me as Pansy fans, and as soon as we started, they looked stunned. They lasted six songs, until the "Hi Honey, I'm homo" line of "The Cocksucker Club" drove them out. When I sang the line "Look what I found in your groovy underwear!" I leered at the cutest one with as much lust as I could muster.

In Canberra we played a posh lesbian bar; they liked us, and supplied our best deli tray ever, but made us play *really*, *really* quietly. In Sydney, we visited the Imperial Hotel, where the drag scenes in *Priscilla, Queen of the Desert* were filmed. We got a private guided tour of the Sydney Zoo, courtesy of a gay guy who worked there. We heard Liz Phair's "Supernova," with the line "you fuck like a volcano," uncensored on daytime national radio. Also, I got to meet and have my photo taken with Evan Dando of The Lemonheads, who I'd spotted but not spoken with at Madison Square Garden two months earlier. By lucky chance I crossed paths with Lindy Morrison, drummer for one of my favorite bands, Australian cult pop outfit The Go-Betweens, and chatted with her for about ten minutes in a postcard shop on Bondi beach.

However, one Australian show was a big dud. It was a

YMCA pool party in a Melbourne suburb where we opened for Boom Crash Opera, an INXS-type mainstream Australian band whose popularity had peaked but were still well known. Our tour promoter had graciously booked this extra show as a way to break even on our tour. However, it was early on a Sunday afternoon, and the place was full of kids and old folks. As our material was primarily risqué then, it was the only time in the history of our band that I felt embarrassed to sing our songs. I cringed through several songs and left out lyrics. Patrick hated every minute of it. I'm not embarrassed about anyone hearing us, or about younger people hearing us, but the setting was wrong.

We played with Aussie bands who were about to be big there: The Mavis's, who had a very out and very cute singer/guitarist, and Regurgitator, who, although straight, had a song called "I Sucked a Lot of Cock to Get Where I Am." I met a number of people from other Aussie bands I liked, and even a few gay musicians.

Australia was a veritable feast for guys. In Canberra, Chris met a man he described as Cockadile Dundee, with the biggest one *he's* ever seen, which later inspired his song "Dick Of Death." After a sound check in Sydney, on gay Oxford Street, I was standing outside the club with a couple of hours to kill when a gorgeous guy walked by. With nothing better to do, I followed him for a couple blocks. I thought I'd see where he went; maybe he'd go into a cafe or something and I'd have to the nerve to say hi. He turned a corner, walked halfway down the block into a building. It was unmarked but didn't look like a residence. On closer inspection, I realized it was a gay bathhouse! Here was my chance! So I paid to go in but couldn't get him to pay me the slightest attention. Oh, well, at least I was scoring at our shows.

Less inspiring was our week in New Zealand. I had been

especially excited about going there because I was a fan of a number of local bands, such as The Bats, The Chills, The Clean, Bailter Space, and Tall Dwarfs. But New Zealanders seemed pretty apathetic, lacking interest in us as well as our enthusiasm for their own homegrown bands. Unlike the one in Australia, our promoter was not professional, showing up late at the airport, barefoot, with a van whose back window wouldn't completely shut. After we'd asked him where we could get good food, he took us to KFC. Afterwards I got so sick I spent a good part of the following day vomiting. (All three times we've had food poisoning on tour it's been from eating chicken.)

Our van, equipment, and soundman were substandard. Our promoter usually toured punkier bands and seemed unprepared for a band who wanted to work at getting a good sound and didn't want fast food. Each club charged a fee for use of the PA, but the PAs were shit. Monitors (which they called "fallbacks") were absent or useless. Practically no one came to the first three shows, and in Dunedin people sat on the fucking floor until the last song. During that show a woman punched some guy in the face and then split, and he danced alone with his head bleeding for a good part of the evening.

We fared better on the North Island in Wellington and Auckland (where we played with Tall Dwarfs singer Chris Knox) and at a glorious gig we lucked into at the last minute in Hamilton. Throwing Muses had canceled their show at the university there, and we replaced them on the bill, headlining for over a thousand enthused students during orientation week. It was Patrick Hawley's first experience with a huge, loud crowd wanting encores and autographs.

One odd incident: in Wellington, I was recognized on the street by someone who remembered me from The Outnumbered! He'd emigrated from Illinois to New Zealand and knew nothing of Pansy Division. I was as floored as he was!

It had been a great trip, one unimaginable for us a year earlier. We had an opportunity and we were making the most of it. Still, we were looking forward to getting home and working with our new drummer.

CHAPTER 13

Long Hot Summer

Back home, we began rehearsing in earnest with Dustin. He had learned some of our songs for the January tour, but now it was time to start learning the new songs Chris and I had written. Never in the band's history had we gone out on the road, perfected new material, and then gone into the studio to record it with the same drummer we'd learned it with. Our goal was to have the songs evolve more organically, rather than record them with someone who learned the songs just to record them. Chris and I had always come up with our songs sitting at home, which gets you different results from creating sound in a room together. Our goal was to nail that live-in-a-room band sound.

Dustin had played in an art-metal band in Michigan called Thought Industry, which had two CDs out influenced by Rush and Skinny Puppy. He said he was into the concept of our band, and wanted to add things to our basic pop format; that was also what we wanted, but once we began working on the first songs with him it was apparent he had no patience for pop minutiae. His attitude was that Chris and I should figure out the details, and then bring in the song. We were disappointed, but hey, we needed a good drummer, so we worked around it. We were so relieved to have a solid drummer that we overlooked the difficulties.

Dustin had moved to San Francisco without a lot of money and wasn't making a lot from being in our band. Chris and I were doing okay because of royalties from our record sales, but we needed to tour frequently to make a living. Dustin wasn't on any of the records, so we suggested he take a temp job when we were off tour, like Chris and I sometimes did. He thought we should support him; he wanted royalties from records he hadn't played on, since he was in the band now. We said that if we gave him money from the records, we'd be giving him money for someone else's labor, money someone else had earned. Also, having just moved to San Francisco, he wanted to stay home more. Now that we'd finally landed a drummer, Chris and I wanted to do the extensive touring an unsettled lineup had prevented us from doing earlier. So many people had seen us with Green Day; we thought, let's go back out there and see how many will come back to see us on our own, and build our career that way.

In May, we played the last shows we've done with Green Day. Our tours with them took us out of town, so we'd never played a hometown date with them. When they asked us to open two nights at Kaiser Auditorium in Oakland, we were thrilled! Eight thousand people a night! Plus, it was a benefit for Food Not Bombs, who feed the homeless. We brought back a couple of our go-go dancers, and had two wild shows. It was great to show the locals what we'd been doing elsewhere. With Dustin aboard, it was the fourth drummer Green Day had seen us with in only ten months.

Before we started our long summer tour we went into the recording studio with Dustin for the first time. We recorded songs for a forthcoming single and did live run-throughs of the new songs we'd been working out. It went quite well (which was a bit of a relief), though we weren't entirely happy with the sound of the finished product. Using a digital ADAT system, it was the first time we'd done a non-analog recording, and we could tell the difference (mainly in the way the cymbals sound mushy). The A-side was "Valentine's Day," an all-too-autobiographical heart-on-the-sleeve rocker about being single on the national couple's holiday; the B-side, as was our custom, had a couple of covers. Chris sang Josie Cotton's "He Could Be the One," which later appeared on a Valley Girl soundtrack tribute album, and we rocked up Depeche Mode's "What's Your Name," renaming it "Pretty Boy" (which is what it should have been called if they'd had the nerve, given the lyrics…but hey, they're not gay, they're just British). It was released the following year just before V-Day in a red sleeve on red vinyl.

We set out on the Fourth of July, seeing fireworks at nightfall while driving through Salt Lake City. The first week of the tour was pretty easy going. We had a fantastic time in Iowa City—almost felt like stars. Due to a cancellation, we were there for two days. Our show went great, and then we did zine and college radio interviews. Walking around town the next day, we were continually stopped and complimented on the street. As we were leaving a food co-op, an employee came racing out to bestow thanks on us for coming to Iowa City. At a gas station on the way out of town, a cute guy in a leather jacket walked by as we were pumping gas, recognized us, said he loved our band, and asked for a sticker. For a day, we owned this town!

We played Kalamazoo, Dustin's hometown, and an avalanche of his friends attended. In Iowa City, he ran into two friends who'd relocated there. I bring this up because almost every single one of his male friends was really cute. Of course I had to ask, but Dustin said they were all straight. The goatee/short hair "new clone" thing so prevalent in San Francisco at that time wasn't happening in the Midwest, and I was loving every minute of it.

The show in Kalamazoo brought up one of the unexpected difficulties of being on tour. There were four bands on the bill, and we went on at 1:30 a.m., way too late, especially for a Monday night. People who'd driven in from out of town couldn't stay, and we only got to play for thirty minutes, instead of our usual forty-five to an hour. So often, the staff doesn't give a shit, and tonight I blew up at the soundman. He was taking his sweet time, and as a performer one can either be mild-mannered or make it an issue. (Or have your manager do it…um, that would be me.) Though the headliner (last slot) makes the most money, it's actually better to play the next to last slot on a three-band bill. We were pretty sick and tired of the battle to get onstage at a decent hour. With all the pent-up energy and frustration, we had one of our wildest shows ever. Nonstop fuel-injected mayhem! Dustin said it was the most people he'd ever seen dancing at a show there.

In summer 1995 the weather was total hell. We were in Chicago the week hundreds of people died from the severe heat. It was 105 degrees at its worst, with 100 percent humidity. We had two shows in Chicago, staying in my friend's non-air-conditioned apartment, where it didn't get below 95 degrees overnight. With no sleep, we drove out to the suburbs to spend the afternoon at a friend's air-conditioned house before going to the gig that night. We never made it. Our van stalled in stop-and-go traffic in the fast lane of the Kennedy Expressway. Traffic was going just fast enough to make crossing four lanes extremely dangerous. It was over 120 degrees inside our van, which we couldn't abandon 'cause it was full of our instruments. We were trapped; we couldn't cross traffic to go for help.

Just as we were feeling desperate and totally bummed out, a car pulled up behind us and stopped. A woman with a five-year-old girl got out, and asked us if we needed any help. Yes, yes, yes! I asked her why she'd stopped, and she said that she was a lesbian, saw the rainbow flag on our bumper (we'd gotten bolder since our first tour), and thought she'd help us out. She drove me back to her nearby apartment and I called AAA for a tow. Overwhelmed with similar breakdowns, they had a four-hour wait. This woman had just moved there from Dallas, but she knew a local guy with a truck who could probably haul us to the gig. She reached him, he was free right then, and for forty-five dollars he came over with his truck. We drove back to the van, which after an hour had started again, and was parked near the exit ramp. We drove the van a few blocks to a repair shop, unloaded our bags and musical gear, and got a ride to the club, the Metro. Though we thanked her profusely and called her our guardian angel, in the haste of events I neglected to write down her name or address. She is one of our heroes. Though we're not big fans of what the rainbow flag has become these days, ever since that day we've made sure we had one on our bumper.

Once we got to the gig, we discovered that the building had no power. The power was on across the street, but not on our side. People kept arriving, but many left. We had to do something, so Chris and I decided to sing songs a cappella for those lingering outside. This became something we would turn to in times of need in the future. Our a cappella version of "Negative Queen" came from this. It went over great; during our fourth or fifth song the power came back on. By the time we got onstage at 1:00 a.m., over half the crowd had split, but we got out our frustration, playing our hearts out to the two hundred or so who remained. Sadly, prior to the exodus it would have been the biggest crowd we'd ever drawn in the United States on our own, but we sweated our asses off for those who stayed.

In Madison we played their Gay Pride event. We did two shows in one day—an afternoon outdoor show and an evening gig at a club. Outdoors, the stage area was separated from the beer tent/dance floor area, which was playing Whitney Houston and The Village People. Though there must have been a thousand people there, only thirty people came over to watch us. Hmph. The bar show that evening was in an old hotel that had been converted into a number of clubs. There was a video bar, a posh salon-styled bar, a bar with a DJ, and a live music club; though considered gay clubs, not all were explicitly so. All the bars within the building were connected by a loudspeaker system, and after it had been announced several times that we were about to begin, we played to no more than fifty people, many of whom weren't gay and had come just to see us. Irritated, we checked out the rest of the place after we played, to find packed crowds dancing to The Village People and Whitney Houston (again). We had just played successful Pride gigs in San Francisco and Los Angeles the previous month to a thrilled response. Were we barking up the wrong tree? Backward Midwestern provincials (my heritage)? The organizers were nice and apologized for the apathetic response. Though it seemed to us like we were the perfect band for such events—pro-gay, pro-sex, damn fun!—the poor response led us to avoid Pride events for several years.

With my grandfather and father, 1963.

As a junior in high school.

For my fanzine *Hoopla*, Dena and I concluded the next big thing to out-punk punk would be Ugly! Summer 1977.

Our first promo photo, December 1991. Me, Chris Freeman, and drummer Jay Paget.

1993 promo shot, drummer David Ward in the middle.

Backstage with Green Day (Mike, Tre, Billie Joe), June 1994.

That's me curled up backstage with Billie Joe. We had discussed doing some fake shots depicting Billie Joe in gay situations, thinking that'd mess with the media. We never got farther than this, in part because it was the last shot on this roll of film. July 1994.

Me and Chris on tour in Brighton, England, summer 1996.

Sweating in the studio with Tre Cool from Green Day, October 1996.

Glamming out, 1997, first photo with both Patrick (far left) and Luis (far right).

Rob Halford from Judas Priest joins us onstage, San Diego, July 1997.

Promo shot for *Total Entertainment!*, 2003.

Jon Ginoli,
circa 2009.

Our van's engine was never the same after its Chicago heatstroke. It broke down six times in six weeks; we repaired it and it kept breaking down. We were fucking miserable. We weren't getting enough sleep and staying somewhere air-conditioned was a luxury. Tempers were flaring, but we did manage to have some great shows. One was in Evansville, Indiana, a last minute gig that turned out to be amazing. Our opening band, who'd driven in from Louisville to play, were so excited to be playing with us they said they hadn't slept the night before. We played a community center on the edge of town surrounded on three sides by head-high cornstalks. It was a great summer night, with tons of kids showing up. After being bummed out about whether our van would make it, a great show was a relief. I felt so good I jumped around and kissed boys in the front row during "Bunnies." One young guy French-kissed me something fierce, and came back for more face-sucking after we finished, saying he was sort of bi. Sort of.

We played Nashville for the first time. We went to Music Row, where old country music stars had souvenir stores. At the George Jones store, we saw rows of Aunt Jemima-style watermelon-eating figurines! We were shocked; we thought you had to go to a museum to see that kind of shit. Our show was at Lucy's, a record store with a large back room for all-ages shows. It was pretty well attended, especially for a weeknight in a new town. Usually when people dance at our shows, they're right up front, but tonight the dancers were in the back of the hall, with other people pressed up against the stage. During the show I noticed a very tall college boy with broad shoulders and an adorable smile. He was making eyes at me, and I started making them back. I blew him a kiss, and he blew one to me. He was dancing in the back but came up front as each song ended to meet my eye. During the "Bunnies" finale, when Chris sprays the crowd with silly string, I jumped into the crowd and gave him a kiss. He shoved his tongue down my throat, and I thought I had a good thing going. After the show, I went over to talk to him. I asked him how old he was, and he said, with gleeful enthusiasm, "I just turned fifteen two weeks ago!" Needless to say, that night I slept alone.

We played at the Grog Shop in Cleveland, one of our favorite clubs, and our opening act was the new British band Supergrass, doing their first U.S. tour. They were in the U.K. Top 5 just then and were opening for us! We had our little van, and they had a bus, which their tour manager said cost five thousand dollars a week. I think they made two hundred and fifty dollars that night. Some of their songs were good ("Caught By The Fuzz"), but that night I felt we were better.

We were particularly looking forward to a few shows we were doing with Tribe 8. We had a show with them in New York City at a club called Tramps, and one in Washington, DC at the 9:30 Club, which I had played a decade earlier with The Outnumbered. I never thought I'd see the place again and was excited to be returning as one of the two leading American queer bands. We had actually discussed doing a whole tour with Tribe 8 but realized that a double bill doesn't earn double the money; neither band was in a position to endanger their finances for an entire tour. Roughly the same audience would come to see each band, although we'd draw more men and Tribe 8 more women. So I felt glad we were able to do at least a couple shows together outside San Francisco.

The excitement in DC was palpable. We drew a large crowd, very mixed between men and women, gay and straight and in between. The New York dyke band Sexpod opened, then we came on, playing one of our best sets ever. We weren't trying to outdo each other (our bands sound fairly different), but we really wanted it to be as great as possible. We played with confidence, and when they played, Tribe 8 were spectacular. It was almost as if we could feel the country changing just a little bit.

The next day, in New York, walking around town, we saw a number of large gig posters wheat-pasted all over lower Manhattan. An all-ages show, we had three hundred people going wild that night at Tramps, including a large number of teens who'd seen us on the Green Day tour, plus a variety of NYC queers of various ages and genders. The sound tech had a DAT player and we paid twenty-five dollars to have the show taped. It sounded so good that we later released a cassette of the show. Again, both bands rose to the occasion; this was a moment we'd all hoped and waited for, and it was here. You're always trying to improve, trying to do better, but this moment was one of satisfaction.

While in New York, we met with a fan who worked at MTV. He took us up to visit the offices, introduced us to Kurt Loder (who had done the piece on queer punk MTV had run a few months before). We were told our only shot at airplay was on "120 Minutes," their alternative program. Green Day and Nirvana's success had blown open some doors, and we were trying to walk through one of them. None of the videos we'd made so far were anywhere near the quality needed to get on MTV, but knowing we had a possibility of being shown was food for thought.

When we played again at Squeezebox in New York City, we met Ned Sublette, the writer of the song "Cowboys are Frequently Secretly Fond of Each Other." We asked him if he was gay, and he said no, but told us if you grow up in West Texas and are the least bit artistic, you are basically suspected of being a fag anyway. He was very nice, and we were quite happy to meet him; we told him how to contact Lookout and collect his royalties.

While in Boston, we did our first (and last ever) Tower Records in-store performance. Though we'd been in direct contact with the store, no one had informed us it was to be an acoustic show. Then, after we arrived, the manager told us he had a problem with our content; there might be kids in the store. I told them they should have brought up all of that earlier; with those restrictions, we would have skipped the gig. But we acted professionally and did the show, toned down a bit, and absolutely hated it. A waste of time and energy and a big hassle.

We played Provincetown, and the culture clash was evident. In a town full of people walking around looking for something (and someone) to do, we drew fifty people. Some San Francisco friends of ours, libidinous drag musician Pussy Tourette, and stand-up comedian Mark Davis, told us the club had censored both of their acts. Who did they think they were getting: importing the freaks from SF? Log Cabin Club Theater? But we were there for just one night and didn't clean up the act.

We had a post office box in San Francisco, and one of my roommates would check it every couple of weeks when we were on the road. He would forward boxes to us at various friendly locations, full of mail orders, fan mail, and San Francisco newspapers so we could keep up with life at home. We'd bring shipping supplies with us, so we could package up orders and ship them out without people having to wait months. We'd do this mainly while in the van, en route to somewhere or another. We hoped being this organized would help us make enough money to keep going as a full-time band and not have to get other jobs.

We found that we had developed followings in some towns where we'd played with Green Day (Detroit, Cincinnati, New York, Chicago, Cleveland, Toronto) but not others (Philadelphia, Montreal, Omaha, Indianapolis, San

Diego). It was very hit and miss, great audiences followed by mediocre or lousy ones. In Charleston, South Carolina, a fan approached us and had me and Chris sign his dick. (I have pictures.) He was pretty cute, and I told him I'd like to see an expanded version of my autograph. He expressed interest but said he'd have to ditch his girlfriend, who was also at the show; sadly, they disappeared before the show was over.

Late one night we broke down somewhere in South Carolina. Our tow truck driver had just moved back there from San Francisco the week before. He said he'd gotten sucked into the heroin scene, and had come home to clean up. He asked if we had any good Cali weed—said the local stuff was terrible—and we smoked him out as a thank-you for helping us out.

Somehow the van survived long enough to get us home. The first time I went to start it after we returned, it wouldn't run; after six repairs and no clear diagnosis, we finally had the thing towed away. In the meantime, Chris and I had come into a bit of money. When we were on tour with Green Day, they told us they were lining up music for a film, *Angus*, and wanted to get us on the soundtrack. They ended up using "Deep Water," and we got ten thousand dollars! The movie wasn't a big hit, but it was shown on just about every cable-TV system worldwide, earning us airplay royalties from places like Singapore, South Africa, Argentina, and Poland. We spent it upgrading to a bigger, more comfortable used van, but decided never to tour again in the summer.

CHAPTER 14

Touring Tensions

We kept our booking agent busy. Jay usually did a good job but would too often procrastinate about securing gigs. Some gigs would be lined up less than three weeks in advance, which aggravated Lookout, who said that wasn't enough time to do proper promotion. We agreed, and talked to him about it, but though we gave him plenty of lead time, way too many things would change at the last minute. But for two and a half years he did our bookings, and his being Canadian was advantageous; we kept returning there and developed a following.

That fall of '95 we did a United States/Canada tour with two Canadian bands, Cub and Pluto. Both had records out on our Canadian sister label, Mint Records, who released some of Lookout's titles in Canada. We also visited cities we'd missed before. About a week into the tour, Dustin announced one day, apropos of nothing, that he was "fuckin' bored." He said it in a threatening way, like, "Do something about it," or "What we're doing doesn't really interest me." This set a pattern for the rest of his tenure in the band—often acting like he really didn't give a shit, but saying otherwise when pressed; it was confusing figuring out how to handle him. I think he was frustrated that he couldn't just step in and do things his way, but we already had a successful style and approach we were happy with and weren't about to abandon. Still, we were as inclusive as we could be considering he wasn't on any of our records; we made sure to mention him in interviews if he wasn't there, and have him meet our friends. We thought that maybe after he did a record with us he'd be happier and feel like a full-fledged member, and we'd be more unified.

Onstage we were going over better than ever, so Chris and I put aside our personal feelings for the moment. On this tour we played Saskatoon, Saskatchewan, which we'd played with our friends Chixdiggit the year before. That time, the response had been so tepid that we swore we wouldn't come back. Though we were on stage in the same room with these people, they'd responded as if we were on TV. For this tour, we bowed to our Canadian friends who wanted to play there again. We decided that we would do *anything* to get a reaction from the crowd, and after our best efforts met with light scattered applause, we resorted to nudity. It woke a few people up, but twice now the audience seemed to lack a pulse. We might not be the best band in the world but we *are* entertaining, and nowhere else has the response been so apathetic.

Speaking of nudity, it was during Dustin's tenure in the band that we acquired a reputation for it. Our lone straight member was always the most eager to remove his clothing on stage; he played so hard that his clothes would be drenched with sweat. This goaded Chris into being more of an extrovert. However, I felt like we didn't need to resort to nudity to be effective, and I held out. The first time I got naked was the first time we played in Chapel Hill, North Carolina, at the famous Cat's Cradle club. The show had been so good, the response so enthusiastic, that I felt it merited something special. Chris and Dustin had stripped off for the first encore; when we earned a second, I followed (birthday) suit. My band mates were as surprised as the crowd! Later, we went to a restaurant where a number of fans were hanging out; when we entered, we got a standing ovation! And I went home with a cute boy as well. It was a perfect day.

During the Canadian part of the tour, we flew from Vancouver to New York to the Gay and Lesbian American Music Awards (GLAMA). It was their first such ceremony; they weren't actually giving awards that year, but held the event to raise consciousness about the number of gay musicians and show some of them off to both the music industry and the public. It was fun, a very nice bit of whirlwind. They flew us in, we did interviews and performed three songs. The nicely dressed, seated crowd was taken aback by our loud performance but applauded politely. Afterwards, we hobnobbed a bit, spent a too-brief six hours in individual hotel rooms, and flew back to resume our Canadian tour. We found out that to be eligible for the following year's awards, you had to apply and pay a fee for each category you wanted to be considered for. Why pay to be nominated? We're gay and American and play music, isn't that enough for a nomination into the Gay and Lesbian American Music Awards? We never applied and thus never won.

We played in Topeka, Kansas, home of the homophobic "God Hates Fags" preacher Fred Phelps, famous for picketing funerals of those who died from AIDS. Our promoter tried to get Fred to picket our show by stapling a flyer to his church's door, but Fred did not show. The creepy club manager assumed (wrongly) that our all-girl opening band Cub were dykes, and he tried hitting on them because he thought two girls doing it was hot…or something.

On this tour we played most of the new songs that would become our next album. We were scheduled to record at the end of November. Because of our busy tour schedule, we planned out the album cover in advance, doing the photography and artwork for the booklet before we actually recorded it. During the tour, the proofs were sent ahead to us for our approval. I had typed up the credits for the album, and when Dustin saw them, he completely flipped out, precipitating a huge fight in the course of which he threw an entire pitcher of water on Chris. He was livid that he had not been given songwriting credits. I told him, well, that he hadn't written any of them! We had given him an opportunity early on to be in on the process of writing the songs and he had opted out, saying he was bored by it and that Chris and I should bring in finished compositions. His opinion seemed to be that if he played it, he had written it, because he thought of the drum part to play on it. We told him that we took songwriting seriously and that playing was conceiving a song, constructing it, and that what he had done was help arrange it. He wanted writing credit on a song ("I Really Wanted You") that I had written a decade before and had already been recorded twice (once with The Outnumbered, and previously with PD as the B-side to "Jackson"). He thought he should get writing credit for cover versions too. Dustin assumed we were dissing his contributions to the band, treating him like "just the drummer."

This was a low point of the band for me and Chris. Though we were sounding great live, we still hadn't found a third member we could truly prosper with. In the end, we ended up giving a credit on the album for arrangements and production, which Chris hated; he thought it too self-congratulatory. That was our compromise to keep Dustin happy.

This cold war went on for four very tense days, playing gigs despite having virtually no communication. On a drive day in Eastern Canada, we stopped at a motel that had rather tacky old-fashioned wood paneling, quite similar to the backdrop for a series of then-current Calvin Klein underwear ads. The ads had very young adults posing in their undies in basement rec room settings. I had an idea—*Why don't we take our own underwear shots?* I got out my camera, and we took turns shooting each other. After four days of near silence it broke the tension, and we actually had fun with each other. As a promo item for the next album, a Canadian friend who made minor league hockey cards made three thousand sets of Pansy Division cards, with the photos of us in our underwear, as well as PD facts and other trivia. Instead of bubble gum, each pack came with a condom.

We completed the tour and went home to record. At this point Chris and I had been in the band together for four years. During that time, our disagreements had been surprisingly few. We had mutual goals and we were reaching them. But the situation with Dustin was very divisive and was the first big fight we ever had. I was upset having to do the record with Dustin; I felt he didn't respect the work Chris and I did to come up with the songs. I wasn't sure I wanted his name on an album of ours. Chris and I considered replacing him. If we really wanted to boot him, we had to do it then, before the recording sessions. A friend suggested a drummer who could step in, and we practiced once with him. We agreed that it sounded really good on one run-through, and I was ready to go through with it. Chris said yes but changed his mind almost immediately. He felt we had started a process with Dustin that hadn't been completed; the project needed to be finished with the person we began it with; besides, we had planned to go on tour right after the record came out in January, and we couldn't do that without Dustin. I was ready to dump Dustin, but Chris wasn't, even though he had the same frustrations. He felt strongly that for the good of the band we had to carry on as is, and that the band was at another make or break point. I gave in.

CHAPTER 15

Wish I'd Taken Pictures

After returning from the Canadian tour, we had a tense meeting where Dustin told us how much it meant for him to be in our band. I wasn't totally convinced, but we plowed ahead and did the album with him. Feeling we had outgrown the studio we had been using, we moved to Razor's Edge, where people like The Melvins and NOFX had recorded. We worked with a good engineer, Tim Daly. It took eight days to do the album, the longest we'd spent.

Considering the rancor that preceded it, we actually had a pretty good time doing the album. We got great guitar sounds, thanks to an amp loaned to us by Kirk Hammett of Metallica (a friend of Dustin's), some Russian brand that sounded incredible. We spent more time on vocals, and I did what I felt was my best singing ever. We brought in an outsider to help get sounds and mix the album—Jim Marcus of Chicago band Die Warzau, a professional acquaintance of Dustin's. Given how different his band sounded from ours, Jim was an odd choice, but different was what we were after. He gave the mixes an odd flavor that felt strange at the time, but which I'm happy with in retrospect. Jim worked his ass off, practically living in the studio over the last four days of production, sleeping on the couch after working long hours (made even longer by the studio's continual equipment problems).

Wish I'd Taken Pictures has a lot of our favorite material. "Horny in the Morning" captures the common but seldom commented upon (in song, at least) feeling of waking with morning wood. "Vanilla" explores someone's (well, maybe my) limits in the bedroom, and was my tongue-in-cheek riposte to "James Bondage." "I Really Wanted You" was a remake of an Outnumbered song, a true-life tale of being hooked on a straight guy only to see him fall into a woman's clutches. "Dick of Death" was Chris's second songwriting effort for the band, and it proved to be a Pansy classic. It's about the joys of picking up a guy and finding out he has a really, really big dick. Some people, reading the title, assumed it was about AIDS; the thought had crossed my mind also, but I felt that gay men shouldn't be defined by AIDS alone, and that we shouldn't be cowed that people might take it the wrong way.

The next song, "Expiration Date," was a noisy, experimental effort that sounded like nothing else we'd done; in a blindfold test, you'd have never guessed it was us. The droning, feedback-laced song tried to capture the noise in my head regarding frustrating relationships. I think Dustin wanted us to do more songs like this; he had a bigger hand in how this one sounded than some of the others. "Pillow Talk" was a bouncy rocker about jealousy in a nonmonogamous relationship. The title song was a wistful, bittersweet remembrance of guys who had gotten away without leaving even a photograph as evidence.

"The Summer You Let Your Hair Grow Out" was my idea of what a gay Everly Brothers song might have sounded like and has been an enduring PD live favorite. I was at home one day cooking, listening to Gram Parsons, when I had the idea for the lyric; I paused the CD, went into my room, scribbled a first draft, finished cooking, ate my lunch while finishing the words, then worked out the music. I mention this in part because I've noticed in general that the songs that come easiest are usually my best ones, and the ones the get labored over more intensely often fall short. The lyric recalls a guy at my high school who I suspected might be gay; the summer after my senior year, we worked at the same department store. He'd grown his hair out and looked great, and I tried but failed to get to know him much better. He'd pique my interest, then backpedal; later he told me he was joining a fraternity, so I noted our diverging directions and gave up.

Side two had a string of more introspective material. I wrote "This Is Your Life" for Chris to sing; it somewhat described his situation at the time, a dilemma about moving in with someone and into that person's settled house and settled life. He heard it, loved it, but rewrote most of it; it was one of our first true songwriting collaborations. Though it's one of my favorite PD songs, we raced through it in the studio; it's a shame it didn't get more subtle treatment. We have never played it live. "Don't Be So Sure" is a moody, soul-baring ballad, about someone who's being strung along and trapped; whether or not the character gets out at the end is not quite clear. Our earliest songs were so full of certainty and conviction; I was happy that our sound and mood had evolved to let in some vagueness, some doubt. Previously we had always spelled things out in our lyrics, and although we would sometimes continue to, I wanted to broaden the range of our songs. Though not as blunt as other songs, it was still emotionally direct. Dustin strongly disliked it; it reminded him of REO Speedwagon! As a result, this song was only played live twice while he was in the band.

"The Ache" was another departure, another song that you wouldn't have guessed was us by the sound of it. Just electric guitar, cello, and light percussion, it tells of a relationship gone stale. "Kevin" is about a guy who everyone thinks is gay but isn't; the song speculates over Kevin's situation but doesn't condemn the character. I felt a lot of gay people could identify with it, as it had been such a common topic of conversation over the years. "Pee Shy," a sardonic rocker, is yet another topic ripe for the Pansy Division treatment, a common but rarely acknowledged reality. "Sidewalk Sale" examines the scene outside a gay bar at closing time and is one of my favorite lyrics I've written, almost documentary in its effect. I wrote this after a show in Portland, when we'd had an early gig and had gone to a gay bar afterwards. We tried to make this as concise as possible, and it came out a mere minute and fifteen seconds long!

Despite the presence of "Horny" and "Dick Of Death," *Wish* had more songs about relationships than sex. I'm not sure we were fully aware of this at the time, but you can see the evolution taking place. Looking back, the biggest flaw of the album was that we played a number of the songs too fast. We finally had a rocker drummer, and we set out to prove that we could rock out. Live, we were playing faster because we could; onstage, songs like "Sidewalk Sale" or "Wish I'd Taken Pictures" became a blur of words, almost completely lost. Such a breakneck pace was appropriate for some songs, but a slower pace would have brought out more personality in others. In later years, I'd play either of these songs as my mid-set solo number, where slowing down enhanced the impact of the lyrics. At the time though, it was just what we were aiming for. Chris had been right. We sounded like a band.

There's a hidden CD bonus track. If you start track one and press pause, then scan backwards, it will take you to six-plus minutes of us reading a list of strung together band names. We did this to amuse ourselves in the van, and we read a list I'd kept, with names like SammyHaGarthBrooks, DuranDurancid, Boo-Yah Tribe 8, Boyz II Men Without Hats. (It sounds funnier than it reads.)

With Green Day's huge success following Nirvana's superstardom, there was a sense at this time that bands plugging away underground might be able to enter the mainstream, get on MTV, and have the proper promotion needed to sell more records. This was a leap for Lookout, who we were always pushing to do more for us, and this time they didn't hold back. We spent $5,200 of Lookout's money to make a video for "I Really Wanted You"—a decent effort—and okayed taking out ads for the album in magazines like *Spin*. Lookout began advertising in *Rolling Stone*. They paid for the Pansy Division card set. Remember, our first three CDs took a total of less than $3,000 *combined* to record, so this was ratcheting things up considerably. Our goal was to get as far as we could by staying indie and not making the major label leap. We knew it was risky, but we thought we'd regret it if we had the chance to break through and we didn't take full advantage of it. The low overhead for the first three albums allowed us to break even early and make some good money from record sales, but this time we went for broke.

In January '96, in between finishing the album and its release, we returned to the studio to cut a single. We'd had an idea for a concept 45, and realized that the only time all year we'd have to do this project was right then. Chris and

Dustin are (or have been at various times) into heavy metal. We'd conceived doing the Pansy metal single, and Dustin came up with the idea of making the cover a parody of AC/DC's *For Those About To Rock…We Salute You,* calling our seven-inch EP *For Those About To Suck Cock…We Salute You*. It contained three songs: my original "Headbanger" (a rather silly fantasy about bedding a long-haired metal dude) and two covers, "Sweet Pain," a Kiss song (Chris had wanted to cover them if we could find the right song) and kind of a sequel to "James Bondage," and "Breakin' The Law," a Judas Priest cover. On the latter, we altered the lyrics and changed it into an anti-sodomy law song. The single sleeve folded open like the original AC/DC LP cover had, and we threw on some random bits of stuff we'd collected at the end of each side. To top it off, we had the idea of including a sticker with the single, of Beavis & Butthead getting it on together on their sofa. A friend of Dustin's drew it (I was never told who) and in the single it went.

The song "Headbanger" called for a heavy metal guitar solo well beyond my means, and I had a friend in mind who would be perfect to play it. Instead, Dustin said, Why don't we get the real thing? Kirk Hammett's amp was still in the studio, he hadn't picked it up yet. We thought, well *sure,* if he would only do it! One phone call later, he'd agreed to do it. (It helped that the studio was a few blocks from his house.) He arrived at the session with his guitar tech, warmed up, and listened to the track. Then we hit the record button, and he whipped off a solo. Great! He did it a second time, an even better solo, and that was that. Amazing! After a half hour, he left, job done. He asked us to use a pseudonym, Al Shatonia, a name he used to check into hotels. Nowhere was his name to be seen. When the single came out, we told Lookout who was on it but asked them to mention only that a mystery guitarist from an actual metal band had done it.

We hinted in interviews but didn't drop his name. Eventually word did spread, and in an issue of the British metal magazine *Kerrang!* he eventually spilled the beans.

Wish I'd Taken Pictures was released in February 1996. Besides the American release, it came out in Canada on Mint Records and was released in Europe through the Dutch label DeKonkurrent. We had spent big (by our standards—it wouldn't cover the cost of deli trays for a major label release) and wanted to get out to support it, so we hit the American highways as soon as it came out. We did two tours—first a month around the Southern edge of the country during February and early March, then after a couple weeks off, six more weeks around the rest of the country. For the first time we took an acquaintance with us on tour as a roadie/merch guy, to create a buffer between ourselves and Dustin. The roadie helped Dustin—Chris and I carried and loaded our own stuff. Even with this extra help tensions still simmered between us and Dustin.

That March we played in Bakersfield, California. A guy who ran an all-ages gay club there had contacted us, inviting us to play. We were curious about the town, and curious about an all-ages gay club in such an unusual place.

There were about one hundred people there, many of whom were not gay. The show went pretty well. For the encore, Chris did his usual bit where he ran out in the audience at the end of "Bunnies" to spray silly string at the crowd, and someone kicked him from behind. He turned around and saw a girl aggressively trying to kick him, and sprayed her in the face and continued through the crowd. Her big, macho-looking boyfriend (I'd noticed earlier the way he was holding "his girl" as a display of his hetero credentials) charged the stage right as Chris had jumped back on it and began landing punches. Chris curled up into a ball to deflect them, and I didn't see what was happening for a few seconds. Suddenly I turned to see Dustin heroically grab a mic stand, and with its heavy base, start hitting this guy in the back with it. When he paused and looked up, Chris escaped (and wasn't really hurt), and others managed to get the guy off the stage and thrown out. People were saying the guy was a skinhead, so we had a large group of people help us pack our things and load us out. We never returned to Bakersfield.

Though we were going over well and having good shows, in April we reached another crisis point and did something we'd never done before—canceled some shows. Because of the tension within the band, we cut about ten days off the second tour leg and returned home early. We were also sick with the flu, which contributed to the decision. Dustin stayed behind with friends in Michigan, so Chris and I traveled home in peace. Dustin returned to San Francisco a week and half later and seemed more civil and happy to be with us as we did a handful of West Coast shows. We thought he might be on good behavior because he wanted to go on the European tour we were planning.

While our dream of playing with Nirvana never happened, at the end of April we came as close as we could, opening for The Foo Fighters at the Warfield Theater in San Francisco. Visiting family the previous Christmas, Chris had run into Dave Grohl—former Nirvana drummer and The Foo Fighters front man—in a West Seattle furniture store. Chris introduced himself, and Dave was very friendly, and mentioned he'd like to have us open for him some time. That eventually came to pass with this benefit show for Rock for Choice at the Warfield. We were bottom of the bill, followed by 7 Year Bitch, Ween, Jawbreaker, and The Foo Fighters. At the end of the night, I got to spend a few minutes alone talking to Mr. Grohl, who was incredibly nice. I'd recently named him my number one dream date in *Outpunk* maga-zine; in the face of godliness, I kept my cool and did not mention that fact (guess I blew my big chance).

CHAPTER 16

Next Stop Europe

Touring the states isn't too difficult; you can get in a van and do it in a fairly DIY manner. Touring overseas is a different kind of adventure. It usually means your band has reached a certain level of success. I had been to Europe once before as a tourist; I had wanted to play there with The Outnumbered, but we were just too obscure. Chris had only been to England and France, and Dustin hadn't been at all.

We were hooked up with Hans, a Dutch booker. We flew in and out of Amsterdam, where Hans and DeKonkurrent were located. We had expressed our concern over who would be accompanying this gay troupe around the continent, and for a tour manager Hans enlisted Oscar, a radical Dutch queer with red dreads and pink Doc Martens. He drove us and capably looked after our finances. We quickly became great friends.

We could have driven ourselves, but Oscar was a good choice. He had been the singer in a politically oriented gay electronic duo called Blind and had toured all over the continent. Having a tour manager who spoke several languages (Dutch, German, English)—as well as someone who had an EU passport—was quite helpful. We rented a Mercedes van that was built for transport, not comfort. It was completely reliable and completely uncomfortable. Larger than our American van, it was laid out all wrong. Too much storage in back, cramped bench seats in front. When we looked around on the motorways, the European equivalent of a cargo van was strangely absent. All we saw were smaller, easy-to-break-into VW vans, or even larger vehicles. This may seem trivial, but as we spent most of our days in our tour vehicle, it greatly affected our mood.

We did six and a half weeks, playing in England, Germany, France, Spain, Italy, Austria, the Czech Republic, Belgium, and the Netherlands. We were concerned about the language barrier. We can project enough attitude to get our intent across, but the words are important. As it turned out, most young people in Western Europe spoke English well enough to understand us. They had the most trouble with slang and colloquialisms, which our songs are full of; to bridge this gap, we took more care to introduce the songs before launching into them.

We started out with four shows in smaller towns in the Netherlands. Before our first show we were interviewed and photographed, and seeing the photo now, which I was awakened for, all I can see is jet lag! The Dutch shows were well received but not hugely attended. Something sadly funny had happened at our show in Utrecht. The stage had a long runway that jutted out from the center. While Chris took over the lead vocal spot for "James Bondage," I took the opportunity, freed from the vocal mic, to wander onto that runway. After the song was over, Dustin called me back to the drums. "Don't ever fucking stand in front of me onstage again," he angrily spat. I was just stunned. I told Chris, who just shook his head.

The first great show was in Bochum, Germany, at a hideously painted sterile university, built in the early '70s in the style of Modern Cement. After being warned to arrive on time (German punctuality, we'd heard about that), we complied, but the PA did not arrive for another three and a half hours. When it did arrive, it was puny. Waiting for the show to start, we were expecting disaster, and even though the power went out a couple of times, it turned out okay. As would prove true elsewhere in Germany, the crowd was enthusiastic and extremely drunk.

We had an okay show in Celle, where I had a platonic experience with maybe the cutest guy I've seen in my entire life, who was *that* far from having a gay experience. In Bremen we played an event in a warehouse where all-night dances were held (we were the early evening's entertainment, for once). Some artists had workspaces there, including a woman who welded giant metal insects out of rusted motorcycle parts, very cool.

In Hamburg we discovered that our promoter had committed suicide two days prior; our show was canceled, but on our day off we were put on a bill with a German rock/folk group called Die Lassie Singers, who were in the Tom Petty/Pete Droge vein. They were good, but played for over two hours. However, they drew eight hundred-plus patrons, and though we were barely billed, the audience greatly enjoyed our set, and they allowed us an encore. This turned out to be the biggest crowd and best reception we had on the whole tour.

We had a day off after that show, and Oscar and I went for a walk around the Reeperbahn. Oscar said to me,

"Dustin is a good drummer." "Yes," I said. "But," Oscar asked, "why is he in your band? He doesn't fit visually, or in attitude or personality. You and Chris are very nice, but he is a dick." Dustin had rubbed him the wrong way, and Oscar had picked up the bad vibes.

In Gottingen, Germany, we had an odd incident. We played in a former squat that had been converted into a youth activities center. After loading in our gear, we were taken upstairs and fed. Some creepy guy ran into the room, grabbed a couple cokes, and ran out. They said he was a local junkie. Later Dustin was walking around the building, which had a lot of rooms, and the creepy guy went into one of the rooms and starting acting very threatening, attacking Dustin, who fought him off. We went to one of the promoters and asked what was going on. The promoter said it was a public building, so they had to let him in. I asked why they let in someone who was stealing and being violent, and they said they couldn't stop him. Oscar, who grew up a few miles from the German border, said that the postwar German left were poor at dealing with authority, given the country's history. They were so fearful of being fascistic that they were ineffectual. We told them that we wouldn't play if they wouldn't stop people from entering the building and causing trouble, especially since, as a gay band, it was paramount having a safe environment for our fans. They reluctantly agreed, and ejected the guy, but he returned later.

The show was all right, but a different obnoxious guy (very drunk) kept wandering onto the stage. He tripped on my guitar cable, unplugging me in the middle of a song. When Chris would wander away from his mic, this guy would step up to it and mumble incoherently into it. When Chris went into the crowd to spray silly string at everyone, the guy climbed back up and started yelling *blah blah blah blah* over and over until I gently grabbed his collar to pull him off the mic. He then toppled off the stage, dragging a monitor wedge with him. It looked like I had shoved this guy off the stage and thrown him on the floor, but I had barely touched him. Now the crowd was mad at me, and I was pissed off because no one would police this guy and stop him from interfering with our show. Totally irritating!

The next morning we ate breakfast at the promoter's house, looking through German language newspapers and magazines. Leafing through a teen girls' mag called *Bravo Girl*, I was suddenly face-to-face with a supercute, fully frontally naked teenage boy. Each month there would be a naked teen boy for the girls to ogle. The boy in question was sixteen. Were we in the states, I could be jailed for having a magazine of nude underage boys, but here it was for sale to girls in supermarkets and drugstores. The mag also had lengthy photo-comic strips that dealt with sexual situations a girl might find herself in. There was also a shot of two men kissing in an article on a new German gay film. It was *eons* ahead of what is allowed in teen girl mags here in the United States. Oscar smiled and said that yes, the magazine had a following amongst gay men. The boy profiled in that issue was from Munich, our next city, so I brought the mag with me onstage and asked if anyone knew how to get ahold of him, but to no avail.

The Prague gig was one of our worst. Some traffic cops shook us down driving into town. Our van was pulled over, and we were told we'd committed a traffic infraction, which could be solved then and there for thirty deutsche marks. Other cars were doing the same thing we were, but only those with foreign plates seemed to be pulled over. Arriving at the club, we were informed that it had been busted the week prior for drugs—in a possible setup by the local police. An American living in Prague who had been there that night told us he'd had a chair busted over his head; he showed us the stitches across his face. Our promoter was conveniently out of town, and the sound system was horrendous. The crowd couldn't hear or understand the words, so we took off our clothes and tried to get the crowd to take off theirs. We got a couple guys down to their undies. Apparently we caused a sensation, but only fifty people came. We were supposed to be paid in deutsche marks, but we got paid less than promised in the local currency. Although as a band we generally avoid McDonald's, we went to one after the gig (it was the only food we could find at 11:30 p.m.) because the food the club had fed us was horrible—lukewarm red beans in an anise-flavored sauce, and hard, dense brown bread. We were happy to see the Austrian border.

We actually enjoyed Vienna quite a bit. Oscar was surprised; he'd called it an "old lady town." The gig was good, with a decent crowd, in a club right along the riverbank, and we walked all over town the following day. We wandered into a beautiful historic church, which turned out to be rife with right-wing literature (Austria is *quite* conservative). As we walked around, Dustin and Oscar had an argument over something trivial—I don't recall what—that escalated into a kind of power struggle, lasting over an hour. Chris and I trailed behind, fascinated at hearing Oscar puncture Dustin's "logic."

When we got to Italy we discovered we were actually popular! We had big crowds everywhere we went; prior to this, we'd had decent attendance, but here we had our biggest crowds in Europe. Since the Communist Party was still influential then, some of the places we played were Communist-sponsored clubs in squats. One, in Turin, had no bathroom, and you had to go across the street and pee in the river. Turin was good for me though—I went home with a cute long-haired boy. We got up the next day, turned on the radio, and heard "Cop Killer" by Body Count—uncensored, played at noon on the big local rock station. Fucking unbelievable!

Rome was one of the best shows of the tour. We played at a former military fort on the city's edge. Terrific reaction. However, they had us stay in what used to be barracks, damp cavelike rooms covered in mildew. When I awoke the next morning, my sleeping bag was covered with condensation. It is amazing we didn't get sicker than we did. And as for the shower…there was unmentionable filth in it, which Chris bravely cleaned up because he *really* needed a shower.

Had two tolerable shows in France, the European country that is most difficult for American rock bands. Both were in the Southeast—one at a skate festival (god help us) in Carcassonne, a beautiful, well-preserved medieval city we explored. The other was in Valence, with American band Gas Huffer as headliners. Spain was better. Certain pockets of Italy and Spain love obscure underground American rock music, more than anywhere else we played in non-English-speaking Europe. They stay up late in Spain; we went on after 2:00 a.m. in Valencia. In Madrid, five or six Outnumbered fans showed up, with records they wanted autographed, which blew my mind! *That* didn't happen anywhere else. The weirdest experience of this tour occurred in Barcelona. Walking around town, we happened down a narrow street. We heard the agitated squawks of a large bird in an apartment high above the street. We walked on. I noticed a shop doorway that had a poster for our show in it. I stepped forward to check it out, as it was the first of our posters I'd seen. As I stepped back into the street, I felt some kind of motion near my head, and then immediately heard *crack!* something hitting the pavement. I looked down at my feet and saw a syringe with a needle two inches long. It missed my head by inches, thrown from some high window. And suddenly, no more bird squawking. Very weird….

England was great; we even got a bit of press coverage, a must there. The London show was at the Garage. We couldn't stand Oasis, then at their peak, with their "new lad" cocky stupidity and rip-off music (everyone has influences, but we weren't impressed with their wholesale theft of riffs and melodies). They were baiting everybody they could, so we thought we'd bait them back; for our encore, we came out wearing white T-shirts that we had written on, one word each, FUCK OFF OASIS!

Tensions with Dustin were still high. We argued about seemingly everything. On the way to a gig in Wales, we visited Stonehenge, while having a ridiculous argument over The Sex Pistols' influence on modern music, of all things. The air was never thicker than that day. Our hope had been that Dustin would appreciate all that was happening to him, but nothing seemed to please him. The tension, however, seemed to be propelling our live shows as we poured our energies into performing.

We struggled through the last few shows in Belgium and the Netherlands. We had a notable gig in Saint Niklaas, Belgium, near the Dutch border. Walking around town that afternoon, we discovered some poster-sized cardboard display ads sitting in the trash next to a cosmetics store. They featured heavily made-up women, so we swiped them, got out our markers, and did a satiric commentary on sexism. We displayed these defaced posters all over the stage (we had almost twenty of them!), and it was a great success.

We hoped Saturday night in Amsterdam would be a big show for us, but we drew only seventy people. We played early because a dance club was happening there later on; we were done by ten or so. We decided to hang around, but Dustin disappeared for a while, then reappeared, and began telling me how much he loved me and Chris, and was so glad we'd had such a cool tour and on and on; I was flabbergasted. After he walked off I *ran* over to tell Chris. "Oh," Chris said. "He just told me he's on ecstasy!" We had one more show the day before flying home, and after the ecstasy wore off he became the same irritating grouch once again. If only we could have dosed him with the stuff every day.

CHAPTER 17

Plowing Ahead

By the time we returned from Europe, our album had been out five months. We had hoped the record would have made more of a dent; European sales had been slight, and we hadn't reached beyond our fan base in the states to find new ones. Despite the comparatively massive amount of money and effort made for *Wish*, it had sold barely half as much as *Pileup*. Not only was this disappointing in terms of our progress, it meant we wouldn't be seeing royalties on it for years. MTV showed the video once on *120 Minutes*, a coup for an indie band, but it had no visible effect. The album made it up to #39 on the College Media Journal (the bible of college radio stations) chart, higher than our others, but you'd have never known by the sales.

Though we'd made what we believed was a superior

record, we hadn't been able to increase on the boost we'd gotten from playing with Green Day, and we'd hit a plateau in both touring and record sales. This impacted Dustin more than the rest of us; we really hoped he'd make some cash from royalties, and life would be easier and less stressful for us all.

Chris was dealing with it better than I was. I'd heard the cliché about that hour onstage being worth all the hassle to get there, and for the first time it seemed to be accurate. I was getting increasingly despondent about having to share that stage with someone whose mutual respect level wasn't there. Our self-imposed work ethic said to keep touring and promote the new album, to tour till we could do no more. I wanted to stop and replace our drummer, but Chris wanted to finish the process we'd started: finish the tour for this album and start afresh next time. The fun was fading for me, feeling trapped in my own band, not wanting to do it anymore.

The *For Those About To Suck Cock* EP was released at this time to good reviews, and also some controversy. The *Beavis & Butthead* sticker had indeed gotten us into trouble. The single came shrink-wrapped to hide the sticker, and there was no mention of it anywhere in the package. We figured it would take months for MTV to find out, but with the advent of the Internet, the time lag was suddenly much shorter. Three weeks after its release, Lookout received a cease and desist letter from MTV. So Chris had to go over to the Mordam warehouse and unwrap and remove all the stickers from the remaining copies.

We organized a fall tour, taking another friend of Dustin's with us as a roadie, an ally of his to keep him occupied. We were finding ways to cope instead of actually enjoying ourselves. Every day was an endurance test. But we were professionals, and we did it, strain and all.

The clear high point of the tour was a Lookout Records showcase we played in New York during the annual College Media Journal convention. We played with most of the best Lookout bands—Cub, The Smugglers, Groovie Ghoulies, Mr. T Experience, and The Queers. We did one of our best shows ever and had so much fun that the bad vibes vanished even though Chris had just come down with a flu and 102 degree fever, throwing up between songs. There was a huge packed crowd, with lots of musician luminaries (several Ramones, Rancid, Lemmy from Motorhead). Tim from Rancid invited us to open up for them sometime. We were in demand.

Then we headed over to Squeezebox for a late night gig as we had done so many other times, and things felt great. Ah, but you can't play New York every day. We did however play Burlington, Vermont, to a small crowd, but fortunately we opened for the popular Devo-goes-surfing band Man or Astroman? We had a mutual appreciation society going, and they said they'd love for us to open a tour for them some-time, which we said we'd love to do.

Around this time we parted ways with our booking agent. We liked Jay a lot, but after giving him several second chances, we had to move on. The last show he booked for us was a doozy. We were to play San Francisco's Exotic Erotic Ball at the end of October. It was a well-paying gig; we'd be sharing the bill with Love and Rockets and The Tubes. We would get $2,500—only the second time we'd made over a grand. Chris and I decided Dustin should play the gig, have a big final payday, and then be let go. Chris and Dustin being huge Bauhaus fans, they were thrilled to play with Love and Rockets. The ball itself was very, very hetero, to our surprise; we hadn't attended before (tickets weren't cheap). The organizers hoped we might queerify the event, but it turned out we didn't. There were many scantily dressed folks, but as is usually the case it was the lumpy old men who were most prone to get nude in public.

After the gig Chris was handed the task of letting Dustin go; we didn't want it to be a two-on-one situation. By the end of our relationship, Chris and I had played good cop/bad cop to ease our strains, so good cop Chris got to tell him the news. Dustin was surprised and unhappy, and eventually ended up telling people he'd quit the band. Which is fine, 'cause the dissatisfaction was mutual. Now that we're not in a band together, we get along much better. Soon after leaving, he formed his dream experimental/industrial band I Am Spoonbender. They've released several albums and have acquired a cult following. That it is so completely, utterly different in sound and approach from PD speaks volumes about his stormy tenure in our band.

I have only one regret about leaving Dustin behind. We had a wild promotional idea that was never fulfilled. As the band with no secrets, I suggested doing a hard-core, XXX porn promo video. In the video, I would be seen having sex with the guy of my choice, and Chris would be seen with his. Since we have very different tastes in men, it would be, you know, diverse! As the straight drummer in a gay band, Dustin wouldn't be getting laid, so he would be jacking off by himself in a bathroom. We thought this would be hysterical and agreed we should do it for the next album. My idea was for me to be in the middle of having sex with someone, then turn to the camera and start lip-synching to the song. Or in the middle of, say, getting a blow job, turning to the camera and announcing, "This next song is 'Wish I'd Taken Pictures!'" and then returning to the action. Sadly, Dustin's (very shy) replacement was horrified by this idea. We mentioned it to Lookout once, and they shuddered at the prospect. Another great idea foiled.

CHAPTER 18

Luis and Patrick

We were considering a short list of drummers. One was a former temp PD drummer, and two others were gay drummers we'd run across on tour. The one who I considered the long shot was the one who won the job. He turned out to be a Pansy Division fan, a crucial factor. Finding drummers who embraced our concept had been difficult, so in the end it took us five years before we could find the missing link. When we called Luis Illades (drummer number twelve) he was surprised and thrilled to be considered for our band.

At the time we called Luis about trying out, he hadn't been playing his drums very much. But when we drove down to San Diego to play together, he played well and it went swimmingly. He drove us down to Tijuana for some authentic Mexican food. We asked him to join that day, and he accepted. He was going to school at San Diego State and would move to San Francisco (he'd already contemplated such a move) at the end of his semester. Since he was gay, the all-gay band concept was finally a reality.

Luis has an interesting background. A Mexican citizen, his mother is an American citizen who has lived in Mexico most of her life, thus making him eligible for a green card. He grew up bilingual, speaking Spanish with his father and English with his mother. He lived in Tijuana most of his early life, then crossed back and forth between there and San Diego. There are many things Luis loves about Mexico, but being gay and out has meant that he's spent his adult life on the U.S. side of the border.

The initial rehearsals with Luis didn't go as smoothly as the tryout, but after several weeks we began to sound like a band. We had made plans to fly to Chicago at the end of January to record with famed underground musician and engineer Steve Albini (who's worked with Nirvana, PJ Harvey, and hundreds of others). We saw it as a trial run for the next album. He had such a reputation for intimidation that a fair number of people asked us if we were really sure he was someone we could work with. Our label, in particular, was worried we had bitten off more than we could chew. I had met him several times when I lived in Illinois, but I barely knew him. Despite his reputation for being a highly opinionated crank, he couldn't have been nicer, and it was great working with him. He was thoroughly professional and a great guy to boot.

We went there to make two singles, our hardcore punk single and our Canadian-themed single. We had asked Mint Records in Vancouver if they wanted to do a single for us, and they said yes. While on tour one day that previous fall, thinking about my affection for Canada (and its men), I cranked out two Canadian-themed songs: "Manada" and

"Hockey Hair." This is unusual in that I rarely get anything written on the road, much less two full songs. And I never get two songs written in one day at home either! For the B-side I learned enough phonetic French to do a Quebecois version of "Manada." We had been in Montreal the day of the referendum on an independent Quebec, and it was sad how there were OUI signs everywhere but no opposing signs in public view. The French version was our small attempt to counter that nationalism. The last song on the single was "One Night Stand," a song by Maow, a Mint Records band we'd become friends with and played with in Vancouver. Their drummer, Neko Case, later became much better known as an alt-country singer and as a member of the great Vancouver band The New Pornographers.

As for the hardcore single…over the years we'd had a seemingly infinite number of interchangeable hardcore punk bands open for us, some of whom were fans of ours, and it struck me one day that we should do our version of hardcore for them. That became the *Queer to the Core* EP, featuring one of our signature songs, "I'm Gonna Be a Slut." Also included was the politically explicit song "Political Asshole"; one of the things that bugs me about hardcore is that the words are so important but they are usually completely undecipherable, so we slowed down the verses to make it clearer. After our fifteen-second thrash "Two-Way Ass" was "Expiration Date 01/98," a revision of the song that had appeared on *Wish I'd Taken Pictures*. At Luis's tryout we ran through it, and it showed off a much heavier, noisier side of the band than before, so we did it for the B-side. Ironically, it's our worst-selling single. Guess the hardcore kids didn't get the message.

We were asked to be on an Iggy Pop tribute album, the proceeds of which went to a New York AIDS charity. Our version of "Loose" turned out to be one of our best covers, and followed in the heavier vein we'd recently discovered. We were quite proud of it, and when the album came out, virtually every review favorably mentioned our contribution, in part because our arrangement didn't seek to copy the original. The label later put out a 45 to promote the album and picked our track for the A-side. The B-side had a Blondie track (under the pseudonym Adolph's Dog) and Joan Jett. We were the A-side, they were the B-side! We were on a single with Joan Jett and Blondie! Gotta step back for a minute sometimes and say, Jeezus Christ, life is good!

Around this time, the *Generations 1: A Punk Look at Human Rights* compilation was released, including among others Green Day. We offered them the appropriate "Breaking The Law," with its commentary on sodomy laws. But the label wanted a new, unreleased track; we had a week to submit one to make their deadline. In a pinch, we whipped up "Can't Make Love," a cover of a Wall of Voodoo song. Though Luis had just joined the group, he was still in school in San Diego and couldn't make the recording. Tre Cool from Green Day volunteered to play drums and record us at his home 8-track studio. In one day we worked out an arrangement, rehearsed it, and recorded it! We mixed it at Billie Joe's home studio a few days later.

By March we were on the road again. We'd played about a dozen shows around California to break in Luis, then headed for the East Coast. Luis had never been on tour before. He celebrated this by staying up as late as possible, except for the part when he got sick. The response to having Luis in the band was tremendous. Not only was he the capable drummer we'd sought, he was also a much-in-demand sex symbol. He was quite shy and reluctant about this designation; on this initial tour he'd take off his shirt during our sets, but after several articles in which a shirtless Luis was the only band member pictured, his modesty prevailed. (We would have been happy for *anyone* in the band to be a sex symbol.) And though guys (and girls) were practically throwing themselves at him, and though he was much more of a party animal than Chris or me, he almost never slept around. Chris and I encouraged his slutdom to no avail.

The response to the new lineup gave us great confidence that we were destined for bigger and better things. Part of the tour was with Servotron, a side project of Man or Astroman? Just before joining the Servotron portion of the tour, we had a nervous moment on the road. Heading east from Houston, we crossed into Louisiana with Chris at the wheel. The van suddenly began to make a horrible noise; when Chris took his foot off the gas, the gears began to grind violently. Finally, he just had to let up, and with a dreadful sound, the van sputtered to a halt and we drifted onto the shoulder. A bad smell lingered; odd fluids were dripping from the rear of the van. We had somewhat conveniently broken down at the exit for Sulphur, Louisiana, so I walked across a field to a pay phone and called AAA. They towed us to Lake Charles, the next large city.

Our tow driver said our options were a Texaco station or a garage belonging to a buddy of his. Having had poor repair experiences at service stations in the past, we opted for the little guy. We got towed in to a dumpy little place in the woods not far from the interstate. Our guy was a Cajun, missing most of his teeth, but he said he was glad to help us, since "the coons who usually come in here don't have any money." We gave each other tight smiles and shuddered. We weren't used to this casual, offhand racism. He gave us an estimate, and said it could take a couple of days, depending on parts. The estimate was high, so I called my mechanic in San Francisco and asked him if it was on the level. Assured it was, we retreated to a Motel 6 about a thirty-minute walk from his garage. This is where we spent three long days.

The mechanic had trouble locating one part. We needed a new rear end, of all things. It was easy and cheap to obtain one for a half-ton Dodge Ram van, but our van was a far less common three-quarter ton. Since our van was eight years old, Dodge no longer had new parts, so we had to rely on scavenge yards. Finally, one was located, but it was across the country and would take a couple of days to arrive. We had to have Lookout wire us two thousand dollars to pay the guy in advance, the only time we ever borrowed money from our label; our garage did not take credit cards, and we didn't have enough cash with us.

We decided to rent a Ryder truck and return on our way home from the tour to collect the van. We didn't want to miss more shows; besides, Lake Charles was driving us crazy. We were bored out of our minds, and called Lookout asking if they had any local contacts. They mentioned a record store, but it was far from us. We called them, and got in contact with some kids back in Sulphur who offered to pick us up and hang out. They had a house full of instruments, so Luis and I spent a nice evening there. The kids were planning to move to the East Bay, lured by the mythology of Berkeley, Gilman Street, Rancid, and Lookout. We got out around Lake Charles a bit, checked out some thrift stores; we took a cab once, and the cabbie's teeth were even worse than the Cajun's. We heard a lot of sirens, saw one car chase; there seemed to be a lot of police activity in our neighborhood.

Renting the truck, we left behind the comforts of our van—no loft bed, no tape deck, uncomfortable seats. We were stuck having to listen to the radio. Luckily, Louisiana had the best fucking radio stations in the country. For more than an hour we listened to the best oldies station I can ever remember hearing, playing underexposed, nonobvious, and obscure '50s and '60s rock and soul oldies with a terrific

DJ. It finally faded out, but we picked up Cajun stations that would alternate French zydeco with Top 40, stations that mixed zydeco with New Orleans classics, and south of Baton Rouge we picked up a great college station from LSU. Over our next two weeks on the East Coast, we heard virtually nothing of interest on the radio. When we returned to Louisiana a few weeks later to retrieve the van (which the racist mechanic had done a great job with), we couldn't find the oldies station but heard other wonders. We were wowed. Ain't no radio like that where we live.

One of the odder nights on this trip was our show in Louisville. We arrived expecting to do a sound check, but our venue was actually two clubs in one, and upon our somewhat late arrival we discovered there was already a concert going on in the much larger room next door—Eddie Money. We checked out his set of clichéd classic rock; a lot of the men were in suits, like they had come directly from the office to the concert. They were raising their beers to the hits; it looked like a Budweiser commercial.

On our previous Louisville trip I had slept with a certain young man, who was there waiting for us. This time, he took one look at new member Luis and brushed me off (nicely). He and Luis ended up getting together, the only time one of us has hooked up with somebody who's been with another band member. We aren't passing the groupies around. (I'm not morally opposed to that, mind you!) The Eddie Money show was running late. There was a guy in the club, already very drunk, kinda cute, who was interested in picking me up. I could tell he wasn't going to last the evening in his condition, so we excused ourselves to the band van for some quick action. The event transpired quickly, and he left—not even staying for the show!—driving home drunk. Sheesh. Not one of my proudest moments, but hey. In my memory, the offstage stuff was better than the gig.

One of the things we were questioning around this time (though certainly not for the first time) was punk rock and our relationship to it. In some ways we were punk (in our minds' idea of punk) but not in others (in the way punk was practiced by fans and musicians). This conflict reared its head in specific ways at two shows near the end of this tour. We played in Omaha at the Cog Factory, an all ages punk club. We hadn't played Omaha since '94 with Green Day, but we knew of this venue from Tribe 8. Though it was difficult tracking down the club (their phone number had changed and they weren't listed), we set up a show. We arrived, and they presented us with the promo posters Lookout had sent them. "Here are your posters," they said. Uh…you're supposed to put them up, to promote the show. Duh. But not only did they not put up those posters, they didn't make any others. Publicizing the event might have caused the wrong kinds of people to come to the show and invade their scene. They didn't have (or want) any listings in the paper. There's no way that anyone uninvolved with the club or outside that small scene would have known about the show. (Especially any nonpunk gay guys who might be curious to check out a gay band.) It's an elitist, bullshit attitude, but try to tell them that. Trying to keep a scene "pure" only hastens its demise.

The result: twelve people attended. And we felt really sorry for them, 'cause it was the worst PA in PD history, completely abysmal, completely incompetent. You couldn't hear the words, the music was a muddy blur. I wonder how many of the six hundred people who saw us the last time we played Omaha would have come if they'd heard about it. This show totally pushed all our buttons about punk rock stupidity: by having such a shitty Z-grade PA system, it's ripping off the kids—all in the name of anti-commercialism. The question of whether to play twenty-one-plus venues or not, if we have a choice, was settled by this experience.

The last show of the tour was quite memorable. Salt Lake City is the kind of city bands play because it's on the way to somewhere else. We had played it three times, with sixty people being our largest crowd. All had been over-twenty-one shows, so this time we used a different promoter to get an all-ages show. He added us to a bill with bigger punk bands Pennywise and Blink 182 in Park City, a resort town twenty miles away. The venue was at a snowboarding site, capacity twenty-four hundred, and sold out in advance.

By 1997, the jock/punk crossover was well underway. Alternative was now so mainstream that it was safe for frat jock types to embrace. Instead of punks being the runts, now jocks were becoming punks, adding a new ignorant macho edge to the scene. As our rather large venue indicated, Pennywise had become one of the bigger bands with jock punk appeal. We were very curious as to what kind of audience would show up, and what kind of response we'd get. Blink 182 I hadn't heard; I had them confused with Blanks 77 and Link 80.

We did our sound check, ate dinner, and set up our merchandise table. The Pennywise merch crew set up their table next to ours; they had twenty-one different styles of shirts and nine different hats. We set up our own table, with our three types of T-shirts, no hats, four different CDs, and some singles. Activity buzzed around their table; a couple people asked if we had free stickers, but that was it. We dismantled our table, and went to play.

We played our set to little notice, despite the packed hall. It wasn't until our ninth song, "Groovy Underwear," that we got any reaction: some booing, some fingers, some remarks. By this point we were just glad they had noticed we were there. After a half hour, we moved our gear aside, and I returned to set up our table again. At shows with Green

Day two years before, crowds sometimes hated us, but there was always a small number of people who'd visit our table, thank us for just being there, maybe buy a shirt or CD. Not tonight. A couple of people bought stickers, and we sold one single. Twenty-four hundred people, five dollars' worth sold. We had never seen this level of disinterest at a show this big.

Meanwhile, Blink 182 took the stage. Of all the professional bands we've ever shared a bill with, they were to me one of the most unimpressive. They sounded like an inferior Bad Religion; the tempos were all the same, way too fast, an undifferentiated blur, devoid of anything unique. They said some really silly and stupid things between songs; I can't remember what, but it struck all of us as being unfunny and pathetic. But the audience was lapping it up; their T-shirt table was quite busy. We were truly mystified and bewildered at what seemed like one of the worst bands we'd ever seen going over so well. If you had told us then that they would soon become so popular, we'd have laughed at you.

After they finished, we hung around our lonely merch table, but as Pennywise began we packed up, loaded the van, and got paid. The promoter at least said he loved us. Ready to head home (this being the last night of our tour), we wanted to see Pennywise before we split for our twelve-hour overnight drive. We'd never seen pictures of Pennywise; there weren't any on their albums. As they took stage we understood why—they looked like a bunch of heshers. One guy I had assumed to be a roadie (he looked like he'd just come off the last Iron Maiden tour) turned out to be the guitarist. It was punked-up metal. For their fourth song, they launched into the world's worst version of "Stand By Me," and we fled.

Some people we know questioned why we'd play before crowds that would hate us. We took it as a challenge, and wanted to see how it played out; until we did it, we couldn't be sure it was a waste of time. After this, however, we tried to avoid playing on bills with Epitaph and Fat Wreck label bands. It did happen a couple more times (sometimes it's hard to say no when you're doing a long tour and the only gig in that town that day is with such a band), but this is where we gave up trying to win over a regulation punk rock audience.

This had been the last show of our first tour with Luis and our last gig as a trio. A few weeks later, we became a quartet.

My basic guitar-playing skills had suited us fine when we were playing simple songs, but in time you repeat yourself. We had considered adding another guitar player before, but it seemed inappropriate to make such a move without being settled on something as basic as a drummer. With that settled, we could consider expanding the lineup.

We had first met Patrick Goodwin in Denver on the Green Day tour, when he had come up to talk to us at our merch table. Later he moved to San Francisco and we met again at the Folsom Street Fair. He said he was a gay guitarist, into stuff like Redd Kross, The Muffs, The Posies, and Kiss (which he and Chris quickly bonded over). I got his phone number and made a mental note. When the time came to call him, he wasn't at that number anymore (the phone was answered by his bitter, unhelpful ex), but we tracked him down shortly after.

Though he had just moved to the city from Denver, he had grown up mostly in Southern California; not the glamorous part of Southern California, but San Bernardino—the redneck "inland empire." His father had been in the military, and he had lived all over the place as a kid. He had been in a Christian metal band in high school, then worked at a hip-hop record store, and ended up in Denver in a guitar pop band. Patrick turned out to be an excellent guitarist and sang well too, so once we started playing with him, we decided to look no further for our new member. With his versatility of sound, our music became more diverse. We spent the next few months writing and learning songs for another album.

From the first gigs, he went over well with our fans. He also added another dimension to the band…bear appeal. Patrick isn't that large, but he's bearded and is attracted to bearish men and is well-established in that scene. Between Luis and Patrick, we had added sex appeal (for decidedly different tastes) as well as musical appeal. Win-win!

Patrick, like Chris, had an interest in metal. When we formed our band, we wondered if we would ever encounter certain musicians that we suspected were gay, or maybe other closeted rockers, who might privately tell us of their appreciation for us. It's only happened once: with Judas Priest lead singer and metal god Rob Halford. In June 1997, on Gay Pride weekend in San Francisco, Chris and Patrick spotted him in a bar. They looked at each other and said, "Is that *Rob Halford?*" Cautiously, they went over to talk to him. He was friendly, and when they told him that they were in Pansy Division, he said, "I *love* Pansy Division!" They were floored. They mentioned that we had done a cover of Judas Priest's "Breaking the Law," and he said he loved our version. Chris told him that if he ever came to see us, we'd play the song for him. He responded by saying that if he ever came to see us play, he'd sing it with us! *That* we had to make happen.

Chris got email and post office box addresses for him and stayed in touch. Rob lived in Phoenix, but often traveled to San Diego, where we were scheduled to play Gay Pride at the end of July. We arranged for Rob to come sing with us then. We had a bar show the night before, and he'd said he'd come to that also. The bar show was at the Casbah, San Diego's finest rock dive, and when we informed the staff who was coming, they were all atwitter and quickly called friends with the news.

When he arrived at the club, he was dressed in shorts and baseball hat, all black. We did a little run-through in sound check. When the time came to do the song (as our encore), he walked up to the stage, and said that he was proud to join "our Hall of Flame." Then, he sang along with the song, including a few new lyrics I had written to make the gay aspect clearer. He was singing *our* version of his song! We were thrilled!

The following night, playing to a larger crowd on an outdoor stage in Balboa Park, we repeated the experience. He went out with us after the show, to a karaoke place, but declined to sing. He was soft-spoken and intelligent, and meeting him was a truly wonderful experience. He later came to San Francisco to sightsee, and we drove him around to our favorite places and took tons of pictures.

This encounter put us in a dilemma. Our view was that the closet was outdated, yet he hadn't come out. He told us that he was going to do it when the time was right, but it wasn't that time yet. So we had to measure what we said to whom. On one hand we had great respect for him, but on the other we didn't feel like covering for someone, either.

MTV News heard about Halford singing with us, and planned to air a report stating that Halford was gay. Since that sort of media disclosure is grounds for defamation, it first had to be cleared with the subject, and approval was denied. I'm not sure exactly how it transpired. At the time he was working on a CD for Trent Reznor's label, with his band called Two. When their album was released about six months later, he did an interview with MTV and came out in the *Advocate*, mentioning us. We were happy for him and relieved as well. It wasn't the kind of secret I wanted to have to keep.

When Two toured in 1998, they played near San Francisco and we were invited to the show. Everybody went but me—I had a ticket for an extremely rare screening of The Rolling Stones' film *Cocksucker Blues*, a film I had been trying to see since I was a teenager in the mid-'70s. There was only one screening and it was sold out, so I made my choice. Shit! The film was fairly dull, its decadent reputation overblown. The others were invited onstage to sing and dance around, and I missed it. They had a late dinner together afterwards, and I arrived at the end of it to at least pay my respects.

It was not our only metal connection. Riki Rachtman, host of the MTV Headbanger's Ball, was an unlikely fan. He liked our song "Groovy Underwear," and invited us on his radio program in Los Angeles. We were on one evening for a half hour; he interviewed us, asked us some questions, and played a couple songs.

CHAPTER 19

The Descendents Story

Some credit The Descendents with being the first pop-punk band. You can hear their influence in Green Day's sound. They put out their first album in 1981; I didn't have any of their records then, but was interested in knowing more about them. Sometime in the early '80s they played in Champaign. I was right up front bouncing around and enjoying the show. Then they played a song called "I'm Not a Loser." Listening to lyrics like "fucking homo buttfuckers" and "go away you fucking gay/I'm not a loser," I quickly stopped enjoying the show. I was so livid, I wanted to grab the mic stand and club the singer over the head with it (I was close enough to the stage to do so). But I thought, if I did this, nobody would understand why I was doing it, and like the time in high school when I didn't want to stand for the Pledge of Allegiance, who would have stood up with me/for me? I felt like I would have been totally out there by myself, and it would be a futile gesture. Fuming, I stormed out of the concert, and decided to never listen to The Descendents again. They might have made music I liked, but I decided I could live without it.

The next time I heard them at any length was when Luis joined the band. He was a big fan and would play them in the van. I told Luis about my experience. He said the lyric didn't ruin his appreciation for them; to him, it was a very Southern California skater kind of thing to call everyone a fag if they were bugging you. After breaking up in the late '80s, they reformed in 1996, and Luis was excited 'cause he'd been too young to see them their first time around. In December, they played the Trocadero in San Francisco, but that was a week before Luis moved up from San Diego to join the band. Later we saw a review of the show, and the accompanying photo showed singer Milo Aukerman wearing a Pansy Division pink triangle shirt! Unfortunately, their opening act had been a loutish, homophobic SoCal punk band called Guttermouth.

Cut to Dallas, March 11, 1997. We are playing at the Galaxy Club, and The Descendents are playing down the street. Luis and Chris went down to their club, but the band members were busy doing their sound check. They left a note backstage, with a *For Those About to Suck Cock* single. About an hour later, their bass player Karl Alvarez came over to say hi and apologize for the song. Karl explained that they were just teenagers then and that they were just being obnoxious. He mentioned that they didn't really know any gay people when they were that age, but they weren't homophobic and that they liked and respected Pansy Division. Luis told Karl he didn't have to apologize, that their music basically saved him in his adolescence. I was happy to hear the apology. We said, "Take *us* on tour, not Gutter-mouth!"

Upon returning home a few weeks later, we discovered The Descendents were doing another show in San Francisco. This time Luis attended. Again, Guttermouth opened. Before one of their songs, their singer said something like, "Are we homophobic? You bet we are." There was no irony (I believe Guttermouth are incapable of it). The audience seemed puzzled. Luis said, "I loved seeing their anti-homo rant fall flat on its face because they were in San Francisco. Like they were expecting people to cheer them, but instead San Franciscans' reaction was more like 'gimme a break, loser...' So who was the *'loser'* now? You could smell the social shift in the air." When The Descendents played, they did "I'm Not A Loser," singing "I'm not a loser/I'm not a *hetero*sexual!"

After The Descendents broke up in the late '80s, three of them formed another band called All. In 1995, post-Nirvana and post-Green Day's huge success, All released their one major label album, *Pummel*. On it is a song called "Hetero." It's an obvious antigay backlash song, written by their drummer Bill Stevenson (who didn't come along to make nice with his bassist). In it he proclaims himself as a normal straight guy who can't get laid, and he's blaming gay guys. What? In his words, "the only way you are cool is if you're gay or dead." Huh? "Maybe I should pierce my butt or get a few tattoos/Maybe I should wear a dress or be a homo like you. Normal, hetero, straight guy yeah, that's right/I'm a straight, normal, girl fuckin' coffee drinkin' titty suckin' cigarette smokin' seal killin' red neck ass bastard from hell." Hmm, I don't think the *gay guys* are to blame for *that*.

Thing is, I didn't know about "Hetero" when Karl came to talk with us, or I would have brought it up. Hearing the song, it was hard not to take it personally, the same way I took "I'm Not A Loser" personally. At the same time I felt sad for the guy who so obviously appeared threatened by gay people having more visibility and acceptance.

CHAPTER 20

More Lovin' from Our Oven

We started working on new songs as a four-piece, enthusias-
tically honing our new sound. We knew that making a new
album would take a while, and momentum felt important;
we didn't want to go another year without an album, as
there still seemed some hope that we could somehow break
through. We had done *Pileup* to clear the decks of singles
and rare tracks, and we had enough to do it again. But
should we release another album of singles so soon? And
if we didn't, would those songs get lost in the shuffle? With
Dustin on half of them and Luis on the other, it seemed like
if we didn't do it now, it might be years before they ended
up on an album, and the music was what we had been doing
lately. So an album it was.

Pileup, which included a ton of covers, went over quite

well, and though there weren't as many covers on this one, we thought it was a good move to make. We'd have rather had a new album with our new lineup, but we were pleased with the music on it—it was quite diverse, and we were at pains to demonstrate we could do more than just the one thing we were semi-famous for.

More Lovin' from Our Oven compiled all the songs from "Valentine's Day," *For Those About to Suck Cock* EP, *Queer To The Core* EP, and "Manada" singles. To these we added some fun extras: our a cappella version of "Negative Queen"; our acoustic version of "The Summer You Let Your Hair Grow Out"; our version of the Undertones's "Male Model" (which we'd done for a tribute album); a great live performance of "Bunnies" from the *Live at Tramps* cassette; and a couple of songs from the first PD demo. We played around with the track order until it sounded like an album; I think we achieved our aim of balancing the humorous and the serious.

My major regret about this CD is that I wanted the songs from the new singles to be listed as the main portion of the album, and the last seven oddball songs (which included different versions of some songs we'd done before) listed as bonus tracks. Otherwise it looks like a bunch of the songs from the previous albums are on there again. As it turned out, it sold barely a third of what *Pileup* had, and combined with what we were hearing and seeing with other bands in our league, it was the first clue that underground/alternative/punk was on the downswing.

Trends come and go, but there was more to it than just that. While on tour in Europe in 1996, we had a chance to watch MTV Europe. Among the bands whose videos we saw was the Backstreet Boys. I had read about them, because they were Americans from Florida who had to go to Europe to become popular. Watching the video, I understood why.

They had tapped into that certain brand of cheesy, contrived pop that England and the continent ate up but that Americans, for whatever reason, resisted. I recall being grateful that we were spared this stuff on our side of the ocean.

As a direct result of the 1996 Communications Act, and the resulting corporate consolidation of pop radio and the rise of Clear Channel, please welcome The Backstreet Boys, Britney Spears, and Hanson. It was a return of the lowest common denominator. Wait, I must admit I like "Mmm Bop." But it seemed clear that alternative/punk was dying in the commercial sense, that the Nirvana/Green Day juggernaut had faded, and what replaced them—virtually overnight, in 1997—was safe, bland, formula pop. It was the revenge of the industry, the revenge of the producer, the revenge against artists having control over their careers. It was all about corporate control, the clampdown on the noncompliant.

But maybe I'll surprise you here by saying that I'm not opposed to manufactured bands or music. It just depends on what's being manufactured. As a kid I loved The Monkees, Herman's Hermits, Lesley Gore, and any of a number of performers whose careers were controlled by managers and producers. I still love them now. It's just that the times have changed and the marketers are far more crass. In 1966, they didn't have the market research analysis tools they have today. Then it was possible for weird and wonderful things to become hits, as the companies hadn't yet gotten a handle on how to exercise complete control over the mainstream music business. That began during the '70s, with the rise of the LP trumping the single and the consequent larger amounts of money needed to finance successful records. The number of labels with records on the charts has dwindled further and further with each successive decade, till now in 2008 we're left with four major labels and no chance whatsoever for any oddball independents to break through.

You could say that all of this is irrelevant; why worry about the mainstream anyway? The bounce that a band like us got from a certain kind of music being popular is not to be underestimated, even if Nirvana begat Pearl Jam begat Candlebox begat Collective Soul, and even though Green Day begat Blink 182 begat New Found Glory begat Good Charlotte. I don't want to dismiss the mainstream, I just want it filled with better music—rock that actually rocks, soul with actual soul, country with actual country in it, and teen pop with actual feeling. It affects millions of people, especially kids, and they (and we) deserve better.

CHAPTER 21

The One-Hundred-Day Tour

I should reiterate the impact of having Patrick and Luis join the band. Both were incredible musicians. It was like the band was really starting over. We finally sounded as good in real life as we had sounded in our imaginations, and we were so optimistic for the band's future. They were fun to play with and fun to be with. We had played to thousands of people over the first six years of our existence, but it was with them in the band that we really achieved our creative peak. It makes me wonder how much more success we could have had if these guys had been with us during the Green Day period; as well as we did then, now we absolutely killed. It was like turning the volume up to eleven.

Dustin had forever complained about having to tour. Because of this, our touring schedule was never as complete as it should have been. With a stable lineup at last, this fall of '97 we got the chance. We did a thorough U.S. tour, going nearly everywhere. Coming from a place that was often overlooked by touring bands, I wanted to play the second-tier towns, because of the loyalty you can earn from fans simply because you bothered to play their city. We set out for one hundred days of gigs.

9.5.97 Portland, OR

Here we are, Day One of our longest-ever tour. This was Patrick's first tour, and he got laid on the first show! Welcome to the road! Played a club called EJ's with our dyke pals Team Dresch. It was a twenty-one-plus show, which worried us, but we drew one hundred and sixty people (as opposed to sixty at our last all-ages show here). Of course, Team Dresch helped with that. Good show, good time. Though road food can be very bland, tonight the club fed us spicy Cajun chicken that was too hot to eat! Had to scrape the stuff off the chicken.

9.8.97 Seattle, WA

Played three shows in three days around Puget Sound. First was an all-ages show in Redmond, out in the Eastside burbs. Seattle is the toughest place in the country to book a decent all-ages show, so we played this show despite the poor money offer. I'm glad we did it, but I wouldn't return to that venue. It was the first of two shows with Supersuckers, who are way more popular than us, but I think we had more fans tonight (their crowd is an older, drinking crowd). The next night at the Crocodile in Seattle, had a wild and excel-lent show, and the 'Suckers drew well. Met Julianne, our new booking agent, for the first time in person since we began working with her. Tonight is probably the best show we've had since Patrick joined. We were well paid and sold tons o' merch too. If only every night (or at least every weekend night) could be this good!

The Sunday show was in Olympia, where we'll probably never play again. Most of our shows in this indie rock epicenter have been disappointing—the gig situations are either half-assed, poorly attended, or both. A local dyke band opened for us, and they threw a lot of PC attitude at us; they drew some fans, none of whom were anywhere to be found during our set. The best thing about the evening was four big hulking guys who had come from Aberdeen to see us; kind of mean looking, they turned out to be enthusiastic fans. They were spending the night on the streets of Olympia before getting the first bus back to Aberdeen at 6:30 a.m. Now *that's* dedication to a band: I'm honored.

9.10.97 Vancouver, BC

Today we returned to Canada. We crossed the border last night, the easiest border crossing ever. Hung out with Dave and Grant from The Smugglers and did karaoke at the Dufferin, one of my favorite gay bars anywhere. We did our version of "Dancing Queen," with the lyrics altered to "Leather Queen." First time up North for Luis and Patrick. Canadian beer is stronger than U.S. beer, but Luis was not aware of this and got *very* drunk. The karaoke was in a small side room, and the larger other room was filled with a wider variety of people than I'm used to seeing in a gay bar. Different classes, races, genders. There was a stripper, but he wasn't a muscled bimbo—he was kind of a skinny guy, average body, like somebody you'd see walking down the street. To me that's a lot hotter. People drank, played pool, talked. For all of its gay mecca status, there's nothing like it in San Francisco; there, gay karaoke means The Mint on Market Street, where attitude may have been invented. After Chris and I touting Vancouver to Luis and Patrick as one

192

of our hot spots, the show itself was a letdown, only sixty people. The promoter actually apologized and promised to make it up to us next time.

9.11.97 Edmonton, AB

Edmonton…is there any use for us to play there again? We haven't had an exciting show since the Green Day tour, and this time was no different. The opener was possibly the worst punk band ever, and afterwards the DJ blared Bad Religion so loud we couldn't talk, and some morons idiot-danced and air skateboarded like the new heshers they are. Feh!

9.16.97 Fargo, ND

Drove all night en route to Fargo, via Montana (first time I'd been through it). Slept damn well, waking up at daybreak and admiring the scenery. We stopped in Bismarck, ND, to buy oil for our van at Wal-Mart, which was festooned with huge ceiling signs that read *Bring It Home America!* (It was all about buying American products. I doubt Canadian Wal-Mart signs say "Bring It Home Canada!") Arriving in Fargo the night before the show, we stayed at a Motel 6 and walked around. It felt great being back in the Midwest; it was a warm, windy night, and we walked around in the big green wide-open fields, looking up at the big sky, and absorbed all that wonderful open space. That's what I miss most about living where I do.

The Fargo show was a big success, our first time there. The club allowed all ages while serving alcohol to adults, the best situation. We had one hundred people on a Tuesday night, quite impressive.

9.18.97 Minneapolis, MN

In Minneapolis we had much a higher percentage of queers than before (it varies so much from show to show), and a cute dreadlocked boy in a Social Distortion T-shirt, the sort of fan we have few of, marched up and bought a T-shirt. All right!

On our way out of town, we had a flat tire. Unfortunately, it was on a very long, high highway overpass that was dangerous to traverse. While we were fretting over what to do, a pickup suddenly appeared behind us. It was a guy from an auto shop, who simply stopped to help us out. He changed our tire and got us back on the road. We had about eighteen beers with us from the previous night's show, and we gave them to him, and he was quite satisfied.

9.20.97 Detroit, MI

After having been told for a while that we should play The Shelter in Detroit, we finally did. A beautiful venue, it's downstairs from a larger club, and I wrongly had visualized it as a dingy basement. The promoter, Maria, was extremely nice, a striking contrast to the staff, who were big-time jerks. They played homophobic stuff between bands (Guttermouth, who else?), and were not pleased when we politely but firmly told them to yank it and play something else. Then we discovered that they were trying to get our show over with as early as possible since much of the staff wanted to see a friend's band elsewhere later that night. They rushed us onstage and tried to stop us from having an encore, despite applause. But the night ended well—we went to dinner with about fifteen people to have Greek food and ended up staying with a bear couple in Farmington Hills.

The next day, a day off, Maria was promoting the David Bowie show at the State Theater, and we got to go for free. Only Chris had seen Bowie before, and this was an intimate venue. He opened up with "Quicksand" from *Hunky Dory*, but it was downhill fast after that. The sound was horribly distorted, as if they'd arrived late and hadn't had a chance to do a sound check. Awful. Even good songs sounded terrible. We went out to the lobby. I asked Maria why the sound was so bad, and she said they'd taken two and a half hours to get it that way. Very weird.

9.22.97 Toronto, ON

Toronto was decent—a fair crowd, quite a good performance—but the club lost money despite extra promotion effort. It being a Tuesday didn't help. It was a fairly queer crowd too; Toronto is one of our favorite cities. Last time in Toronto I had a wild time with a certain young man who I hoped would appear, and he did...with his new monogamous boyfriend. But all was not lost! I met a supercute Scottish lad on his last night in Canada and had sex with him in the van, parked outside where we were staying on Queen Street West. When he came, he sighed, "Aye." It was one of the sexiest things I've ever heard.

9.26.97 Quebec City, QC

Onward to my favorite day of the tour so far. We played Quebec City for the first time, a difficult town for English-language bands. Our friends Maow got us in touch with the right folks, and we were thrilled by the town and the club, L'Arlequin, is close to perfect. Spacious, vividly decorated, with a huge stage, it had the biggest video collection I've ever seen, over seventeen hundred VHS tapes lining the walls from floor to ceiling in the control room. Through their computer you could look up their contents, and we discovered they had nearly every indie/obscure rock video you could think of, things we'd never ever heard rumors of existing! Many had been taped off of Much Music's excellent show "The Wedge," and others from collectors. They even had our videos! We spent a couple of hours before the show watching rare footage on their big screen.

Our performance was rather sloppy (the monitors were weak), but the crowd was crazy and the vibe was great. During the opening band, a young guy came up to the merch table and in broken English volunteered his willingness to strip, especially if we would as well. He also claimed to be straight...hmm, all right. So we had him come up and strip for "Groovy Underwear," which we played in our undies, but he had gotten drunk enough that he got naked for the last song. He also fellated a blow-up doll that someone had brought to the show, and Patrick captured the whole thing on his camcorder, which he had set up on the side of the stage.

We were invited to stay after hours watching vids, but we had a twelve-hour trip ahead of us so we opted for the overnight drive. Before we did, however, I coaxed our dancer into the van for a quickie, where he joined the Cocksucker Club. What a blast!

9.27.97 Halifax, NS

En route to Halifax, the highway in eastern Quebec is littered with sleazy looking sex motels, all the small towns named after obscure Catholic saints. We stopped in St. Louis-du-Ha!-Ha! (the best ever city name?) to watch the sun rise.

Like last time, Halifax was awesome. Our second time for the Halifax-on-Music festival, we played a packed, sold-out show, with a bunch of requests for the seldom-played "Headbanger." Playing later the same night was Yo La Tengo, one of my favorite bands, who were amazing, mesmerizing. I play them in the van constantly, and I'm glad Chris got to see and enjoy them.

9.28.97 Moncton, NB

I feared Moncton would be anticlimactic after Halifax, but it proved to be worth the while. The crowd was a bit apathetic, but we got one hundred people for a last-minute gig on a Sunday. One bad thing though—the singer for our opening band stuck the mic up his butt at the end of their set. As I was setting up onstage I could smell it. This is why we carry our own vocal microphones with us (though I used the antiseptic mouthwash I carry with me for such situations to clean off the mic). Since we started doing that, we have gotten sick on tour far less often.

10.2.97 New York City, NY

In New York, we opened for Kelley Deal, from The Breeders. Backstage we ran into Sebastian Bach of Skid Row, a friend of Kelley's (they'd done some recording together—what an odd combo). Chris and Patrick talked to him. He was in a leather Motley Crüe tour jacket, and had an elaborate, goofy handshake. Chris asked him about the anti-AIDS remarks he'd made around 1989, and Bach apologized, saying he was really young and didn't agree now with what he'd said then. I guess this is our year to collect apologies from reformed homophobes.

10.8.97 – 10.13.97 Man or Astroman? Tour

Our chance encounter with Man or Astroman? last year led to opening a week of shows for them this year. They are an instrumental band who started out surfy and evolved into something similar to Devo. Their stage show was like a science fair, all these cool electronic contraptions they built themselves (two of them were electrical engineering majors). Based in Atlanta, they were far more popular in the South than us, so we decided to hook up for a week of shows in that weak rock and roll state, Florida, plus a final show in New

Orleans. Great musicians and a really good time, opening for them we reached beyond our usual audience and made a bunch of new fans. Three things are notable from our week with them: 1) In Tampa I finally laid a long-haired headbanger boy, who said he'd been a roadie for Deicide. 2) Our Gainesville gig was a large outdoor festival, headlined by Blink 182 (we skipped their set). Walking around the festival, a PD fan appeared who we'd met at previous shows revealed himself to be quite racist. You want to be polite to fans, but we said we didn't agree with him and tried to lose him. We also saw one of the ten worst bands we've ever played with, called Stuck Mojo. They had large amp cabinets on stage; later they destroyed some of their equipment, but it turned out the cabinets were empty and there just for show. Too bad. 3) We had a day-off adventure in New Orleans. Our show there with MoA? also included the band Delta 72, who we'd shared a bill with earlier that year in Canada. The highlight of our set was Luis falling backwards off the drum riser during a song. On the following day we indulged in one of the most drunken days in band history, downing numerous hurricanes and getting thrown out of several bars. I have a video of me doing a gay version of Lesley Gore's "It's My Party" in a heinous karaoke bar, which alienated our Jimmy Buffett-loving MC. (One of the Astroman guys tried to get the MC to show him his dick. He pulled his own out, saying, "C'mon, we're both guys." Then he put the mic down his pants at the end of his karaoke version of "Whip It" and made the MC pull the mic back out.) We returned to where our van was parked, in front of the club we played the night before. Drunk and tired, I crashed out briefly in the back of our van, only to be awakened by the commotion of one of the Astromen being chased out of the club completely naked. (This was the same guy who'd baited the MC, so I guess he was really into showing off his dick that day.) Luis and the others jumped in the van, yelling, "Go, Go! Let's get out of here *right now!*" Apparently another drunken member of MoA? (who is shorter than me) had punched out a bouncer. So we tore out of the neighborhood and caught up with the other band's van about a mile away.

10.18.97 St. Louis, MO

I'm so sick of road food. In Louisville, we hunted for a Denny's to no avail. Stopped at a Waffle House. The service was so bad we walked out. Stopped later at a Big Boy. Food was horrible. St. Louis was better; we had a fun show, and Patrick's bear friends were having a barbecue. Our dinner consisted of grilled pork and corn on the cob, and nothing else. (Do real bears eat vegetables?) One of our hosts worked at a gay bathhouse, so we got free passes. Only Patrick and I went; neither of us found what we wanted there.

11.1.97 Chicago, IL

Chicago was a respite, a great show, and some spicy food. I ate as much spicy food as possible since Cincinnati was our next stop. We lucked out though, staying with Michael, a political activist who runs a theater company, and he took us to a good restaurant. Ohio has the blandest food and the most overweight population we've seen. To be fair, Cleveland was great, one of our best cities, and a fan who works at a posh hotel got us rooms for free. Ohio was good for us sexually (even for hard-to-get Luis).

Meanwhile, our relationship with our label had deteriorated. Lookout Records co-head Molly Neuman (of Bratmobile fame) told me on the phone one day that our tour was too long and they couldn't keep up. (Please note: labels *never* say this, because touring is by far the best way to sell records.) We had done a video for the song "Manada" (paying for the whole thing ourselves) and gave them the tapes right before we left. They did nothing—didn't copy them, didn't send copies, even to Canada, where they were meant to help our tour. I really felt they were dropping the ball, and after pondering other label possibilities we settled on Touch & Go in Chicago as our best bet. While in Chicago we'd set up a meeting with Corey, the label owner, and had a nice chat. They seemed interested and wanted to hear what we were going to do next. When we met Corey, he had just bought a copy of *More Lovin'* to check out. He said he liked the CD and was astonished to discover we weren't just a generic punk/hardcore band with gay lyrics. That was our reputation; the word *queercore* was having negative connotations.

We didn't consider major labels. We figured that we'd be at the bottom of the totem pole at any major label we were on, and we were concerned that our unique qualities just wouldn't work in that kind of system and we would be easily lost in the shuffle. We had made a friend high up at Reprise Records and asked him to give his honest evaluation of what moves to make. His assessment was that we should stay on an indie, saying we'd get chewed up and spit out at a major.

Mid-November…Somewhere on the East Coast

Chris, usually a very together person, had a meltdown. He freaked out and didn't speak for almost a week; it was a byproduct of being on the road so long and some personal stuff he wouldn't talk to us about. It made the rest of us closer. (Later we found out his aunt and an ex of his had died.) Seeing friends in the various cities cheered us up; three days in a row in New York City helped too. We went back to New York for a college show, plus a wonderful gig with Tribe 8 as a party for the NYC Mix alternative queer film festival. We played Baltimore and Silver Spring, outside Washington, DC, which was great because we got to stay with some friends there for three days in their wonderful house. Staying in the same place for a few days, at this point, was welcome relief from road fatigue. We had not been on tour continuously for so long before, and our nerves were getting frayed.

We had a lot of off days towards the end—way too many days where we had to pay to keep going instead of getting paid to perform. It makes you think, what am I doing here? If I'm not playing shows, just why am I sleeping on floors and eating crappy food? Our booking agent told us that we had been out on tour for too long, giving us the impression she had lost interest. Most agents would encourage us to tour our asses off, since it builds an audience and that's where the money's at, but ours didn't appear to want to do the work that went along with it. She only wanted us to play the cities she had contacts in but we wanted to expand our audience beyond the usual places. We felt a harder-working agent would go out and books shows anywhere she could; instead we ended up booking a number of shows on our own, feeding info back to her when we had it and essentially doing her job.

12.4.97 Santa Fe, NM

I had a birthday in Santa Fe; the guys got me Dr. Seuss *Cat in the Hat* slippers; I loved them. Also in Santa Fe, an old boss of mine from the record store in Illinois appeared at the show (in a gleaming gay bar), but she had gotten divorced and was now a new-age dyke!

12.6.97 Tempe, AZ

Playing Phoenix near the end of the tour, we got to stay at Rob Halford's house. We had been invited previously but had never been through town when he was around. His house, in a well-to-do suburb, was large but not a mansion. It was sparsely furnished and very white—white carpet, white walls—rather Spartan, but quite nice. It was very, very neat; his music room was the only clutter. He had guest rooms and was a great host; he lived there with his ex-Marine boyfriend. We asked if he had a dungeon, and he replied yes; perhaps a bit sheepishly, he shared it with us. It may have been a cement block room off his garage, but we saw Rob Halford's dungeon. *We saw Rob Halford's dungeon!*

12.12.97 Las Vegas, NV

The Las Vegas show was memorable, if not particularly pleasant. We opened for The Vandals, the long-running Southern California punk/hardcore outfit. The band themselves were really nice to us, but their audience...oh, my. We played the Huntridge Theater, a real theater (capacity around one thousand), and some of the crowd pulled the wooden armrests off the theater seats and chucked them at our heads. They missed, but it was like playing dodgeball. They also threw full containers of cheese and nachos at us (sticky yellow cheese all over the grille of my amp). But near the end of our forty-minute set, their mood changed, and they started getting into it; the elements of the crowd that were into it got louder, and contested the moronic response. Some of the guys who'd been throwing stuff at us were dancing by the time we got around to "Groovy Underwear."

Sitting at the merchandise table tonight, witnessing numerous displays of macho behavior, I saw boys wearing a slew of band T-shirts. The most popular were Lag Wagon, Unwritten Law, Dead Kennedys, Operation Ivy, Pantera, Metallica, and of course The Vandals. Also seen: Black Flag, Bad Manners, Pennywise, NOFX, No Use for a Name, Flux of Pink Indians, Rancid, Misfits, Guttermouth,

Madness, FYP, Screeching Weasel, Good Riddance, DFL, Tool, Brutal Truth, Sepultura, Blink 182, Sublime, Ten Foot Pole, Jughead's Revenge. Most girls weren't wearing band T-shirts; two that did were wearing Weezer and Radiohead, far lower on the testosterone scale. To compensate for that was an ugly man in a SHUT UP BITCH shirt, and one genetically spliced metal/punk guy with Iron Maiden and Ramones patches on his denim jacket with Rollins Band stitched into the back, topped off by a poofy blond '80s hesher 'do.

Though Vegas has grown into a large city, the music scene is strictly hicksville. A friendly Vandals roadie reported that some skinheads carrying metal pipes were waiting outside for us; he helped guard our van and helped protect us when it came time to load out.

12.13.97 Costa Mesa, CA

The tour ended well with some Southern California shows, then we limped home to San Francisco. I could not wait to get in my own shower and sleep in my own bed, something I had been fantasizing about for weeks.

Following this tour we didn't see each other for a while. For Luis and Patrick, being gone so long was more than they had bargained for, and they were especially glad to resume life beyond the band. The extra days off along the way weren't helpful financially, either, and at the end of the tour we now had to split the money four ways instead of three. Since we did about as well as usual, it meant less money per person to go around, and temp jobs while we were home.

During January 1998, we were waiting for a phone call. The year before we had played a couple of shows with The Supersuckers. One of their crew was on tour with Smash Mouth, who had played the same night as us in Dallas at the end of November. The Supersuckers guy showed up, with members of Smash Mouth in tow, just in time for our two-song encore. Afterwards, their singer Steve Harrell introduced himself and told us he *loved* it. He asked if we would like to open for Smash Mouth. They were riding quite high right then with their first hit "Walking on the Sun" (the only song of theirs we'd heard). They were going on tour with local Bay Area corporate/faux-alternative rock stars Third Eye Blind, who we couldn't stand. We said yes, it would be *quite interesting* to play in front of their audience. But he had only seen two songs, so we figured he was just blowing smoke. But he gave us a number, and we followed up on it.

We figured they wanted us for the what-the-fuck factor, or perhaps for some needed indie cred. We'd gleefully take another shot at infiltrating the mainstream crowd. Still waiting as the tour dates loomed, we were finally told we hadn't been selected. We have no idea what went on behind the scenes, but I can't believe Third Eye Blind would have had any of it (our mere presence mocks them). In the end they chose Imani Coppola, a then-new major label act. This was probably fortunate—Smash Mouth turned out to be possibly even worse than Third Eye Blind, and Imani had just one album before vanishing.

In January, we played Lookout's tenth anniversary party in San Francisco, doing a forty-five-minute set of songs from the upcoming album—no old favorites, no hits. We were fantastic, we just burned. People could see how much we'd grown as a band; we succeeded in putting some distance between the band we had been and the band we had become. We had something to prove, to our label, to our local peer group, and to ourselves. Patrick and Luis were making us into the band I'd always hoped we'd be. For me, it was one of the most satisfying gigs ever.

Our new songs had been road tested and proven worthy.

We had been working on songs for our album for almost a year, and after adding a couple new ones in winter rehearsals, we were off to Chicago to record it in early March.

CHAPTER 22

Absurd Pop Song Romance

Pleased with the results of our previous Steve Albini recording adventure, we returned for our first full-length release with Patrick. We spent nine days making it, our longest time given over to making one record. We stayed with Steve at his new residence/studio. He'd purchased an old industrial building on Chicago's North Side by the Chicago River and fitted it out with two complete recording studios. On the middle floor was an apartment where he and Heather lived. There were small individual guest rooms where we stayed—with futon bed, radio/CD player, TV. We shared their kitchen and cooked meals together. The sessions went pretty smoothly. This was the first time we'd totally sequestered ourselves during the recording process, so the days were productive.

We had achieved a certain prowess live and now had made an album that was equal to that, but different. On our previous albums, most of the songs were fun or funny, but there would be several more moody or introspective ones. This time, the ratio was reversed—a couple of laughers, but overall a more serious themed and darker sounding record. The album opened up with "February 17," written by Chris for Billie Joe's surprise twenty-fifth birthday party (where we had premiered the song). It's partly written for him, but mostly it reflects the dilemma of growing older versus growing up. It opened up with Luis's drums alone, 'cause we finally had the drummer we needed and wanted to put him right up front.

"Sweet Insecurity" followed, a song of mine. After having written so many literal lyrics, here I tried to capture a mood. The riff Patrick wrote over the chord progression was like icing on a cake, making it complete. To us, it was a hit single; with Albini's clear mix and great drum sound, it sounded like it would be perfect on the radio. It was followed by "It'll Never be the Same," the most rocking song Chris had written but not a punk rock song. Chris had wanted to be more of an equal songwriting partner, and with songs like this he'd really succeeded. After having so many sex-positive songs, the lyric was a dose of reality that helped balance the scales.

When we began the band, we wanted to hear songs where the guy got the guy, because we hadn't heard that. After having done that, we were at the point where we felt the need to see the other side. "Too Beautiful" was a true story about somebody I was never going to get, a downer. "Better Off Just Friends" was more upbeat but still not rosy.

Then, four songs in a row that just might be the peak of our band. "Luv Luv Luv" is comical, but cynical too, probably our second-most popular song (after "Bunnies").

Summing up the kinds of ideas about love that we grow up with, and the misconceptions that pop songs give us, its universal appeal—and chanting chorus—made it a hit from the first time we played it. A lyric from it supplied the album's title, *Absurd Pop Song Romance*. Tonally, it was the only song on the album that sounded like our earlier records (perhaps because Chris and Luis switched instruments, for that ragged but right feel), a link from past to present. Next up was "The Best Revenge," as in Happiness Is…. This is our hardest rocking moment on record, an elastic song that goes up and down and back and forth and really lifts off at the end. Patrick in particular shines here (again).

After listening to the mix, I felt that the end of the song needed just a little extra something, an extra gritty edge to put it across. Steve's suggestion was to take the final section of the song, record it onto a cassette (maxing out the input), then record that part off the cassette back onto the master tape, losing a generation—the resulting distortion adding the crowning touch that was needed. It's a great example of how Albini works. Instead of imposing his own ideas, he offers a suggestion based on his extensive recording knowledge to solve a problem that the musician has identified. We were repeatedly impressed at the great job he did.

"Bad Boyfriend" was a punk song with horns. Instead of complaining about a bad boyfriend I'd had, I pointed the finger at myself. (It's easy to always blame someone else.) Albini described our music (and this song in particular) as "romantic punk, like The Only Ones or The Saints." I love those bands, and they aren't obvious influences, unlike The Ramones, whose sound so many of our Lookout label brethren could not escape.

Following that was the second song on the album about friendship, Chris's "You're Gonna Need Your Friends." So many pop songs are about love, not enough are about friendship. (Who else is going to listen to you complain, and what's life without complaining?) A more subtle approach from Patrick, combined with fuzzed-out tones from me, makes it right. This is another staple that lasted in the live set for years.

The next few songs are a cut below. "Tinted Windows" is the most lightweight song on the album, a fun bit of fluff with a real bare bones arrangement and spartan mix. "Glenview" is a melodramatic ballad with strings, an interesting diversion, nakedly sincere. I have a hard time listening to it now. "Used to Turn Me On," another lament from Chris, is a good song that goes on too long; I prefer the shorter, punchier demo version that later came out on a Lookout compilation.

The final two songs pick it up again. "Obstacle Course" was the last song written for the album, another one where the boy is elusive and the situation difficult. It starts a bit slow but really nails it. Though it and "Too Beautiful" were rarely played live, I rate them as two of our most successful recordings. Playing the downer stuff live just didn't go over, but on the album I think they really hit their mark.

The album ended with "Vicious Beauty," a hard-rocking, noisy song with a post-punk disco beat during the verses. The riff was something I stumbled on during one of our first practices with Luis as a three-piece, and it carried on the occasional heavy noise tangent we'd stumbled upon. The lyric concept was discovering your high school bully on the cover of a gay porn video. Fun to play live, it was our set closer at that time.

Interspersed between a few songs on the CD were skits and other odd bits. Luis and Patrick were particularly into having these on the CD, akin to the kinds of between-song bits you'd find on hip-hop albums. They're there in part because we were trying to have all the band members influence the overall presentation of the album. That said,

I think they prevent the album from being played straight through—they're like little roadblocks, and unlike the songs, they don't stand up to repeat listenings. I'd be satisfied never to hear them again.

The only other regret I have about the album is its cover. We simply could not agree on it. I wanted a band shot on the front, 'cause we'd never done that and I was proud of our new lineup. I also wanted people to see that it was a new lineup, something different. The end result was a compromise that none of us really like. It's designed to look like an old pulp paperback, but it's not particularly attractive.

It also contained another hidden bonus track. During this period, we played "Melba vs. Gay Day" by Brother Russell just prior to taking the stage. Russell had released a CD of prank phone calls to Christian talk radio stations, using the persona of a sweet old lady named Melba. Melba called into one program claiming she'd gone to Disney World on their "Gay Day," and that homosexuals had recruited her nephew. It was great satire, and we wanted to share it with our fans (there was a note about it inside the CD booklet).

There it was—our sixth album, complete. We were branching out and it felt right. We'd evolved but stayed true to our ideals. Upon hearing the completed recording, we thought it sounded commercial, in a good sense. We always thought we had hit-caliber songs, but now we had the recording quality to back it up. As people seemed to be tiring of punk, we'd thought its commercial prospects were good, good enough to put us in a better league. We envisioned a new audience responding to something different.

However, we weren't sure who would release the record. Eventually, Lookout courted us back into the fold. We knew our record didn't fit the exact profile of what people expected from a Lookout label record, but we knew that Lookout had also hit a sales plateau, and that our evolution could mirror theirs (as our ascent had mirrored theirs). They seemed enthusiastic about the album and promised extra radio and press promotion. We didn't really want to leave the label; we just wanted them to do us right.

The record was mastered by late spring, but we wanted to prepare for a big college radio push (thinking this album might do better there than earlier efforts had), so we held it back for a September release, to coincide with the fall semester. (Interestingly, the album's release date was the same as that of another band—The Outnumbered! A best-of compilation was released by the Illinois indie-pop label Parasol.) The intervening time was to be used to get interviews and reviews lined up and prepare for the best. We did some shows in a few off the beaten path California cities, and two pride shows of note.

First up was San Jose's Gay Pride, fifty miles south of San Francisco. Apart from us it was an all disco lineup—Ru Paul, Kathy Sledge of Sister Sledge, and Evelyn "Champagne" King. We drove our van; the other performers arrived in limos. We played our instruments; the others sang to tapes. Ru Paul didn't even sing, but lip-synched. Nobody was allowed anywhere near the stars (including us). After our set, we had our usual merchandise table, where people came up to actually talk to us in person. I hate the whole diva mentality, whatever the musical style; on this occasion we witnessed the "Gimme the check and get me the hell outta here!" thing. We're such the fish out of water at these events. We did go over well, and did have a good time, but there was a definite alienation factor. On the other hand, if we hadn't played, there would have been no one to offer a musical/cultural alternative to the pre-sold gay lifestyle.

Then there was San Francisco Pride. We were supposed to play on the main stage but didn't. We were listed on the cover of the Pride Guide that was distributed all around town, yet we were allocated a mere fifteen minutes onstage. The event was so disorganized that ultimately we didn't even have that much time. It ran far behind schedule and all the local San Francisco queer rock bands lined up for the end of the day got bumped. After waiting around nearly four hours we felt it was a real slap in the face. Our very own Pride Committee was showing some legendary incompetence. They had promised us things would not be as bad as in previous years, but alas, they were. They even misspelled San Francisco on the souvenir programs! The one good thing I can say about the whole experience is that we had fun meeting Chumbawamba, who played a short acoustic set.

CHAPTER 23

Road Warriors

In early September, we set off on a six-week U.S. tour, and after a week off, an eight-week European tour. We were anxious to show off our new baby, to blow the minds of earlier fans and impress new ones. We were kept busy with interviews before and during the tour, thanks to Yvette Ray, a publicist we'd hired. As usual, I kept a diary.

9.14.98 Los Angeles, CA

Four days out on the road and it's been a breeze so far. Usually after we've been out this long we've covered a lot of mileage, but by going to Southern California first and playing four shows there, it's been easy. It doesn't feel quite like a real tour yet, not enough driving. We played outdoors at University of Southern California on Friday at noon, in front of the statue of the USC mascot, Tommy Trojan. We didn't even make any jokes about it (we figured they'd already heard them). We played in the bright sun (it's the first time I can remember wearing sunglasses onstage—can The Sisters of Mercy say that?), for a decent lunchtime crowd.

That same night, we played across town at Spaceland in Silver Lake. One of the opening acts was The Glitter Panthers, a new band formed by two out gay musicians who've played the major label game, Brian Grillo (ex-Extra Fancy) and Bill Tutton (ex-Geraldine Fibbers). I liked their sound much better than Extra Fancy—more melodic, not hard rock sounding, and they had some really good songs. Our performance was okay, though we played a lot of songs too fast, which is something we hadn't done in a while. Our set was heavy on the songs from the new album, tilted a little too heavy that way in retrospect; I think we played two thirds of it.

The next night we went behind the "orange curtain" to play at Club Mesa in Costa Mesa, Orange County. This club has a clientele of white rednecks and middle-aged Latino men, plus some really skeezy characters hanging out in the parking lot. On Sunday, we did a pretty wild and spontaneous all-ages show in the valley, at a place called The Smell. The place is so tiny it should really be called The Small; it was so narrow we faced the side wall, and the crowd gathered around us in a semicircle. But it doesn't get more intimate than that, so it made for a fun night.

One show we didn't do this weekend was an in-store at the Virgin Megastore. In 1996, a fan of ours working at the Virgin in Costa Mesa scored us an in-store appearance there. We did it to get exposure in populous but conservative Orange County, a free performance for people who shop in chain stores. We had one hundred and fifty people, about half of whom were there to see us. We got a crowd, the store got more customers, and everybody was happy. The fan told me that when the L.A. store on Sunset Boulevard heard we were playing, people there were jealous! So I made a note to contact them once we had a new record to promote.

Now was that time. I went through the proper channels, attempting to secure in-stores at both L.A. and Costa Mesa. However, this time Virgin insisted that our label take out expensive ads in the *LA Weekly* and the *Orange County Weekly*; those two ads would have amounted to over 40 percent of the entire promotional budget for the new record. Here was an illustration of what I felt had gone wrong with "alternative"—now everything had a price tag. The Virgin policy meant that only labels with large promo budgets could get in-stores for their bands. Instead of being thankful that a band performance might bring customers into their store—for which the band was not even getting paid—they just try to squeeze out every dollar they can.

Another Orange County show we didn't do was at the UC-Fullerton campus. Last year we'd been tentatively scheduled there but were canceled a month in advance. A small but vociferous group of right-wing students complained loud and long about public money being spent on a gay band. (Since gay people don't pay taxes, their position makes sense.) The student group booking the shows chickened out and canceled us. They feared that such enemies could shut down their group entirely. There had been a large protest over the showing of *The Last Temptation of Christ* on campus, and the student group wanted to avoid more controversy. We were pissed off—we wanted the chance to defend our position and have the debate. Let us at least have the protest instead of silencing us preemptively.

9.18.98 Columbia, MO

One of the top ten PD shows ever! College towns can be iffy for us, but Columbia has always been a good one (it was also good for The Outnumbered a decade before). Every night, you roll into a town and wonder what the reaction will be like. You hope the venue will be full of people going crazy, and tonight it was. Though our CD has been out for a mere ten days, people knew the lyrics to the new songs and sang along. We played great, a cute boy came up to the stage during the set and gave me a hell of a kiss, and a different one was all ready to take me home afterwards, but we decided to do the all-night drive and have a whole day off in Chicago. Deliriously happy.

9.20.98 Chicago, IL

Five years we've been touring now, and it has become clear that our best city is Chicago, and our best venue is the Fireside Bowl, on Fullerton. It's a dilapidated bowling alley, no longer available for bowling; bands play on the area in front of the lanes (which are cordoned off). The wall behind the stage has ugly water-damaged wood paneling. It's an all-ages club, but with a bar up front (which the under twenty-ones are not allowed into), probably the reason it still exists. It's a dump, but it's our dump. Year in, year out, we get hundreds of fans, have a great show, and sell tons of merch. That's what happened again today. I love it and look forward to it every year. Because I have so many friends in Illinois, it's a big social event for me. I am in my element. I have a great life.

9.23.98 Toronto, ON

Because we're going to Europe, we didn't have time to do a whole Canadian tour this year. For a band like us, it doesn't pay to just do a handful of appearances, due to the cost of work permits, so we snuck up to Toronto for one show, leaving all our stuff behind in Detroit and borrowing our opening band's gear. We traveled up in two cars, with a few fans of ours, in case we looked like a band and they checked our immigration histories.

We got in okay, and when we got to Toronto, our Canadian publicist Yvette told us a commercial radio station there was playing "Sweet Insecurity." This station hadn't even been sent a copy of the CD. We went to the station, did an interview, and thought, hmm, maybe this album is actually happening! It was still too soon to tell; it had only been out two weeks.

10.15.98 Portland, OR

Tonight we opened for Rancid in the beautiful Crystal Ballroom, a vintage 1920s-era hall built for ballroom dancing with spring-loaded wooden floors that visibly bounce up and down. Though it's great to play in front of a bigger audience, they didn't respond much. We played with Rancid again the following night in Seattle to another lackluster but peaceful response. Though I'm pretty tired of punk rock right now, and find their anthemic posturing trying at times, tonight Rancid were truly great. I was really impressed, and they were extremely nice to all of us. A cool experience. We played a second show in Seattle at a new club, The Breakroom, with our friends Chixdiggit. I feel so lucky right now.

CHAPTER 24

France Is the Indiana of Europe: European Tour Diary

10.21.98 Amsterdam, the Netherlands

The first of forty-one shows of our mammoth eight-week European tour took place here. We met up with our booker Hans again, got our rented band gear, and met our Belgian driver, Greet. Our beloved guide from the previous tour, Oscar, now has a job that won't permit him to have such extensive time off. With Greet along, there are five of us traveling across the continent together; four seemed crowded last time, so we'll just have to grin and bear our yellow Mercedes truck/van. Alas, it was a fair-to-middling crowd…shouldn't Amsterdam be a big city for a band like ours?

10.22.98 Naarden, the Netherlands

In 1995, we bought our van from a dealer in Sonoma,

California, about an hour north of San Francisco. On the wall of this dealership was a photo of a very cool-looking town surrounded by water. I asked the guy if he knew where the picture was taken, if it was in California somewhere, and he told me it was a small Dutch town called Naarden. It's only twenty miles east of Amsterdam, so on the way to our gig today we stopped to sightsee. It was as beautiful as the photo.

10.23.98 Duisberg, Germany

It's no secret that Germans like beer, but I've never seen a crowd at one of our shows get this obliterated. The show was at the University of Duisberg, sponsored by the campus gay group, many of whom wore black leather pants (very popular in Germany). Very friendly crowd, most of them toasted before we got onstage. Sitting in the gay group's office before the show, a girl puked loud and long right outside the window. During the show people were passing out, falling over the monitors. The show ended fairly early, so people hung around afterwards and drank even more; in the hallway outside, there was puking galore and people face down on the cement. I had my eye on a guy who had flirted with me during the show; I saw him seated on a chair passed out as I was talking to some folks and later noticed liquid dripping from the bottom of his pant leg. I thought maybe he'd peed himself, but on closer (not too close, mind you) inspection I saw that he'd puked so voluminously down his shirt that it had dripped all the way down his leg to the floor. Only us Americans took notice; the locals seemed quite used to it.

10.28.98 Oslo, Norway

Oslo was a really good time. After our sound check, the promoter took us to a university radio station for an interview. The interviewer was friendly and knowledgeable about our band. They played a couple of our songs. At the end, a shopping bag was brought into the studio with great fanfare. Inside the bag were two large mason jars containing our interviewer's shit, presented for our reaction. He was conducting an experiment to see how long it would take to break down. Or something like that. It had been in there for months. He'd put little bits of food in once to see how long it took to be eaten up by the decaying shit. Patrick recalls that it stunk, but I remember being relieved the stuff was in well-sealed jars. I remarked that winters must be very long up there. The promoter said Norwegians have a very anal sense of humor. I believe him.

We had a larger than usual amount of time to kill prior to showtime, so I explored downtown Oslo. Motorhead was playing down the street, and the other guys briefly went to check them out. We were near the central train station, so I had a very civilized time sitting by myself (a rare event) in a restaurant drinking tea. At a bus stop outside the station, nearly all the people there were chatting on cell phones. (In 1998 in San Francisco you would very rarely see such a thing—I remember a yuppie woman in a power suit marching down Valencia Street with one, she looked so ludicrous. In Oslo it was commonplace, and by a year later, it had become so in the states too.)

The venue was fairly large, but the crowd was small, about sixty people. In the crowd I noticed an extremely cute young guy. After we were done, he came over to our merch table with a cute friend and we got to talking. They had traveled eight hours on the train from Bergen to see us. They were both bi, and had a history together, and were both interested in me. But I couldn't take them back to the hotel with me—I was sharing a room with Patrick, where would he go? So we spent some time making out on a sofa, and some time in a bathroom stall, but if they couldn't come with me they had to go to a friend's house, and she was leaving (and I couldn't go with them). As it turned out, Patrick ended up getting laid and going to that guy's place. I had the room all to myself—but by then they were gone! I missed having the cutest three-way imaginable, drat! Learning the lesson of my own song, however, I did remember to take pictures.

10.30.98 Goteborg, Sweden

After an exciting show in Stockholm, we arrived in Goteborg to find our show canceled. The day before, there had been a fire in a discotheque there that killed sixty-three people, all of them teenagers. Over two hundred people were treated for injuries. The whole city was in shock. We hung around the venue for a bit and decided to drive back to the ferry ahead of schedule. Before leaving, Patrick and Luis liberated a dozen beers from the club. Drinking them later on the overnight ferry, they noticed that they weren't getting drunk. Discovering they had stolen non-alcoholic beer, they were bummed out and amused at the same time.

We are enjoying Greet's company. She's no-nonsense (firm, but with a sense of humor), from Gent in Belgium, and has the proper requisite anti-Americanism (or more precisely, skepticism about America) that so many young Europeans have. She understands, of course, that the group she's accompanying is the polar opposite of the things she hates about America, 'cause they're the things we hate too. She drives all of the time, keeps us on schedule, collects our money, sells our merch, and sometimes does our sound.

11.5.98 Antwerp, Belgium

Sometimes you just get lucky with a crowd. Tonight we were booked onto an already popular club night at a bar called Cartoons; though we'd never played Antwerp before (and don't seem to have that many fans in Belgium), we had a huge, fun crowd that dug the show. Had it been any other night of the week, we'd have had only a fraction of the audience we did. It was great winning over a group of people that wasn't there to see us in particular.

11.7.98 London, England

I was pumped up for this show. We played the Garage, at Highbury Corner, a great venue, on our first tour and we were stoked to return. We met Crissy, the British publicist Lookout had hired for the tour; we had no such perk on our last trip and were hoping for a big turnout. We got it, and we played great. Our set took place at a decent hour 'cause there was a rock disco afterwards; they played great Britpop and indie stuff, and the crowd was mixed between gay and straight. There's nothing like this in the gay scene in the United States, except possibly Squeezebox (which is a much smaller place). It was great hearing Pulp's "Do You Remember the First Time?" played over a big sound system in a room full of queers rather than the usual club crap.

We went to Tower Records, where they had several of our CDs in stock, but not the new one. The number one U.K. hit at the time was Cher's "Believe," which we heard everywhere in London. It wasn't a hit in the U.S. until the following spring.

11.10.98 Manchester, England

Had one of the best shows of the tour tonight in a city I have wanted to visit for years (we didn't play there on our '96 tour). The bar staff was incredibly nasty, before and after the show, but the crowd was enthused and the place fairly packed. After finishing, a couple of crazed fans tried to steal my effects pedals right off the stage; I barely caught them. I ended up going home with a cute guy who was obsessed with

222

Courtney Love. He lived in a suburb called Bolton (that's Notlob to Monty Python fans) and we had a swell time; in the morning, I took a train back to Manchester to rendez-vous with the band. I had some trash to throw away, and I walked around the station looking for a trashcan. Thanks to IRA bomb fears, the entire station had no trash receptacles. In fact, a huge IRA bomb blast had occurred there while we were on our 1996 European tour.

Manchester is the home of some of my most beloved bands (The Buzzcocks, The Fall, and Magazine), and having the next day off I walked around and saw landmarks and neighborhoods mentioned in their songs. I actually saw our new CD in a HMV shop in the city center; we hadn't seen our records in many shops (same as our first Euro tour) but didn't really do much record shopping anyway.

That night Tom Robinson was performing in town (we'd had breakfast with him in London a few days before), and it was great seeing one of our predecessors play. After the show we went to another indie rock disco that played great music, with a mainly queer (but mixed) crowd. We chatted with a few people who'd been to our show. When you entered the club, they gave you a "shag tag" with a number on it. There was a bulletin board where you could leave notes saying you liked #57 or find people leaving notes for you. I'd never seen this before, what a terrific idea!

11.13.98 Edinburgh, Scotland

The worst show of the tour. The usual Edinburgh promoter was on holiday, so our promoter took the show as a favor, and his lack of enthusiasm was apparent. Suppos-edly an all-ages show, the club's proprietor wouldn't let in the kids who showed up and was a total dick about it. We had to throw a fit to get him to live up to his end of the bargain. Before the show, a drunk woman stumbled up to

Chris and told him she was going to shag someone in Pansy Division. Chris told her she was a bit unclear on the concept and escaped. But there she was front and center, lifting her dress salaciously, exposing her underwear, and rubbing her crotch. During the third song she stumbled into the stage and knocked the mic stand against my teeth, at which point Patrick stepped in front of me to head her off. She was on the ground, and Patrick stepped over her; she stood up, resulting in Patrick almost riding her piggyback. She spent the last half of the set passed out on the floor, and as we were leaving we saw her downstairs flirting with the ugly jerk of a proprietor.

11.18.98 Munich, Germany

We were nearly a month into our tour. Patrick was sick with walking pneumonia. We had played a show in a cold, unheated squat in Amsterdam a couple of weeks earlier, and he had become ill and never quite recovered. Traveling around in our cramped van in cold weather, he needed more sleep (we all did) but was unable to get any on the long drives we were making. He was pretty grumpy, and we had almost another month to go. The Munich gig was kind of so-so, but we met Elliott Smith and Janet Weiss; Janet is the drummer for Sleater-Kinney, and also has the band Quasi, who were backing Elliott on his tour. On their night off they were told our bar would be a good place to hang out, not knowing who was playing. Elliott had been in a band called Heatmiser, who had a gay guitarist named Neil Gust we'd met in Portland once. When we were looking for a lead guitarist, Luis thought we should ask Neil; Luis called him up, but he politely declined. Elliott told us Neil was flattered to be asked, which was a nice story to hear.

11.20.98 Winterthur, Switzerland

Stayed in a hostel with the Swiss Army! They had booked

this entire hostel except for our rooms; however, they were all asleep when we got to our rooms at 3:00 a.m., so there were no saucy stories to tell.

11.22.98 Basel, Switzerland

A fun show in a dank basement with a riot grrl band called Re-Sisters. They had long blonde dreads and were like an early Chumbawamba. We met some really cool people in Basel, and we were able to go back and stay with them for a couple of days following our other Swiss shows. Having a spacious, comfy place to plop down for a time was a relief. We watched Wallace & Gromit videos with them and talked a lot. I had an intense two-day platonic relationship with one of the housemates, some very intense and wonderful conversations, but nothing physical. On the last day, we went to a local park where the artist Christo had wrapped several dozen trees in gray canvas material. I expected it to be kind of cheesy, but I was stunned how beautiful and wonderfully playful it was. It was getting dark as we left, which heightened the effect.

11.23.98 Turin, Italy

Played to a smallish crowd, in a dusty venue full of dogs (and dog hair). The most memorable thing was the preshow pasta and broccoli meal. They fed us and about twenty other people at a long, long table. I saw them making the food—a big pot of boiling broccoli and large pots of pasta. Though hungry, I was fairly dreading the meal, which looked like it would be a cheap mass meal. It was so unbelievably good, just broccoli and pasta. Italian food is the best, I don't know how they do it. I tried to replicate this meal at home after the tour, and it had none of the magic (and I'm a decent cook). Italy, I bow to your cuisine.

Perhaps France is a rival for the food crown, but we

wouldn't know—we didn't play any gigs there. We drove through it three or four times; as far as rock music is concerned, France is the Indiana of Europe. Centrally located, you just cross it, but it's not your destination—it isn't interested in you.

11.25.98 Rome, Italy

This show was a highlight of the tour, the kind of total fun that briefly makes you forget how tired and weary you are. It was reminiscent of the crazed shows from our previous Italian tour, wild! Chris stripped down to a glittery dress near the end of the show, and someone reached up onstage and stole his favorite tie. We threatened not to encore unless someone returned it, but even though it didn't happen we played on anyway. I had hoped that we could find someone to drive us into central Rome after the show (our club was on the outskirts of town, and I'd never seen the sights), but since we were due in Milan in the afternoon to do a TV show, my plan was foiled.

11.26 Milan, Italy

We arrived on time, but then spent two to three hours drinking cappuccinos, waiting for them to be ready for us. Oh, for more sleep! We did three songs plus a short interview, and I think the show was broadcast later that week. We played to the film crew; they later filmed a studio audience when we weren't present and edited it to look like they were watching us. Our Milan gig was just okay, but we got to meet some of the people from *Speed Demon* magazine, an excellent Italian queer zine that had extensively covered us (and many other obscure queer rockers).

11.28.98 Genoa, Italy

Tonight more people attended a Pansy Division show

than any other show we've ever headlined on our own—six hundred and fifty people. It was fun but hardly a top venue. It was in a dirt floor Communist party squat that lacked toilets (there were two holes in the floor, behind shower curtains) and was very dusty (gave me an asthma attack). The building had no electricity, just a generator, which went out a couple of times during the set. The crowd listened, danced, moshed, formed a pit, stayed through the whole show. At the end...nothing. No noise, a smattering of applause. But they didn't leave. As we learned (afterwards), the tradition of the encore is not well established in Italy. This happened a few times that week in Italy, at well-attended shows. The encore is a pretty silly tradition, a cliché, but sometimes they can really mean something. They expected us to play more but didn't clap for more.

12.4.98 Tomelloso, Spain

This small town has a '60s obsessed rock club called Beat (whose stickers have a picture of the Beatles and their famous logo on it without the last three letters). Before the bands began, I enjoyed several hours of VHS bootlegs of 1960s American TV music shows—"Hullabaloo," "American Bandstand," "Shindig" type of stuff; Paul Revere & the Raiders, 13th Floor Elevators, very cool. Like everywhere else in Spain, the show began late. It was fun, but we are so weary. The Spanish hotels have tile floors, not carpeting, so I was awakened several times during the night by people walking down the hall.

A photo I took the morning after this show exemplifies the weariness we felt at this point in the tour. As we awaited our bread, cheese, and coffee European breakfast, we look like we'd rather be anywhere else. It was about to get worse.

12.5.98 Valencia, Spain

Drove to the coast on a brand new four-lane interstate-type highway that had opened the day before. Smooth ride, almost zero traffic (it helped that it was a Sunday). Following sound check, Greet stepped into a hole next to a tree and broke her ankle. Ouch! Conveniently, she did this in front of a hospital—so she limped right in. We stayed with her for a bit, until when she got in to see the doctor. Then we wandered off to find food. We'd been in better moods. The show was pretty good—the show here in '96 had been a good one too. We went back to the hospital afterwards to confirm that her ankle was broken, and she had a cast on it.

Her fortune could have been much worse—the tour was almost over, and our next show was in Belgium, and her apartment was our next stop anyway. She couldn't drive; none of us are particularly good on the stick shift, but we got Greet home. On the drive across France, we were stopped and searched twice at French toll plazas. During the tour we'd had a little bit of pot and hash but never much and never for very long. They had German shepherds but found nothing (Chris swallowed the tiny amount of hash he had left).

12.9.98 Eindhoven, the Netherlands

In the meantime we'd called Oscar, our driver from our previous Euro tour, and asked him if he'd want to drive us around for four or five days. His days off lined up with our Dutch dates, and he was able to do it. It was great hanging around with Oscar, an infusion of new blood when ours was pretty anemic.

Every Wednesday this club had a band and a movie, so our opening act was The Village People film *Can't Stop the Music*. I'd avoided it for years (it would regularly play in San Francisco at the Castro Theater), but it was a camp classic, far more entertaining that I would have expected. The show was really fun; it was strange having the crowd get up from their tables and seats and walk into the next room to watch us.

I don't recall who we stayed with after the show, but I remember their house. They showed us around, and asked us if we'd like to see the garden. Um…sure. The garden was indoors—a large bedroom completely full of pot plants! It was a growing operation; it's not exactly legal in the Netherlands, but it's "tolerated." So we got really stoned. The sad thing was, Chris had found a date that night, so he missed out on it, and he is *by far* the biggest pothead among us.

12.12.98 Sneek, the Netherlands

We had a good show in Rotterdam, where there is a cult around the Lookout Records brand of pop punk, but only had twenty people in the Hague. Still, it was cool to visit these dots on the map. Our last show was in Sneek, in the northern part of the country. I was interested in taking certain routes there and back, so we could go through parts of the country I hadn't yet seen—Flevoland, a farmland province reclaimed from the sea, and the Zuider Zee barrier dam. Driving across the Zuider Zee, there was a place to stop and check out the dam. Getting back in the van, I slammed the door on Luis's hand. He started screaming, "*Open the door! Open the door!*" It was possibly the worst moment of my life. We were trying to make it through one more show and get home, and now it was unlikely we could even do that. Luis sat there in pain, and I could not have felt worse.

When we arrived in Sneek, we dropped off our gear and went to the hospital, our second visit in a week. Miraculously, his hand was not broken, just bruised, and under the influence of Motrin he even played the show. God, what a trooper! He wasn't too happy, but he wasn't nearly as mad as he could have been. We played with two hardcore bands, and it was not much fun on any level. We crawled back to Amsterdam and finally flew home the next day. Home never seemed more inviting.

Once back, we still had two more shows! We played a local morning TV show (we had to arrive at 5:30 a.m., oh, were we cheery!), and then a show in San Francisco that we had no energy to promote. It was about as cold in the city as it ever gets there, and the crowd was meager. What exactly was it we were torturing ourselves to accomplish?

CHAPTER 25

At a Crossroads

We had finally settled our band lineup and sounded better than ever. We had transcended our early sound and evolved into a stronger band and made an album that displayed true growth, a real achievement. But returning from Europe, we had never been so exhausted. We didn't talk much that first month back. Both Luis and Patrick felt like they couldn't take it anymore and wanted to leave the group, but after a month they had reconsidered.

We wanted to know how our CD had fared, given how hard we were working to promote it. The answer was not encouraging. It had sold just over 5,200 copies, continuing our slide. Visiting the Lookout office, I looked over the reports submitted by the radio publicist we'd hired. There was a lot of resistance to us; many stations said things like

"We've already played them," or "We used to play them a few years ago." A few said they "never liked them" and many just plain weren't interested. We did have a core of stations that still aired us, but we had clearly not made the breakthrough to the nonconverted. We wondered if we'd stayed with the right label; maybe a change of scenery would have enabled us to reach a different audience or have people view us differently.

Mostly, we were bummed out. We reinvented ourselves and few had noticed. We felt like if we were to have much of a future, this record had to get through, and it hadn't. The reaction we got from people who wrote us was mixed but generally favorable. Many praised the evolution, saying it was overdue. Some people missed the funnier, dirtier songs (we still played them live). We didn't expect everyone to like it; however, I think if we'd put out that same CD under a different band name or a different label it might have received more consideration.

I think *Absurd Pop Song Romance* was KO'ed by timing more than anything else. But it was hard to complain about that too much—our group had appeared at a moment that was so opportune, you could never have planned for it. The moment that allowed us in was over, and the door was hitting us on the ass on the way out. Punk rock now had jock appeal (Blink 182 was now more popular than Green Day). Alternative had burned out in a wave of lousy bands. Coming up from the punk underground was emo, the most whiny, unmelodic, self-absorbed manifestation of punk yet. Ska (the third wave) crashed in and had already peaked. The Swing revival was at its peak, and it crashed even faster. Commercially, teen pop was huge, and so was rap metal, the worst music ever (Limp Bizkit, the worst band ever). With all these new bands, it seemed all the incremental gains made through riot grrl and bands like us had hit a wall at high speed. You could hear the *SPLAT!* Except for Hole and The Breeders, the women in alt-rock had received far less radio play than the men, and by now those bands were falling apart. Forgetting our own fortunes for a minute, it was bad in general, a very dispiriting time for music.

We pondered our next step. For the moment, touring was ruled out. The rest of the band wanted to stay home, especially Luis and Patrick. We played a mere three shows in the first five months of '99. One show was at South By Southwest in Austin, where we played a Lookout Records showcase. Instead of touring to get there, we flew in for the one show.

We had been a really ambitious band. Around this time we realized that no matter how well we played, or what we might do, we'd probably never be as popular as we had been, unless something unlikely happened—some band asking us to open for them, or some other occurrence out of our control. We'd done a lot of work, fun though the work was. At this point, we lowered our sights. Cut back on our exposure. No recording for a while. Instead of the band dominating our lives, it was going to take a backseat.

Though we were glad to be home, home had changed. The dot-com boom was at its peak in San Francisco—in early '99, the Dow Jones hit 11,000—and people like us simply couldn't find anywhere to live. If you were lucky enough to have an established lease with cheap rent (like Chris and I), you were a prisoner, you couldn't move. The influx of techies had driven rents sky high, and people we knew were getting evicted and being forced to leave the city. Leslie from Tribe 8 lived around the corner from me the whole time I'd known their band, and she was evicted. Almost everyone I knew had such horror stories. The bohemia that defined San Francisco was being threatened, and our friends were ground zero.

During this time at home we finally launched a Pansy

Division website. A couple of web-oriented people had put up pages for us in years previous, and one had even built a small site for us. However, he didn't update it for almost two years, and we realized we needed to take control of the situation. When we'd been on tour with Man or Astroman? their drummer Brian told me they'd chucked their 10,000 strong mailing list in favor of email. That sounded ludicrous to me at the time, as I wasn't yet online, but once we got the website set up I understood. Our mailing list had 4,400 names; it cost a thousand dollars each time we wanted to do a postcard mailing. We did a final mailing in which we asked people to join our newfangled email list (or write us telling us they didn't have computers). For a while we had a tracker on the site, where we could see which countries our web viewers were from. They were from nearly everywhere in the world, from such far-flung places as Pakistan, Russia, and Indonesia.

Not touring meant finding other income. Everyone got jobs except me. Instead, I had discovered eBay. I had lots of records, some of which I'd kept 'cause I knew they were worth more than what a good used record store would pay me. So for several months, I made a killing off my record collection. Who'd have thought all that punk/indie vinyl would appreciate so much? I temped occasionally, but eBay got me through the year.

I spent a lot of time on the phone that year trying to secure a return visit to Australia. I had a good promoter interested—she even faxed me her proposed itinerary—but then she got the chance to book Australia's Big Day Out, their Lollapalooza equivalent, and she had no more time for little tours. Things had fallen into place so easily at one point; now things were slipping away from us just as easily.

I sulked over the lack of touring. After five years of it, I had grown used to the lifestyle of constant travel. Even if the CD had sold disappointingly, it wasn't a total bomb, and we still had fans. If we weren't going to tour, I decided I would! Not to play music, but to visit some of the friends I would normally see in a season of touring. I bought a thirty-day Greyhound bus pass; I flew to Chicago, and had a great time wandering around the East, Midwest, and South for a month. Between St. Louis and Little Rock, some ex-con dykes sat behind me (one of whom had just been paroled) chatting for a couple hours. *Tough* grrlz. I was fascinated and scared; they took absolutely no responsibility for their crimes—it was always someone else's fault.

I returned from my trip in early June, when Gay Pride events start heating up. We were getting offers from people to fly us in to such events, and so that year we went to Boston, playing on Boston Common. The day after, we played San Jose's Gay Pride, opening for none other than Joan Jett—no disco divas this time! We had a fun show Pride weekend in San Francisco, and instead of agreeing to perform on the main stage after the last Pride fiasco we played on a float in the parade, which was much more fun. It had taken half a year, but we were enjoying playing again.

After spending some time at home, the others agreed to tour, under certain conditions: do shorter tours, and make sure we have the relative comfort of our van (*i.e.*, no European tours). We did a week of shows in the Northwest (including a few Canadian shows), came home for a week and played two local shows, and then went back out across the United States and Canada for a month. Both local shows were part of a festival thrown by Lookout ("The Lookout Freakout"). It was spread over three days and included a fun ten-band daytime outdoor show at a miniature golf course in the East Bay.

I was excited and relieved to be back out on the road.

The new songs were going over as well as the old ones. It seemed like we had plateaued; still, there was only a slight drop-off of live show attendance, compared to CD sales. The three most exciting shows of the tour were the weekend of the College Media Journal convention. They were three of our best shows ever—New York/Boston/Philly. We shared a bill with other Lookout bands, opening for The Mr. T Experience and The Donnas. In the friendly competition, we were in peak form. We were so good, the admiring sound guy at the CMJ show in New York asked, "Jesus Christ, why aren't you guys *huge?*"

The show was pretty well attended but could have been more so; this was the day that Mayor Giuliani "closed" New York City because of a hurricane. We pulled up to the Holland Tunnel not knowing this but figured something was up because there was *no* traffic. We pulled right up to the tollbooth, and once in the city, parked in front of the venue. Not our typical New York experience.

Boston was probably the best show this band has *ever* played. We just *killed.* Everybody around us noticed. When we got to Philadelphia, we knew it would be hard to top it, but we came close. Having those larger crowds really fed us. Such a blast!

Back in Canada, we encountered a number of people who told us they'd seen us with Green Day and had been waiting to reach legal drinking age and see us again. Calgary was especially fun. Instead of just the usual club show, we did a TV program as well, a breakfast show the morning after our gig. We were not well rested but whipped through two full songs and portions of two others. It went fine, though I later found out the station had gotten complaints about "Luv Luv Luv" with its "Sex! Sex! Sex!" chant.

This led to our having an evening off. The editor of a local gay paper had offered to take us out…on a Tuesday night in Calgary. (Sounds like a punch line, doesn't it?) He claimed there was a fun weekly gay club that hosted an amateur strip night. So we went, and it was actually fun. After a few drinks, Luis came over to me and said, "I'll enter the contest if you will. I just don't want to do it alone." "I don't know," I said. "There's a hundred dollars prize money, and let's say we'll split it if one of us wins." Also, it wasn't a strip contest, it was a Hot Butt contest, so all you had to do was drop your pants. I said okay. The obvious implication was that, as band hottie, Luis would easily win.

Six people entered. They divided us into two groups of three, and we stood behind a partition showing us from the waist down. Luis and I were in the same grouping. After shakin' it, I was declared winner of my heat. Luis looked at me with *total shock*. He paused, then recovered and said, "Right on, go for it!" Chris, who'd been watching from the audience, told me I had really worked it, while Luis mostly just stood there. After another heat, it was time for the finals—me and a local guy. In the end, the applause was pretty even, but I won by a butt hair. The loser was sore, said he was counting on the money (he had won the contest before). Woo hoo! At age thirty-nine, I won the Hot Butt contest in Calgary. I had never won (nor entered) anything remotely like it before. Buying drinks all around, we spent most of our winnings at the bar.

We played more college towns this year and did better in them than before: Charlottesville, Bloomington, Ann Arbor, Easthampton, Ames. In Nashville we stayed with some older teens whose out-of-town parents were in the music biz—Dad was on the road with The Oak Ridge Boys, and Mom was on tour doing clothing for The Backstreet Boys. They showed us a pair of pants that Howie had worn, which they gave to a fascinated Luis (we'd been making fun of their song "I Want it that Way" throughout the tour). So yes, you can say that the drummer of Pansy Division got into the pants of one of The Backstreet Boys.

It was another successful tour. We could have still made a living off our band if we wanted to tour half the year and make a concerted effort to play more colleges. Perhaps we would have driven ourselves into the ground, but it could have been viable had everyone wanted to continue that way. When the tour concluded, I got a job at Amoeba Music in San Francisco. For five and half years I'd lived the musician's dream—playing music for a living and not having to work a regular job. That was over (it was almost unbelievable that it had happened at all), and a new reality was beginning. It also meant I'd be getting a raise; apart from 1995, when I'd made thirty thousand dollars (largely because of royalties from Lookout), I had been making between seventeen and nineteen thousand a year as a full-time musician.

CHAPTER 26

Drift and Renewal

We still hadn't answered the bigger questions about the band's future. Topping *Absurd* would take a lot of hard work. This was the first time we'd openly discussed not continuing with the band. If Chris was considering it, it was serious. Though we all agreed to keep going, nobody wanted to put that much effort into making things happen. I was still writing songs but wasn't sure what to do with them.

So we stayed together, if adrift. We played a mere eleven shows in 2000—Gay Pride events in Toronto, Detroit, San Diego, and San Jose (this time with Cyndi Lauper, who sang to pre-recorded tracks), and the Folsom Street Fair in San Francisco. The day before San Diego's Pride, we did a club gig opening for El Vez, the Mexican Elvis, whom we all love (and who Chris later did a tour with, and who Luis traveled with as well). One of our odder shows was in June, at a midnight screening of *Beyond the Valley of the Dolls.* For the first time ever, we performed in drag, as the film's fictional female band The Carrie Nations. We learned just one and a half of their songs, a short performance. Patrick even shaved his beard for the show, the only time he's done that since joining the band.

Traveling during this time we had some lively debates about Eminem. Chris and Patrick were pro, Luis and I were con. Chris liked the storytelling aspect and enjoyed the music. I found his voice annoying and couldn't get past the homophobic stuff. People like Eminem 'cause he's a white trash underdog. What bugs me is that, having been put down and bullied, he learns no wisdom—he just turns around and bullies back, repeating the cycle. To me he's the hip-hop Axl Rose, using homophobia to sell millions. (Elton John has appeared onstage with both Axl Rose and Eminem. If we did a homophobic song, would Sir Elton duet with us?)

There was also change afoot at our label during this time. Lookout switched their distribution from Mordam, their longtime home, to the much larger R.E.D., an indie distributor owned by Sony. This was part of Lookout's attempt to run their label more professionally; Lookout had trouble getting their CDs into chain record stores, where a larger percentage of record sales were occurring. Making this switch was quite disruptive—if stores wanted to return their old product, they would have to do it then, so Lookout was flooded with returns. Plus, to make enough money for their new distributor, they were forced to raise their CD prices by three dollars, from ten and eleven dollars to thirteen and fourteen. One of Lookout's advantages had been their low prices; I'd rather makes less per record and sell more copies. As Internet downloading was just beginning to kill sales, Lookout's CD prices suddenly went up 30 percent.

Bad move. Some indies were lowering their prices, especially on catalog titles, but Lookout was slow to react.

I was against the move. In some ways it was a natural progression; however, Lookout had already lost the bigger selling bands that would benefit much from a bigger push (they'd been successful selling records in large extent by word of mouth), except The Donnas (whose manager was Lookout co-owner Molly Neuman). It seemed a risky gamble.

Part of Lookout's identity was that it was more of a seemingly homemade label than its more successful indie punk counterparts Fat Wreck Chords and Epitaph. The R.E.D. deal was meant to give Lookout the chance to excel on the level of those labels, which had gold records and bands on MTV. Rancid had sprung from the ashes of Operation Ivy on Lookout to huge success on Epitaph. Lookout already had problems, and they worsened from this point forward.

Lookout were still paying us our ever-diminishing royalty checks, even though they were invariably late. They weren't the kind of label that would pressure us to crank out another record (although until recently we'd cranked them out as fast as we could without any prodding from them). This had been our quietest year in nine years, and our first year in eight without a major tour. I was settled in at my job, but restless. I would have to wait.

Chris Freeman had moved to San Francisco in 1987. By 2000, he was over it. He'd been complaining about it for a while; the dot-com boom had changed the city so much, and he wanted a change of scenery. In his spare time he was playing with another band, and with dot-coms cannibalizing every available building for office space (at market-peak prices) they got kicked out of three rehearsal spaces in one year. He announced that he was moving to Los Angeles.

He wasn't quitting the band; he promised to come up

dutifully for rehearsals. The year before, Chris was probably the one least enthusiastic about continuing. Chris has
always been good for his word, but the handwriting was
on the wall. You might say you'll come back regularly, but
even if you mean it, things can change. He wasn't letting go
of PD, but it seemed like he was beginning the process of
putting it behind him.

In March 2001, Chris moved. A temp job in San Francisco, doing financial aid administration for small colleges,
led to a similar position in L.A. He was turning forty, and
he wanted a more reliable income and stable future. He was
living in Silver Lake and very happy.

But after arriving in L.A., something happened that
surprised Chris. He won all kinds of unexpected praise for
having been in Pansy Division, enjoying a bit of "celebrity"
status. All the props he was getting for PD reinvigorated
his enthusiasm for the band. Not because it stroked his
ego (okay, maybe a little), but because it revealed to him
people's depth of feeling. When he came back up North a
while later, he was gung ho to move ahead. This was good
timing, since I was starting to think maybe it was time to
let go of the band.

We had done six albums between 1993 and 1998, but
had now gone three years without one. When we began
making *Absurd*, Patrick had just joined and we hadn't yet
seen what he could do. This time we wanted him and Luis to
be more involved with the songwriting process, and to come
up with more songs as a group. To do this, we'd tape our
practices and just play, then go back and take the good parts
and construct them into songs. We'd done this occasionally
in the past, but now we wanted to utilize this method to
vary our results and tap into their good ideas. This didn't
work out so well. The first few practices didn't yield much,
and with Chris making the effort to do a twelve-hour round-

trip drive per visit, we needed more substantive results. Part of this is down to Patrick, who's very talented but hard to motivate. There had been some unfinished songs he'd been handed to work on, but it was like pulling teeth getting him to do his homework. We wanted to include him in more, but he didn't jump at the chance. I had written a bunch of songs, so we began working on those. We made a bit more progress, but it wasn't really taking off. Luis always seemed to be exhausted, and overall the low energy was pervasive.

One day we were working on one of my more introspective songs, and Patrick said, "You know, this really isn't that much fun…this isn't really what I joined Pansy Division for." I countered that both Luis and Patrick had said in the recent past that they were tired of some of our funnier songs, which I took as a hint to write more in the vein of the songs on *Absurd*. I wanted to be mindful of writing for the group's desires as a whole. I said, "I've got all kinds of songs I never play for you guys 'cause I thought that's not what you wanted to hear…in fact, I've got a song called 'He Whipped My Ass in Tennis, Then I Fucked His Ass in Bed.' but I thought you wouldn't like it!" As we fell about the floor, Luis practically screamed "*Yes! Yes!*" We learned it at our next practice, and a corner was turned.

Something else surprising happened to us that summer. In stark contrast to the previous year, we were suddenly in demand. In our indecision we'd retreated from public view, and suddenly we had lots of gig requests and a much higher volume of emails from fans asking when we'd be doing a new album, and when were we going to tour their city again. At the height of our inactivity, the *SF Weekly* ran a cover story on us. We got mentioned on an episode of "Queer As Folk." (They never did use any of our music on the show, though twice they solicited us for songs.) As someone explained to me, we had achieved "classic" status by lasting so long, and in our absence people missed us. As any musician will tell you, it's nice to feel wanted.

We didn't play too many more shows than the previous year, but we got to open for a number of bands we admired—Old 97s, The Posies, Rocket from the Crypt, and an "unplugged" set opening for queer rock pioneer Tom Robinson. We did Pride gigs in Minneapolis and Oakland and played a fun queer rock festival in Seattle where many of the bands were friends of ours.

There was one tour we would have done this year. The Pet Shop Boys attempted to organize a queer Lollapalooza called Wotapalava, including themselves, Soft Cell, Sinead O'Connor (she was a lesbian that summer), Magnetic Fields, and Rufus Wainwright. To us, what was missing from that bill was queer *rock*. So we made our pitch to be the opener, or be on the second stage; with no reply, we sent them another email, describing who we were and why we wanted to play. Their reply, indicating that the Pet Shop Boys were "very aware of Pansy Division," was amusing, but in the end advance ticket sales were poor and they canceled the whole thing.

We continued working on the new songs. They were mostly songs of mine; Chris wanted to hear the tone my songs set and find songs of his that would complement them. As the year rolled on, we made great progress; the new songs were getting a great response live. We rejected more songs in the making of this album than ever before, focusing in on the ones that fit together best. By the end of the year, the album was taking shape. Working at our own pace, we contacted Lookout to tell them what our plans were for the forthcoming year. That's when the trouble began.

We had emailed our plans for 2002 to Lookout in mid-December 2001, but received no reply. We waited until after the holidays and did the same, and left phone messages. No response. They were dodging us. I told Chris I didn't think they wanted to put out our record, and he just couldn't believe it. We'd been on the label for almost ten years—there was loyalty involved. Finally, we got through to Chris Applegren, one of the three people who ran Lookout, and scheduled a meeting to talk about these issues. It took until the first week of March for this to occur.

The meeting was a big runaround; Applegren was very noncommittal. He didn't seem too interested in hearing about what we were up to. At the beginning of May (almost five months after the initial email) we got the official no, which by then we knew. You don't treat people that way if you're interested in working with them, but because of our history we gave them the benefit of the doubt.

There are a number of reasons Lookout dropped us. We had ideas about what a label should do for a band (even a small label), so we were sometimes pushy in asking them to do things for us. We were older than most of the bands on the label and had more experience in making a band run smoothly. We were a hardworking band and competent people, and in turn we expected the label to work hard and do a competent job for us. This sometimes ruffled a few feathers. But compared to the babysitting and hand-holding they had to do for a number of the bands on the label, we felt we were fairly low maintenance.

None of the albums or singles we released on Lookout lost money. We made a profit and were paid royalties for every release. Compared to the sales of some of their newer signings at this time, we were a more solid bet, even with indie record sales declining. I think part of it was that we'd been signed to the label by Larry Livermore, who was long gone. In fact, Larry, who was always one of our biggest boosters, had been urging us to leave the label since the year after he split, saying some other label could do a better job. In retrospect, he was probably right. What kept us from throwing in the towel earlier was Lookout's stated desire to evolve; we had evolved right along with the label. They saw it differently.

Once word got around that we'd been dumped, we started getting emails and calls from insiders—former label employees, bands, and people who worked with but not for the label. They all had the same message: be glad you're gone. These were people who hadn't dished dirt earlier because they wanted our band to succeed and didn't want to poison our relationship with the label. The first thing people were anxious to tell us (from numerous sources) was that our label's publicist absolutely hated *Absurd* and barely lifted a finger for it. She was vocally unhappy about having to work that album, which makes sense now. She was friendly to our faces, which was disappointing. (It's lucky we hired someone outside the company to do extra publicity for the tour and for gay press, or it would have been worse.) We heard a lot about Lookout's poor management, inept business practices, overstaffing, poor signing decisions, time and energy wasted on cockamamie pursuits (like trying to get Lookout releases on airlines' in-flight playlists), and bad faith. As a member of another Lookout band later said, "If you're incompetent for that long, it becomes malicious."

A record either finds its audience, or it doesn't; you can't always blame other people for your lack of sales. Our feeling was that we had given them an album they *could* have used to build a greater audience, and the fact that it didn't happen was a blow to our band.

After a decade, we were free agents once again. We decided to plow ahead with the recording, then approach labels with the finished product. We had set a recording date: June 2002.

CHAPTER 27

Total Entertainment!

We had a theme and a title song: *Total Entertainment!*
Despite our enthusiasm for Steve Albini, we wouldn't be
working with him this time. We had neither the budget (self-
financed, as usual) nor the time to travel to Chicago. For
the first time we used a producer—Chris Xefos, a friend
of Patrick's, who had been in the band King Missile (best
known for their MTV hit video "Detachable Penis"). He
was gay and had recently opened a studio in San Francisco.
Listening to some of the work he'd done, we thought he
would do a good job. We did a demo session at his house
in January. In the end we opted to do the basic tracks in
a large studio and do the overdubs and mixing at Chris
X's studio (in the basement of his house). The basics were
done at Studio 880 in Oakland, where Green Day had

recently recorded their *Warning* album. Using engineer Aaron Prellwitz, we did three days of recording and it sounded great.

The longest we'd spent making an album from start to finish was nine days. *Total Entertainment!* took six months. The other albums were done in intense bursts; TE was done leisurely, on evenings and weekends and in everyone's spare time. Instead of charging us by the hour, Chris X charged per song. The others were made with all of us present; with Chris X at the controls, he worked with us individually. It wasn't as much fun doing it this way, being able to weigh in with your opinions as things happened, but Chris X got terrific results.

The album opened with "Who Treats You Right," a unanimous choice for the first track. We all agreed it was one of the best things we'd ever done. It rocked, but it wasn't very punk rock (depending on where you file Joan Jett). It had some odd chords for a PD song, lyrics about trying to date a jock, and a very catchy chorus. Add some stunning Patrick guitar work, and Luis sounding his very best, and it sounded like a hit to us.

Following was "Blurry Down Below," a song about waking up to find out your bits have been blurred out like on a TV show. It had an intentional Motown feel; we wanted to make a more up-tempo and upbeat album than *Absurd*, and the key word was bouncy. We wanted the songs to be fast but have a little more groove. "When He Comes Home" is a good Chris pop song, which was followed by "Too Many Hoops," another Motown-ish track. "Hoops" originally had a straightforward lyric, but it seemed staid, so I substituted ridiculous references and rhymes, making it a very fun song to play. Up next was one of Chris's best songs. Highlighted by a cascading Patrick riff, "Spiral" told the story of his ex, who had gone down the spiral of using crystal meth. Its sunny sound belied its subject matter.

After five up-tempo songs, we switched gears for a slowie. "Saddest Song" was the first song we learned for the album, and again Patrick's versatile guitar tone works wonders. This is as close as we'll ever get to Galaxie 500, whose elegant simplicity was an inspiration for starting PD in the first place.

Another big curve was "No Protection." There had been some articles the year before about rising HIV rates among younger men in the American gay meccas, and as a safe-sex proselytizer and former ACT-UP member I found this very, very frustrating. Gay guys in their teens and twenties hadn't witnessed people dying from AIDS, and as a result weren't taking precautions. I had written a song about this, an angry rant, but all it did was vent. I wasn't happy with it, and I discussed the subject with Chris. He wrote this song, which I then sat down and rewrote. It's one of our rare fifty/fifty songwriting efforts.

For quite a while we'd half-jokingly talked about doing some kind of dance song, using Blondie's "Heart Of Glass" and The Kinks's "Wish I Could Fly Like Superman" as our models, and now we were ready to give it a try. We thought it would be good to combine this dance song idea with a safe sex message, and voila! The lyrics are about a guy who is into another guy until he finds out the guy won't use condoms or practice safe sex. Though there is some synth on the song (played by Chris Xefos), what sounds like a keyboard is actually Patrick's guitar.

It was fun adding the "Cher" vocoder sound to the chorus, using the device on the lines that the anti-condom guy would be singing (making the unsafe sex character sound more evil!). Again, the tone of the music is happier than its lyric, and the message is wrapped in humor. A more serious tone can sound like a scold. I think this could be a big hit if some dance diva would record it. Come on Crystal Waters, Gwen Guthrie, or Martha Wash (or their current equivalent), take a chance!

We followed the slickest moment on the record with the rawest. "Alpine Skiing" is a slab of '60s-style garage rock that just might be my favorite PD song. The title came from a conversation with Patrick, who used the phrase to describe jacking off two guys at once. I love capturing that vernacular in song, and in an instant I knew just how I wanted it to sound—like a '60s dance craze, "C'mon everybody, let's go alpine skiing!" It rocks in a way that is totally stoopid, and I can't get enough of it. I only wish I had the vocal chords to scream like this at length; we have to play it at the end of our sets or my throat will be shredded for the rest of that set. I wish we had a whole album of songs like this.

Almost as raw is "Not Good Enough," an extremely brief, tough Chris rocker, followed in short order by fairly un-Pansy sounding rocker "Scared to Death," Chris's memoir of his first time. "I'm Alright" is about an insecure guy standing up for himself; Luis spoke up for this one when deciding what songs needed to be on the album. Patrick's crunchy chords and Luis's fills make a good song pretty great.

The following two are my least favorites on the album. In the process of working the album's songs, mine were gone over with a fine tooth comb, Chris reworking things more than ever and earning writing credits. On his songs though... he thought they were perfect and didn't need any touching up! After what I'd submitted myself to, I was a bit let down how protective he was about his. Both are good songs I think could have been better if we'd had more time and Chris had been a little more giving. "Sleeping in the Cold" is based on one of Patrick's riffs that Chris heard potential in, and I like it. "First Betrayal" is a good ballad, but both of these songs are too long for me. They also steer the balance of the album away from the more up-tempo aspect; I had given up pushing for a couple of songs of mine that were slower, only to have Chris's show up instead. Still, "First Betrayal" managed to get onto the soundtrack for *Hellbent*, the first gay slasher movie.

The album ended on an up note with "He Whipped My Ass in Tennis, Then I Fucked His Ass in Bed" and the title song. "Whipped" is as close to country punk as we come, with friends contributing pedal steel and banjo to the track. It was placed near the end of the album because it's just *so* what people expect from us and just too over the top to stick up front. The title track had the longest and most arduous route to the album; in an attempt to really work in Patrick's material, it was rewritten and overhauled several times. Meant to be an anthem, it didn't quite succeed, but thanks to Patrick it does sound as close to a Cheap Trick/ Pansy Division blend as you could want. It has a full sound and it rocks out, man.

We wanted to make an album of no more than forty-five minutes, one side of a ninety-minute tape (what an archaic reference). It came out almost exactly that long, but we had a surprise in reserve. To amuse my band mates, once in a while I would pull out an old song of mine (from the late '80s) called "At The Mall." It had many verses and went on and on, but it was dumbly catchy and had some clever lines. Luis had suggested we all write verses for it and do a marathon version of it as a hidden bonus track. I kept reminding everyone to finish their verses, but by the day of recording, no one else had written any. I asked everyone what they wanted the song to include, quickly threw more verses into the pot, and we were off. We had done the instrumental track leaving room for fifteen verses and did the vocal in one take—over twelve minutes total. If you've ever wondered what Patrick sounds like when he's really drunk, listen for his contributions. (He also muttered to himself a lot, which is the low mumbling you can hear in the background.) Some people said it was their favorite song on the album! There are probably people who still don't know the song is there (it's not listed anywhere on the cover).

It took longer to complete the album than expected, and in the meantime we'd booked a modest tour. We wanted to get our feet wet again after three non-touring years. When we did our first tour in 1993, we did a modest three-week jaunt around the country to see how it went. That's what we did again, nineteen shows in twenty-three days coast to coast, to see who was paying attention to us—no publicist, no label help. We brought with us an opening band, The Plus Ones, with whom Luis was also drumming. Led by Joel Reader, who had been in The Mr. T Experience at their peak, their Badfinger/Beatles-inspired pop rock was quite compatible musically. Luis insisted he could play two sets per night, and he did it, but by the last three or four shows his fingers were like hamburger, held together by tape. He's a hard hitter, and some nights he looked exhausted during our set, but he made it through. It was good having another band's van around, as we discovered on consecutive days in Michigan when the Pansy van had a flat and the Plus Ones van had engine trouble.

The tour itself showed some erosion in attendance but went well. No duds, except for New York, where we'd never had a bad show. We played the wrong venue, we were told; some friends weren't even aware of it until after the fact. Good times, some wonderful shows, and we made money.

After the tour, we finished the last few overdubs and completed the mixes. By early December the album was finally complete.

We mailed copies of *Total Entertainment!* to thirty different indie labels, large and small. We spent about three months waiting and hoping for bigger indies to bite; talked with a few, but alas, no go. We ended up where we almost went in the first place—Alternative Tentacles. A smaller label than in years past, when they still laid claim to the Dead Kennedys catalog, A.T. was run by DK's front man Jello Biafra. After losing out to Lookout a decade earlier, he liked our album and was glad to finally get us on his label. He had signed Tribe 8 and released five CDs by them; he really *got* our bands. Oddly enough, he loved "At The Mall," saying it was the kind of funny observational song I did best. A.T. had Mordam distribution and would release the album in August 2003.

We wanted to tour to support the album, so we played very little prior to its release, only four shows in the first seven months of 2003. We got the album artwork together, took photos for it, the usual stuff. During this time everyone was involved with outside band projects. (Our band played so seldom, *we* were now the side project.) Chris was in four bands in L.A., most notably The Gay-Gay's, an all gay Go-Go's tribute band. He'd also produced a good album by queer L.A. band I Am Loved.

Patrick had released a CD with his metal band Dirty Power, recording it with Nirvana/Soundgarden producer Jack Endino. (Though Dirty Power was three quarters gay, Patrick was averse to making it a selling point; none of the lyrics had any gay content, and he wasn't trying to make an issue out of being gay like PD had.) Luis had The Plus Ones and had joined The Avengers, a great '70s-era Bay Area punk band whose main members had regrouped; Luis and Joel from The Plus Ones were their rhythm section. I had formed a band called The Planning Commission, whose satiric songs were based around local San Francisco politics; I wanted a band that wouldn't have to tour!

We flew to Dallas to play a gay street fair called Razzle Dazzle Dallas. This is notable in that we shared a bill with The Village People. They had one original member (the Indian) and sang to prerecorded tracks. Tribe 8 were flown in too; they played on a different stage. We stayed in a nice hotel. Chris, the only member of Pansy Division who has the shopping gene, is also quite the bargain hunter and very thrifty. He always takes the shampoo and soap from his hotel visits and recently claimed, "I haven't bought soap in seven years!"

San Francisco's Gay Pride seemingly got their act together this year. We agreed to play, and it was worth waiting for, in order to open for Marc Almond (cool!). Chris got Marc to autograph all his Soft Cell albums.

It had been five years since we'd released an album. We planned to do a fair bit of touring but split into two trips with a two-month gap between. We'd do four weeks from August into early September and do four weeks from November into early December. I booked the tour; I had reached the point with booking agents where doing it right meant doing it myself. It was a lot of work, but thanks to the Internet it was far easier than it used to be.

CHAPTER 28

The Final Tour?

8.19.03 Arcata, CA

Humboldt County is almost halfway from San Francisco to Portland. Eureka/Arcata is kind of a graveyard for bands. It's about five hours north of San Francisco but there's no interstate highway. It's pretty darn isolated. However, we have played up here several times over the years, and much to everyone's surprise, we've never had a bad show, and most have been great; this was no exception.

The directions to the club were a bit frightening: go over a bridge on the way out of town, take a right, make another turn, and you'll find a building out in the middle of nowhere. We arrived a little late and found a hundred people waiting for us. The club was a community center in a former school, and we received a tremendous reception. It was one of those nights where a non-jaded crowd really appreciated our presence. The promoter, a twenty-year-old guy, said he had been flyering for over two months, and his persistence paid off. We ended up staying with people we knew up there (who were about to move away—they'd gotten all the way through college at Humboldt State waiting for us to come back to town) and smoked hellaciously strong weed.

8.25.03 Spokane, WA

Thought we'd give this town a try after an eight-year absence. Had a fun time on a Monday night, and notably got a few older gay guys out, a nice mixed crowd. The first band, Horrible Disaster, had possibly the best musician we've ever seen in one of our opening bands. The band was okay, too emo for me, but their drummer was lights out phenomenal. We stood there in awe, watching him play. He totally captured our attention. And he was only nineteen! They later moved to Portland, but I have lost track of them. Make that guy a star, now!

8.26.03 Missoula, MT

As we arrived in town, our van was making a weird noise, kind of a high-pitched whine. It was similar to the sound it made before we broke down in Louisiana a few years ago, but milder. The van has well over 200,000 miles on it…how much more money do we sink into it?

We were looking for a Laundromat and an Internet cafe, and we found both right next to a high school. I walked past the front door of the school and saw that it was called Hellsgate High School. That is the best name for a high school ever! Can you imagine how cool it would be to go to *Hellsgate*? I wanted to buy a T-shirt, but school didn't start for another week. Damn!

By far this was the drunkest show of the tour. Jay's

was about to close—it had been the cornerstone of the underground music scene here for two decades—and the bartenders were extremely generous with the liquor. We had several trays of flaming shots delivered to the stage. All of us were several drinks beyond the pale. We played badly but *we had a great time* and so did the audience, some of whom drank for free as well. We played songs from our back catalogue we swore we'd never play again; band members who had said they'd never play certain songs again were requesting them!

We didn't see any record stores there, but there were pawnshops full of good CDs. I think everyone made a purchase. Oh, and there was no cell phone service for our three days in Montana. Nothing on I-90 between Spokane and Fargo. People in Missoula had cell phones, why didn't ours work? Somebody's got a network there…

Thanks to Chris's shopping skills, on this tour we had pink cowboy hats that we would don for "He Whipped My Ass in Tennis, Then I Fucked His Ass in Bed." Yee ha ha ha!

8.29.03 Fargo, ND

We made it across the plains, but our van sounded asthmatic. After a wonderful show across the river in Moorhead, Minnesota, we stayed with a fan in Fargo. I rose way too early so we could try to get the van fixed and still make it to Minneapolis tonight. The van runs, but it feels like it could give up the ghost any moment.

I set out to find a mechanic. I tried a number of places, large and small, but none would take our van. Everyone was planning on closing early to get out of town for Labor Day weekend. Visiting various repair shops, I finally heard the famed Fargo accent. We hadn't heard it at either of our shows here, but all the mechanics and gas stations clerks had it.

So I gave up, and returned to the house. I said we needed to talk. We were going to continue driving the van though something was wrong with it. I also said that it probably wouldn't last much longer, and that I had enough money saved on my own to buy another van for the band. (I had bought our second van with my own money; the band didn't have enough to buy a decent van at this point.)

Chris spoke up. He didn't want me to do that. We had worked hard on this album, and he wanted to put in the effort to promote it, but he said he was tired of sleeping on floors and didn't want to do any more tours. He'd had a decade of sleeping on floors and needed a higher level of comfort in order to still enjoy it. He wasn't tired of the band, or even tours per se; if we were traveling on buses and staying in hotel rooms, it wouldn't be an issue. He had been planning to say something at some point, but this became that point.

I was fairly shocked, but how could I be upset? He'd totally earned his position. But it meant we were probably on our last tour.

9.3.03 Indianapolis, IN

After a satisfying weekend of shows in Minneapolis, Chicago, and Cincinnati, we drove to Indy after the show (it's only one hundred miles from Cincy) and got a cheap motel room for our off day. Again I rose early to find a mechanic. This time I was successful; the guy said to check back by noon and he'd have an answer for us.

So I walked around Indianapolis, got breakfast. I saw a building that gave me pause; it was almost too anonymous looking, even though it was in an unremarkable industrial area. Turned out to be a gay bath house, and it was open. Is that gaydar? I didn't go in though.

The mechanic told me that the problem was that the

crankshaft needed grease; the rear end had gotten hot from lack of lubrication and caused that whining sound. Did you catch that? Our rear end needed lubing. (I wouldn't make this up.) He applied the lube and charged us thirty-four dollars. Because we had driven so far in that condition, he warned the whine might not completely go away, but it was *much* improved. We breathed easier...until the next inevitable van drama.

9.5.03 Denver, CO

In college, a friend lost her virginity to a guy I knew from the student newspaper. She said the guy had a startlingly large cock. Later, this guy joined the Marines, and at a certain point came out as gay. Then, he moved to Denver and started doing gay porn. Eventually he had gotten back into journalism. After a few years he and I had gotten in touch again, and I had asked him to recommend one of his videos; his cock sure was big but nothing unusual for porn. What was cool about the video I saw was that his personality came through—he actually *had* personality, and even smiled during his scenes. He was at the show, and after the show I was pissing at the trough in the men's room when he had to do the same and whipped it out. We smiled at each other. It *was* really big.

9.6.03 Salt Lake City, UT

Since our debacle opening for Pennywise and Blink 182 six years earlier, we had not returned to Salt Lake. This is a weird town for bands—liquor laws are arcane and all-ages shows had been nearly impossible. But this year a zealous fan recruited us to play here; he told us of a newer all-ages club, Kilby Court, and helped arrange the gig. Then he promoted the hell out of it for three months. The result? Over one hundred people came (doubling our previous crowds), and it was an enthused crowd at that. Philip, the owner, runs the club in a community-oriented way and has made something out of nothing for kids in Salt Lake. We had so much fun, were paid well, and felt the show had really accomplished something. This was the last show of the first leg of the tour, so we drove home on a great note.

Returning home, Patrick was feeling job pressures. It didn't look like he'd be able to do the second part of the tour without losing his job. He said he was quitting the band but would be still be available to play the occasional gig; he just couldn't do the touring we'd agreed to.

We had an inkling of this. Patrick's other band Dirty Power had made a CD, which in retrospect probably contributed to his inability to do more writing for the last album. But Patrick's not the type to speak up until absolutely necessary (which was sometimes later than ideal). As we'd had a good six-year run with him, we had no desire to replace him, but when the time came, we had a candidate.

We had seen Bernard Yin play with several L.A. bands in the '90s, including The Glitter Panthers. Having seen us a bunch of times, he was really excited about having the chance to play with us. He was able to do the tour, woo-hoo! We sent him a list of songs to practice and then rehearsed in L.A. for three days before hitting the road. Oh, yeah, now half of our band lived in L.A., half in San Francisco. Our guess was that he was gay, but he turned out not to be—he's a self-described "male fag hag." He's also the only person I know to have a birthday on February 29.

11.8.03 Lawrence, KS

We drove halfway across the country to this show, our first with Bernard. We weren't expecting a lot from it; we'd played the Replay once before and it was just okay. This time we had a full club. Somehow we overcame our exhaustion and put on a damn good show. Then we got a normal night's sleep (no twelve-hour catch-up sleeps), and we were off again.

11.12.03 Ithaca, NY

College gigs are the best-paying gigs we do, but are sometimes not that much fun. This was a good one, a great turnout on a weeknight. We played in the Cornell University student union. A good story: a student walking down the hall, hears the music, peeks in. "Who's playing?" he asks. He's told it's Pansy Division. He's astonished, thrilled. He asks, "What does it cost?" It's free, he's told. Again he can't believe it. He is nudged in (he's still flabbergasted), and loves the show. Good thing he went for a walk when he did.

Bernard is fitting in great. He's an even-tempered guy, fun to be with, a good driver too. His guitar playing is different than Patrick's; Patrick's a natural rocker, and Bernard sometimes needs to be coaxed. There would be times when I'd think he just doesn't sound as good as Patrick, then he'd turn on a dime and do something Patrick would never do that would be totally cool. Also, he brought a theremin with him, and we worked that into a couple of songs with good results.

11.13.03 New Haven, CT

We're now officially on the East Coast. We noted this today when we had to call the club for directions. The guys on the phone had that classic brusque rudeness that just rolls off the tongue like nowhere else but the Northeast. I don't know if any of them was named Vinnie, but they sounded like Vinnies.

It was an exciting show in a club with a tiny stage and a number of drunken gay guys acting very silly. Crowds at our shows have been noticeably gayer this year. I think it's partly 'cause "the kids" aren't listening to us as much as they used to in the '90s, and also 'cause younger gay guys have fewer of the cultural hang-ups that older gay guys have about what gay culture should be.

It was reported on MSNBC.com that George W. Bush's daughter Barbara was at our show in New Haven (she goes to Yale) and that we dedicated "Political Asshole" to her. This is not exactly correct. The club we played, Rudy's, has a front room, then a hallway leading to a back room with a pool table. We played in front, she was in the back room. I don't know if she saw any of our show, but she was in the building at the time. And we dedicated "Political Asshole" to her *father*, not her.

11.14, 11.15, 11.16.03 Boston/New York City/Philadelphia

We stopped to have our picture taken outside the Cathedral of the Holy Cross in Boston, where the Catholic priest molestation scandal originated. Then we had three killer shows in four days. All were with the fabulous Les Sans Culottes as our openers (imagine a garage rock band with French lyrics channeling The B-52s and Serge Gainsbourg—perfect!). Last year's gig in New York City was a dud; this year was the opposite, filling up the middle room in the Knitting Factory, a dancing frenzy. Michael Stipe and Lukas Haas were there...to see Crooked Fingers, who were playing the larger room upstairs. In fact, Crooked Fingers (featuring Eric Bachmann from Archers of Loaf, doing an Americana/ Leonard Cohen kinda thing) were traveling virtually the same tour route as us for about two weeks; in Boston the night before they also played a different floor of the same club we played. We were unable to play the clubs we wanted to play in DC and Phoenix thanks to them!

Philly on a Monday didn't sound too appetizing; we skipped Philly on our 2002 tour. How wrong we were!

Opening band V.I.P. have clearly heard Gravy Train!!!!; a bunch of gay fake gangsta rappers, their ultrafilthy raps were hilarious and totally over the top. I think every person they've ever known showed up to the show, which made it our biggest Philly show in years. Les Sans Culottes played again so it was a perfect evening.

11.24.03 Bryan, TX

Somewhere between Houston and Austin is College Station, Texas, home of Texas A&M University. Bryan is the town next door and has a virtually deserted Main Street downtown. In the midst of this is a sparkling new gay bar, The Halo, where friends of ours who had moved there from Austin arranged for us to play.

We seldom play gay bars—the patrons want dance music, and most gay bars have sounds systems inadequate for live music. But our opening band, Gays in the Military, came from Austin with their PA and it worked out fine. What was so cool about this night was that it brought people from various subcultural groups together in one place where each could see that the other exists. Queers, punks, students, oddballs, and a wide range of gay men and women of various ages. It really felt like a community event rather than your garden variety rock show. Also, they had video monitors throughout the club, so during our set we had them play *Showgirls*. Since I could see the video monitor while singing, I got distracted a few times—I wanted to watch it!

11.25.03 Austin, TX

We played Emo's on our first tour ten years ago, and year in, year out it's the only place we've ever played in one of our favorite cities. I think this was our tenth time. Even though school was out (pre-Thanksgiving), and it's a big college town, we still had a big crowd.

We had really fun opening bands— Gays in the Military again, and Yuppie Pricks, who pretended to be nostalgic for the Reagan '80s and dressed in tennis whites and made remarks taunting the homosexuals. They also had tennis rackets and hit tennis balls at members of the audience. Onstage the very cute lead singer dared us to kiss his very cute ass (which he revealed to us) but retracted his offer when he decided the crowd would probably like that. Which we would have.

Weird and wonderful things happen to us in Austin. This time, I went for a walk after I got up in the morning, through a residential neighborhood, and what did I see at the end of the street but a castle! It belonged to a female sculptor who had cast many famous Texans of the late nineteenth century. She was originally from Germany and had built a Germanic-looking castle which has since been turned into a museum. And it was open!

11.26.03 Houston, TX

It had been years since a guy at a show has asked me to sign his dick, but tonight it happened twice. Houston can be a good show for us if we plan carefully; tonight we got the right band on the bill with us—local punkers 30 Foot Fall—whose exhibitionist singer go-go danced at our first show in Houston ten years earlier. Hooray!

But the reason we *love* Houston is the presence of some terrific friends of the band (via Luis) who have a nice house with a pool. We stayed with them, and the day after the show they treated us to a hearty vegetarian Texas Thanksgiving. We drank prickly pear margaritas all day, listened to Texas music (and The Buzzcocks) and luxuriated.

11.29.03 Dallas, TX

Okay, Dallas: after a pretty big crowd at Razzle Dazzle Dallas in June, our attempts at securing a gig this time around weren't paying off, so we consulted one of our opening bands from the summer. They said they'd had good gigs at the Hard Rock Cafe...they also recommended avoiding the usual club area, Deep Ellum, 'cause there had been problems with gangs and some gay bashings. We hesitated, since Deep Ellum is pretty much all there is to do in Dallas, but thought different might be good, and the Hard Rock was much closer to the gay neighborhood.

The minute we walked in I realized we'd made a mistake. I hadn't been in a Hard Rock Cafe in five years. The atmosphere was just so wrong. It wasn't just the Spin Doctors and Bon Jovi guitars mounted on the wall next to the stage. It wasn't just the staff, who looked upset they didn't have jobs at the mall. It wasn't just that the bartenders all looked like (and acted like) football players. No, it was buying a shot of Southern Comfort and being charged $5.69. It could have been $5. It could have been $6. That would have been okay. But $5.69 just seemed ludicrous. It just seemed punitive, something that no one who actually worked in a bar would think of. Why $5.69? I guess $5.67 or $5.75 would have just been stupid. It just had to be $5.69.

A few fans of ours showed up. They looked uncomfortable. We looked uncomfortable. Our opening band drew most of the patrons, and we thank them for trying hard and doing the legwork to make it happen. When the promoter wasn't there at the end of the night, and they refused to pay us what we agreed to in advance, we remembered why we try to avoid this corporate crap. (The rest came in the mail later, thanks to our openers.) I wanted to get a story out of playing there, but this wasn't the one I wanted. This was the last show of the second part of the tour (sort of—we had a couple shows in California after being home for a few days), and unlike the first part of the tour it ended with a thud. Ah, well.

12.6.03 San Diego, CA

Luis's hometown. We were booked at a club we love but in a town where our draw is mediocre. We were opening for The Hanson Brothers, a bunch of hockey-obsessed Canadian punks. The artist who did the poster for the show was well aware of this but for fun made a drawing of those other Hanson brothers, the "Mmm Bop" ones. His depiction of that other set of Hanson brothers caused a number of advance tickets to be sold in error. The club was understanding, and some hilarity ensued...what were those ticket buyers thinking? However, it *would* be fun to play with the other Hanson someday; maybe when one of them comes out and renounces the Oklahoma Christian lifestyle....

CHAPTER 29

Beyond and Back

We'd battled back and done an album. We'd gone out on the road and had a good tour. But afterwards we faced the fact that from now on our band would merely be a hobby, with us playing occasionally, but not really blazing any new trails. No more albums, no more tours.

March 2004 marked the end of an era. We sold our van, with 240,000 miles on it. (In fifteen years, our three vans drove approximately 250,000 miles.) We played ten gigs in 2004 (one of which was opening for Chris's old friends Mudhoney, which we had been trying to make happen for a long time), and just four in 2005. We attempted organizing a short European tour but were unable to make it succeed (too much time had elapsed since our previous visit to make it viable).

Still, it wasn't as if things had ground to a dead halt. We released a split 45 with the queer Vancouver band Skinjobs on Mint Records, using a couple of *Total Entertainment!* outtakes. Chris Freeman had a role in a gay film called *Luster*, directed by Everett Lewis. Chris and Luis were interviewed in a movie about the Christian rock scene, an excellent, evenhanded film called *Why Should the Devil Have All the Good Music?* We're in there amongst a handful of skeptics, including Steve Albini. An interview with Chris appears on the extras DVD to the recent re-release of *Beyond the Valley of the Dolls.* In 2005, a song of ours was used in "The O.C." on Fox. Which song? About a minute's worth of "At The Mall," fer chrissakes!

Bernard Yin left to play with Astra Heights, who signed with Universal and recorded an album with veteran producer David Kahne. Replacing him is Joel Reader, who had subbed for Patrick once at short notice and done a great job. It meant we no longer had an all-gay lineup, but at this point it's not something we're worried about.

In January 2006, we released *The Essential Pansy Division*, a thirty-song best-of CD with an accompanying DVD. Now when people ask which CD they should buy, we finally have the definitive answer. In February 2006, in the wake of the success of *Brokeback Mountain,* Willie Nelson's version of "Cowboys are Frequently Secretly Fond of Each Other" made the *Billboard* charts, getting us some press attention. But in 2006 we played only three gigs; between January 2006 and April 2007, we played only one gig, and it felt like the band was fading away.

I had pretty much stopped writing songs by this point. I didn't want to form another band, or be a solo performer; I had done a few solo gigs and hadn't enjoyed them very much. However, I had two songs I'd written a while ago that I thought were great Pansy Division songs and was disappointed that there wouldn't be an album they could call home. I decided I wanted to record them anyway, for posterity's sake, and at least put them on our website. I asked everyone in the band if they wanted to help do them; if they weren't interested I would have gotten other friends to help me out. I was slightly surprised when everyone said yes.

Luis had been curious about living in New York for quite a while, and at the beginning of 2007 he moved to Brooklyn. (In early 2007 he became a U.S. citizen.) Like Chris when he moved to Los Angeles, Luis said he didn't want to quit the band. He was also still a member of The Avengers, and as luck would have it, he would be flying back for a gig with them. So in April 2007, we opened for The Avengers in San Francisco, and then recorded the songs that weekend.

In addition to my two songs, Chris wrote a new one, plus we had been laughing so hard about one of my other songs we decided to do that one too. We recorded four songs in two days, and the experience was so enjoyable, so productive, and the results so exciting, that it made us want to do more. In fact we were so thrilled by how they sounded we decided these songs would be the start of another album.

During this fallow period, Chris had been combining full-time work with getting a film degree. (He'd already been working at the film school as a financial aid administrator.) Nearing graduation and needing to do a documentary, he decided to do it on Pansy Division (in collaboration with another student). The weekend we recorded, a crew came up to film us in the studio, as well as interviewing individual band members. Chris edited the film throughout the year, declaring it done in early October, a full-length feature titled *Pansy Division: Life in a Gay Rock Band*.

Chris was scurrying to get his film done not only so he could graduate but because a mostly unlikely situation had arisen. The Avengers, who in their thirty years of existence had never done a coast to coast U.S. tour, decided to do one in October. It seemed natural to ask us to open, and because Chris was now out of school, we were able to say yes. It all came together very suddenly—and then we were on tour again!

We didn't have a van, but Joel had The Plus Ones's van. The Avengers (including Luis and Joel) rode in that van and carried most of our equipment. I rented a car for Chris and me to travel in, and as a result had one of the most comfortable tours ever. We began in L.A. and ended in New York. (Joel had moved to Boston that summer—how much more spread out could we get?—but his van was still in the Bay Area.) We did sixteen shows in seventeen days (a short tour by our standards); we did five days on, one day off, and then did two shows the final day in New York.

I *loved* being on tour again. In some ways being the opener was preferable; playing earlier, we had the chance to meet people after our set, and each night I watched The Avengers's set. Also, their booking agent organized the shows, so I was spared the workload I'd shouldered on the last few tours. Each of our bands has a cult following, and by combining our audiences we usually did pretty well. Most people there for one band stayed and enjoyed the other.

We played some of the new songs, so it wasn't totally a blast from the past. Chris had bought a Bible (Southern pronunciation: bobble) at a 99¢ store and had been waving it around on the second verse of "I'm Gonna Be a Slut." In Austin he tossed the bobble into the crowd, and they tore it to bits. After The Avengers's set had ended, there were still shredded bits of bobble pages strewn about the floor in front of the stage.

A noticeable change from past tours was the small number of teenagers, despite most shows being all ages (and despite a raft of young MySpace friends). In Chicago, where we customarily draw a large teen audience, the audience was entirely adult. Instead, we got ex-teen fans, like the twenty-five-year-old guy in San Diego who excitedly bought a copy of *Wish I'd Taken Pictures* on LP, replacing the copy his mother had taken away from him, when he was fourteen. Seeing our album made her inquire as to whether he was gay (he isn't) and caused her to throw out most of his record collection (which she deemed incompatible with their church-going lifestyle).

We noticed that more of the crowd this tour seemed to be into punk as a lifestyle—people attired in punk band T-shirts and accessorized in a way that is obviously "punk." This is kind of weird to us—it's not our lifestyle, just some music we like. I'm glad they show up though.

The best shows were probably the last two days of the tour. In Boston (Cambridge, to be exact), we played the larger downstairs room at the Middle East for the first time since our great show with The Donnas and The Mr. T Experience almost a decade earlier. Combine perfect stage sound with a slew of crazed, screaming fans right up front who knew all the words, and the result was probably the best show of the tour. New York was great too—at the Knitting Factory with The Avengers, and then a semi-secret late-night show at an East Village club night called Queers Beers & Rears. The crush of weekend revelers on the Lower East Side is already pretty crazed, but add Halloween to it, and it made New York feel all the more overpopulated and wonderfully out of control. Because our tours usually go in a circle, starting and ending in San Francisco, ending it in New York—usually a peak of any tour—meant an unusually festive conclusion. Not since we ended our big tour with Green Day, which also ended in New York City, has the finale of a tour felt so wonderful and satisfying. At the end, Joel drove the van home to Boston, Luis was already home, Chris flew back to L.A., and I drove the car back across the country, visiting my parents and a few friends along the way, and reacquainting myself with Interstate 80, the band's lifeline for so many tours.

In January, a friend (and benefactor) of the band flew Luis and Joel out to play a show at Gilman Street in Berkeley, where we again opened for The Avengers. It was our nine-hundredth show. We also recorded seven more songs for the next album, tentatively titled *That's So Gay* (after one of Chris's new songs), and we're very pleased with them. We completed four more songs in June and July, and mixed the whole album in September. The new album should be released on Alternative Tentacles in spring 2009.

We've played in forty-five states (still missing: Wyoming, Mississippi, Delaware, Alaska, Hawaii) and seventeen countries. We continue to get emails thanking us just for existing and wondering when we're going to come play Sweden or Australia or Texas. People are still discovering us, stumbling onto us by accident or being recommended by someone in the know.

When the band was beginning in 1991, it struck me that the kind of music we were playing was, in a sense, folk music. Not that we utilized acoustic guitars or sang traditional songs, but because the sources we emulated—certain styles of guitar-based rock and punk—were already historical. The early '90s surge of Nirvana's popularity, and the corresponding mainstreaming of punk, meant that was no longer true. However, fifteen years later it feels true again; our music has little relation to what teenagers see on MTV or hear on lame rock radio today. There are more openly gay musicians on major labels, but few fall into the rock and roll category. (The main exception is Rob Halford, in the reformed Judas Priest, but I doubt he'd be in that position if he was starting out today.) I guess I expected more progress by now. Queer musicians are now more common on the indie/underground scene than when we began, but that is still nowhere near to where things should be.

Before I ever had a band, I had an idea of what it would be like, and ideals about how I would do things—like if we got to make records or do tours, we'd take a certain attitude or approach. What's satisfying about our experience is that we pretty much did things the way we set out to do them and were successful doing so. Our best-selling albums, *Deflowered*, *Pileup*, and *Undressed*, each sold between 22,000 and 23,000 copies; *Wish I'd Taken Pictures* sold close to 15,000, *More Lovin' from Our Oven* sold 7,600, *Absurd Pop Song Romance* sold 5,200, *Total Entertainment!* about 2,500, and *The Essential Pansy Division* is around 3,000 and counting (not bad in the era of ever-diminishing record sales). Because we never got really big enough that our popularity got out of control, we never had to deal with certain real world issues—fame, the prospect of large amounts of money, jealousy, record company pressures—that can upend a group's idealistic vision. It helps too that we weren't kids.

That I'm here at all writing this still astounds me. I actually got to live out my rock and roll dreams. Perhaps some people's dreams would have been grander, for greater stardom or riches, but part of me is still that kid from Peoria—a place of more modest hopes and ambitions. For a long time I felt that I had something to contribute to the culture at large, like a lot of people do. I feel lucky that I was able to actually make that mark, because many who try don't succeed. From a young age I had a vague sense of wanting to achieve something, so there's a sense of relief too, that I haven't wasted my time and effort.

I live in San Francisco with my boyfriend. I still get performance royalties from the appearance of "Deep Water" in the *Angus* film. (As Chris likes to say, "Green Day is the gift that just keeps on giving.")

Regrets? I've had a few, as they say. But then again, you've heard them mentioned. Not too many really. It's been a great ride. After almost twenty years, we're still at it. We don't intend to stop—it's just too much fun.

DISCOGRAPHY

A L B U M S
Undressed Lookout 3/93
Deflowered Lookout 6/94
Pileup Lookout 2/95
Wish I'd Taken Pictures Lookout 2/96
More Lovin' from Our Oven Lookout 8/97
Absurd Pop Song Romance Lookout 9/98
Total Entertainment! Alternative Tentacles 8/03
The Essential Pansy Division Alternative Tentacles 1/06
That's So Gay Alternative Tentacles 4/09

S I N G L E S
"Fem in a Black Leather Jacket" Lookout 11/92
"Bill & Ted's Homosexual Adventure" Outpunk 2/93
"Touch My Joe Camel" Lookout 11/93
"Nine Inch Males" EP Lookout 2/94
"Jack U Off" Empty 8/94
"Jackson" K Records 12/94
"James Bondage" Lookout 1/95
"Valentine's Day" Lookout 1/96
"For Those About to Suck Cock" EP Lookout 8/96
"Manada" Mint (Canada) 4/97
"Queer to the Core" EP Lookout 4/97
"Loose" Royalty 4/98
"Dirty Queers Don't Come Cheap" EP Mint (Canada) 7/04

G I G O G R A P H Y
See a complete list of Pansy Division performances at
http://www.pansydivision.com/Pansy_Division/Gigs.html

W E B S I T E
www.pansydivision.com